Colin Feltham's wide-ranging and thoughtful book, *Depressive Realism*, is written in his characteristically engaging and accessible style. This makes for an easy read on a topic that many people find difficult to contemplate.

David Benatar, Head of the Department of Philosophy
at the University of Cape Town, South Africa

Life is to a first approximation depressing and without meaning. In his latest book, Colin Feltham takes the reader on an interdisciplinary journey through this dark worldview of 'Depressive Realism.' Feltham's conversational prose is engaging and encouraging, shepherding the reader gently but confidently through a masterful tour of the reaches of Depressive Realism. Feltham patiently guides the reader through historical and current applications of Depressive Realism to the realms of religion, philosophy, literature, film, psychology, psychotherapy, politics, and science and technology. Feltham's latest offering is the best one-stop review of this worldview and its applications and implications. Learning about the depressive meaninglessness of life has never before been so entertaining and enjoyable.

Todd K. Shackleton, Distinguished Professor and
Chair, Co-Director, Evolutionary Psychology Lab,
Oakland University, United States of America

Depressive Realism is a welcome antidote to the happiness industry. Through deep and rich investigation, Colin Feltham explores how Depressive Realism is threaded through psychology and philosophy, and in art and in science, in poetry and in politics, in history and in health. Feltham's book will be a revelation for anyone interested in the redressing of this imbalance, in realising how the negative is a critical component of our existence.

Jacky Bowring, Professor of Landscape Architecture,
Lincoln University, New Zealand

A brave and challenging examination of the human condition that refuses to take refuge in a false optimism about our prospects. Probing into areas of our experience that most of us are reluctant to acknowledge openly, Feltham boldly recasts depression as both an unavoidable, and a necessary, part of social existence. A book to make you reconsider your worldview.

Stuart Sim, author of *A Philosophy of Pessimism*

Depressive Realism

Depressive Realism argues that people with mild-to-moderate depression have a more accurate perception of reality than non-depressives. Depressive realism is a worldview of human existence that is essentially negative, and which challenges assumptions about the value of life and the institutions claiming to answer life's problems. Drawing from central observations from various disciplines, this book argues that a radical honesty about human suffering might initiate wholly new ways of thinking, in everyday life and in clinical practice for mental health, as well as in academia.

Divided into sections that reflect depressive realism as a worldview spanning all academic disciplines, chapters provide examples from psychology, psychotherapy, philosophy and more to suggest ways in which depressive realism can critique each discipline and academia overall. This book challenges the tacit hegemony of contemporary positive thinking, as well as the standard assumption in cognitive behavioural therapy that depressed individuals must have cognitive distortions. It also appeals to the utility of depressive realism for its insights, its pursuit of truth, as well as its emphasis on the importance of learning from negativity and failure. Arguments against depressive realism are also explored.

This book makes an important contribution to our understanding of depressive realism within an interdisciplinary context. It will be of key interest to academics, researchers and postgraduates in the fields of psychology, mental health, psychotherapy, history and philosophy. It will also be of great interest to psychologists, psychotherapists and counsellors.

Colin Feltham is Emeritus Professor of Critical Counselling Studies at Sheffield Hallam University. He is also External Associate Professor of Humanistic Psychology at the University of Southern Denmark.

Explorations in Mental Health series

For a full list of titles in this series, please visit www.routledge.com

Books in this series:

Therapeutic Assessment and Intervention in Childcare Legal Proceedings
Engaging families in successful rehabilitation
Mike Davies

Trauma, Survival and Resilience in War Zones
The psychological impact of war in Sierra Leone and beyond
David A. Winter, Rachel Brown, Stephanie Goins and Clare Mason

Cultural Foundations and Interventions in Latino/a Mental Health
History, Theory, and within Group Differences
Hector Y. Adames & Nayeli Y. Chavez-Dueñas

Indigenous Cultures and Mental Health Counselling
Four Directions for Integration with Counselling Psychology
Edited by Suzanne L. Stewart, Roy Moodley, and Ashley Hyatt

The Comprehensive Resource Model
Effective therapeutic techniques for the healing of complex trauma
Lisa Schwarz, Frank Corrigan, Alastair Hull and Rajiv Raju

Respect-Focused Therapy
Honoring Clients Through the Therapeutic Relationship and Process
Susanne Slay-Westbrook

Depressive Realism
Interdisciplinary perspectives
Colin Feltham

Depressive Realism

Interdisciplinary perspectives

Colin Feltham

Routledge
Taylor & Francis Group
LONDON AND NEW YORK

First published 2017
by Routledge
2 Park Square, Milton Park, Abingdon, Oxon OX14 4RN

and by Routledge
711 Third Avenue, New York, NY 10017

Routledge is an imprint of the Taylor & Francis Group, an informa business

© 2017 Colin Feltham

The right of Colin Feltham to be identified as author of this work
has been asserted by him in accordance with sections 77 and 78
of the Copyright, Designs and Patents Act 1988.

All rights reserved. No part of this book may be reprinted
or reproduced or utilised in any form or by any electronic,
mechanical, or other means, now known or hereafter invented,
including photocopying and recording, or in any information
storage or retrieval system, without permission in writing from
the publishers.

Trademark notice: Product or corporate names may be trademarks
or registered trademarks, and are used only for identification and
explanation without intent to infringe.

British Library Cataloguing in Publication Data
A catalogue record for this book is available from the British Library

Library of Congress Cataloging-in-Publication Data
CIP data has been applied for.

ISBN: 978-1-138-82354-9 (hbk)
ISBN: 978-1-315-74199-4 (ebk)

Typeset in Bembo
by Apex CoVantage, LLC

Contents

Abbreviations		ix
Acknowledgements		xi
Epigraph		xiii
	Introduction	1
1	Big history, anthropathology and depressive realism	10
2	Religion, spirituality and depressive realism	23
3	Philosophy and depressive realism	35
4	Literature, film and depressive realism	53
5	Psychology and depressive realism	68
6	Psychotherapy and depressive realism	80
7	The socio-political domain and depressive realism	99
8	Science, technology, the future and depressive realism	118
9	The lifespan, everyday life and depressive realism	132
10	Arguments against depressive realism	156
11	Lessons and possibilities for individuals and society	172
	Index	189

Abbreviations

BCE	Before the common era
BPS	British Psychological Society
CERN	Conseil Européen pour la Recherche Nucléaire
CBT	Cognitive behaviour therapy
DNA	deoxyribonucleic acid
DR	Depressive realism; depressive realist
DSM	Diagnostic and Statistical Manual of Mental Disorders
IAPT	Increasing Access to Psychological Therapies
ISIL/ISIS	Islamic State of Iraq and the Levant /Islamic State
JRF	Joseph Rowntree Foundation
KYA	Thousands of years ago
LGBTQ	Lesbian, gay, bisexual, transsexual, questioning
LSD	Lysergic acid diethylamide
MYA	Millions of years ago
NHS	National Health Service
NICE	National Institute for Health & Clinical Excellence
NLP	Neurolinguistic Programming
OCD	Obsessive compulsive disorder
PDR	Personality dependent realism
PTSD	Post traumatic stress disorder
REBT	Rational emotive behaviour therapy
STEM	Science, technology, engineering, mathematics
TMT	Terror management theory
ToM	Theory of mind

Acknowledgements

Those who have actively and personally helped in either small or larger ways in terms of support, ideas and references include David Benatar, Rune Lacroix Hansen, Andreas Nilssen Moss, Rachel Msetfi, Matt Sarraf, Todd Shackelford, Chip Smith and Gisle Tangenes. Michelle David Hansen has proved a loving presence, sounding board, curious interlocutor and practical help throughout. I am grateful to everyone at Routledge who has assisted in the publication of this book. Finally, my thanks to all those 'sorrowful investigators' now and throughout history, who have held on to and passed on their dark insights. Thanks are due to Bloodaxe Books for permission to quote from Frieda Hughes' poem *The Reason for Not Being* from the collection *The Book of Mirrors*.

'Abandon all hope, you who enter here.'

Alighieri Dante, *Inferno*, approx. 1314

Introduction

One could declare this to be simply a book about pessimism but that term would be inaccurate and insufficient. A non-verbal shortcut into the subject could be had by listening to Tears for Fears' *Mad World* or Dinah Washington's *This Bitter Earth*, or perhaps just by reading today's newspaper. Depressive realism is the term used throughout this book but it will often be abbreviated to DR for ease of reading, referring to the negative worldview and also to anyone subscribing to this worldview (*a* DR, or DRs). DRs themselves may regard the 'depressive' part of the label as gratuitous, thinking their worldview to be simply *realism* just as Buddhism holds *dukkha* to be a fact of life.

Initially, it may seem that this book has a traditional mental health or psychological focus, but it draws from a range of interdisciplinary sources, is pertinent to diverse contexts and hopefully of interest to readers in the fields of philosophical anthropology, philosophy of mental health and existentialism and psychotherapy. I imagine it may be of negative, argumentative interest to some theologians, anthropologists, psychologists, social scientists and related lay readers. Although more implicitly than explicitly, the message running throughout the book is that the kind of world we live in, and that we *are*, cyclically determines how we feel and think. We will disagree about what kind of world it is, but I hope we might agree that the totality of our history and surroundings has much more impact on us than simply what goes round in our heads.

Depressive realism can be defined, described and contextualised in several ways. Its first use appears to have been by Alloy and Abramson (1979) in a paper describing a psychology experiment comparing the judgements of mildly depressed and non-depressed people. It is necessary to make some clarification at the outset about 'clinical depression'. I do not believe that depression is a desirable state, or that those who are severely depressed are more accurate in their evaluations of life than others (Carson et al., 2010). This is not a book advocating suicide as a solution to life's difficulties, nor am I advocating voluntary human extinction, nor is the text intended to promote hatred of humanity. The DR discussed here should not be mistaken for a consensual, life-hating suicide cult even if it includes respect for the challenging views of Benatar (2006) and Perry (2014). Nor can one assume that all 'depressives' necessarily

2 Introduction

have permanently and identically pessimistic worldviews, nor indeed that the lines drawn by the psychological professionals between all such mood states are accurate. But one can ask that the majority worldview that 'life is alright' be set against the DR view that life contains arrestingly negative features (Ligotti, 2010). The strictly psychological use of DR has now expanded into the world of literary criticism, for example, in Jeffery's (2011) text on Michel Houellebecq. It is this second, less technical sense of DR on which I focus mainly in this book, that is, on the way in which some of us perceive and construe the world in dismal terms and believe our construal to be truer than competing accounts. Inevitably, within this topic we find ourselves involved in rather tedious *realism wars* or epistemological battles between yea-sayers, nay-sayers and those who fantasise that objective evidence exists that can end the wars.

Insofar as any term includes 'realism', we can say it has a philosophical identity. In the case of DR, the philosophical pessimism most closely associated with Schopenhauer may be its natural home. Existentialism is often considered a negative philosophy, and sometimes wholly nihilistic, but in fact it includes or allows for several varieties of worldview. DR receives the same kind of criticism as existentialism often has, which is that it is less an explicit philosophy than a mood, or a rather vague expression of the personalities, projections and opinions of certain writers or artists. Depressive realism as it is translated from psychology to philosophy can be said to refer to the belief that phenomena are accurately perceived as having negative weighting. Put differently, we can say that 'the truth about life' always turns out to be more negative than positive, and hence *any* sustained truth-seeking must eventually find itself mired in unpleasant discoveries.

We then come to synonyms or closely related terms and ideas. These include, in alphabetical order, absurdism, anthropathology, antihumanism, cynicism, depressionism, disenchantment, emptiness, existential anxiety and depression, futilitarianism, meaninglessness, melancholia, misanthropy, miserabilism, nihilism, pessimism, radical scepticism, rejectionism, *tedium vitae*, tragedy, tragicomedy or *Weltschmerz*. We could add saturninity, melancology and other terms if we wanted to risk babellian excess, or flag up James Joyce's 'unhappitants of the earth' as a suitable descriptor for DRs. We could stray into Buddhist territory and call up the concepts of *samsara* and *dukkha*. I do not claim that such terms are synonymous or that those who would sign up to DR espouse them all but they are closely associated, unless you are a semantically obsessive philosopher. Dienstag (2006) denies any necessary commonality between different intellectual expressions of pessimism, and Weller (2011) demonstrates a connoisseurship of nuances of nihilism. Kushlev et al. (2015) point out that sadness and unhappiness are not identical. But Daniel (2013) stresses the *assemblage* of melancholy, and Bowring (2008) provides a very useful concise history, geography and semantics of melancholy.

Here is one simple illustration of how the shades of DR blend into one, not in any linear progression but pseudo-cyclically. The DR often experiences the *weariness* of one who has seen it all before, is bored and has had enough; the *melancholy* of the one who feels acutely the elusiveness and illusion of happiness, the impermanence of life and always smells death in the air; the *pessimism* of one whose prophetic intuition knows that all proposed quasi-novel solutions must eventually fade to zero; the *nihilism* of one whose folly-spotting and illusion-sensing radar never rests; the *depression* of one whose black dog was always there, returns from time to time and may grow a little blacker in old age; the *sorrowful incredulity* at the gullible credulity of hope-addicts and faith-dealers; the *deep sadness* of one who travels extensively and meets many people whose national and personal suffering is written all over their faces; and the *bleakly aloof fundamentalism* of one who believes his epistemology to be superior to other, always shallower accounts. In some cases an extreme form of DR may tip into contemptuous or active nihilism, for example, DeCasseres's (2013) 'baleful vision'. But DR need not be, seldom is, a state of maximum or unchanging bleakness or sheer unhappiness, and many DRs like Cioran, Beckett and Zapffe could be very funny, as is Woody Allen. But grey-skies thinking is the DR's natural default position and ambivalence his highest potential.

A broad, working definition of depressive realism runs as follows: depressive realism is a worldview of human existence as essentially negative. To qualify this, we have to say that some DRs regard the 'world' (everything from the cosmos to everyday living) as wholly negative, as a burdensome absurdity, while some limit its negativity to human experience, or to certain aspects or eras of humanity or to sensate life. 'Existence is no good at all' probably covers the first outlook (see Ligotti, 2010), and 'existence contains much more bad than good' the second (Benatar, 2006). We might also speak of dogmatic DR and a looser, attitudinal DR that seeks dialogue. Critics of DR, of whom there are many as we shall see, often joke lamely about the perceived glass half empty mentality underlying this view, and tirelessly point out the cliché that a glass half empty is half-full. DR may not deny that life includes or seems to include some positive values, sometimes, but it is founded on the belief, the assertion, that it is overall more negative than positive. And, depending on what the glass is half-full *of*, the DR may regard it as worthless, tasteless, poisonous or ultimately futile to drink.

The succinct ingredients of DR are perhaps as follows. The human species is over-developed into two strands, the clever and inventive, and the destructive and distressing, all stemming from evolutionarily accidental surplus consciousness. We have developed to the point of outgrowing the once necessary God myth, confronting the accidental origins of everything and realising that our individual lives end completely at death. We have to live and grow old with these sad and stubborn facts. We must sometimes look at the vast night sky and see our diminutive place reflected in it, and we realise that our species' existence itself is freakishly limited and all our earthly purposes are ultimately for nought. We can never organise optimal living conditions for ourselves, and we realise that our complex societies contain abundant absurdities. World population increases, information overload increases and new burdens outweigh any benefits of material progress however clever and inventive we are. We claim to value truth but banish these facts from our consciousness by all manner of mendacious, tortuous mental and behavioural devices. The majority *somehow* either denies all of the above or manages not to think about it. But it unconsciously nags at even the most religious and optimistic, and the compulsion to deny it drives fundamentalist religious revival, capitalist growth, war and mental illness.

Depressive realism may generate a range of attitudes from decisive suicidality or leaden apathy through to cheerful cynicism, eloquent disenchantment and compassionate or violent nihilism. We can argue that everyone has a worldview whether implicit or explicit, unconscious or conscious, inarticulate or eloquent. Wilhelm von Humboldt is credited with the origins of the concept, using the term *Weltansicht* (world meaning), with *Weltanschauung* arriving a little later with Kant and Hegel. DR may contain idiosyncratic affects, perceptions and an overall worldview, the scale of negativity of which fluctuates. It may be embodied at an early age or emerge later with ageing and upon reflection, or after suffering a so-called 'nadir experience', and may even be overturned, although this event is probably rare. Often, we cannot help but see the world in the way we happen to see it, whether pessimistically or optimistically, even if our moods sometimes fluctuate upwards or downwards. Typically, no matter how broad-minded or open to argument we consider ourselves to be, we all feel that we are right. The DR certainly fits this position, often regarding himself as a relentlessly sceptical truth-seeker where others buy into complacent thought and standard social illusions. The person who has no particular take on existence, who genuinely takes each day or moment as it comes, is arguably rare.

We should ask what it is that is depressed in DR and what it is to which the realism points. Melancholy was once the more common term, depression simply meaning something being pushed downwards, as in dejected spirits. This downwardness places depression in line etymologically with the downwardness of pessimism, not to mention countless metaphors such as Bunyan's trough of despond. From the 17th century depression gained its clinical identity but the roots lie in much earlier humoral theory. Whichever metaphor is employed, however, we might ask why 'upwards' is implied to be the norm, and in what sense 'downwards' should be applied to 'unhappy consciousness'. Heaven has always been located upwards and hell downwards. More accurate metaphors for depression might involve inward or horizontal states. But this would still leave the question of why outwardness and verticality should be regarded as more normal, or the view of the depressed, melancholic, downward, inward or horizontal human being as less acceptable or normal than its opposite, unless on purely statistical grounds.

I think it is fair and proper to make my own position as transparently clear as possible. In spite of critiques of writing from 'the view from nowhere', most academic writing persists in a quasi-objective style resting on the suspiciously erased person of the author. Like most DRs, my personality and outlook has always included a significantly depressive or negative component. I was once diagnosed in my early 30s in a private psychotherapy clinic as having chronic mild depression. I have often been the butt of teasing and called an Eeyore or cynic. I am an atheist. I have had a fair amount of therapy during my life but in looking back I have to say that (a) none of that therapy has fundamentally changed the way I experience life, and (b) my mature belief is that I was always this way, that is, someone with a 'depressive outlook'. Only quite recently have I come to regard this as similar to the claim made by most gay people that they were born gay, or have been gay for as long as they remember, that they do not think of themselves in pathological terms and they do not believe homosexuality to be a legitimate object for therapeutic change. I do not mean to say that people who experience clinical depression should not have therapy if they wish to, nor even that it does not sometimes help. Rather, I believe the assumption should not be made that depressive or negative views about life and experience necessarily correlate with psychological illness. Since I have worked in the counselling and psychotherapy field for about 35 years, I have some explaining to do, which appears mainly in Chapter 6.

Appearing in the series *Explorations in Mental Health* as this book does, I should like to give a brief sense of location here. In truth this is an interdisciplinary subject that by its nature has no exclusive home. On the other hand, given my academic background, there are some clear links with psychology, psychotherapy and counselling. On the question of mental health, the contribution of DR is to re-examine assumptions about 'good' mental health and in particular to challenge the standard pathological view of depression as sick, and with therapists as having a clinical mandate to pronounce on everything with depressive or gloomy connotations. The line between so-called existential anxiety and so-called death and health anxiety can be a fine one, and we should question the agonised revisions and diagnostic hyperinflation by the contributors to the *DSM* over such matters (APA, 2013; Frances, 2014). DR seriously questions the standard assumption in cognitive behaviour therapy that depressed individuals must have cognitive distortions, and indeed reverses this to ask whether DRs might have a more objective grasp of reality than others, and a stubborn refusal to embrace illusion. In conducting this challenge we are taken well beyond psychology into ontology, history, the philosophy of mental health and other disciplines. The mission of this book is hardly to revolutionise the field of mental health, but it is in part to reassess the link between perceived depression, pessimism and negative worldviews.

But a book of this kind emerges not only from a personal position and beliefs. I may experience my share of low mood, insomnia, conflict and death anxiety, but my views are also informed abundantly by wide reading, observations of everyday life and friends. Mirroring the 'blind, pitiless indifference and cruelty of nature' (Dawkins, 2001), I see around me a man in his 80s passing his days in the fog of Alzheimer's, another in his 70s with Parkinson's disease, a woman suffering from many sad medical after-effects of leg amputation, another woman suffering from menopausal mood swings, couples revealing the cracks in their allegedly smooth relationships, several young men struggling gloomily to find any fit between their personalities and the workplace, colleagues putting a brave face on amid insane institutional pressures and the list of merely first world suffering could go on and on. The sources of this common brutalism are biological and social. The examples of suffering easily outnumber any clear examples of the standard optimistic depiction of happy humans, yet this latter narrative continues to assert itself, backed up by cheerful statistics and miserabilism-countering examples. I argue that human life contains many glaringly tragic and depressing components and the denial or minimisation of these adds yet another level of depression.

The lead characters in DR will emerge during the book. It may be useful here, however, to mention those who feature prominently in the DR gallery. These include Gautama Buddha, Arthur Schopenhauer, Giacomo Leopardi, Philipp Mainländer, Thomas Hardy, Edgar Saltus, Sigmund Freud, Samuel Beckett, E.M. Cioran, Peter Wessel Zapffe, Thomas Ligotti, John Gray, David Benatar and Michel Houellebecq. One of the admitted difficulties in such billing is that those still alive might well disown membership of this or any group. Another problem is who can really be excluded: for example, why not include Kierkegaard, Nietzsche, Dostoevsky, Kafka, Camus? As well as the so-called greats, we should pause to remember more minor writers, for example, the Scottish poet James Thomson (1834–82) whose *The City of Dreadful Night* captures perfectly many DR themes (see Chapter 4). Sloterdijk (1987) included in his similar 'cabinet of cynics' an idiosyncratic trawl from Diogenes to Heidegger; Feld's (2011) 'children of Saturn' features Dante and Ficino. In truth DRs may be scattered both interdisciplinarily and transhistorically (Breeze, 2014). To some extent questions of DR membership are addressed in the text, but it is true to say such discriminations are not my main focus.

This book is structured loosely by disciplines in order to demonstrate the many sources and themes involved. My treatment of these disciplines will not satisfy experts in those disciplines and must appear at times naïve, imprecise or inaccurate, but these fields impinge on us, claim to define how we live and suffer and what remedies might exist. In another kind of civilisation we might have no such epistemological divisions. I look at how these disciplines inform DR but also use DR as critical leverage to examine their shortcomings. Hence, Chapter 1 excavates some of the relevant evolutionary and common historical themes. Chapter 2 looks at some religious themes and the theologies explicating these, as well as the contemporary fascination with spirituality and its downsides. In Chapter 3 I examine a number of philosophical themes connecting with DR. Some examples in literature and film are analysed in Chapter 4. Psychology comes into focus in Chapter 5, to be complemented and contrasted with psychotherapy and the psychological therapies in Chapter 6. In Chapter 7 socio-political themes are scrutinised insofar as they illustrate DR. I then move on to science, technology and the future in Chapter 8, again in order to depict the dialectic between these and DR. The 'lifespan and everyday life' is the focus of Chapter 9, which takes a partial turn away from academic disciplines to the more experiential. Arguments against DR, as comprehensive as I can make them in a concise form, comprise Chapter 10, while the final chapter envisages the possible utility of DR.

One of the many things DRs find depressing about the societies we live in is that those of us shaped ironically by twisted educational systems to think and write about such matters, and lucky to find a half-accommodating employment niche, are likely to be in or associated with academia. This institution has survived for many centuries and in spite of its elitist niche remains somewhat influential, although far less influential than its personnel imagine. In its current form it is being ravaged by the so-called new public management but at the same time in its social science, arts and humanities departments is defiantly dominated by left-wing academics whose writing style is often highly symbolic, obfuscatory, arguably often meaningless (Sokal, 2009) and designed for coded communication with a mere minutiae of the general population, that is, academic peers. On the other hand, academia can also suffer from a kind of censorship-by-demand-for-evidence, meaning that common observation, subjectivity and anecdote are erased or downgraded and a statistics-inebriated tyranny reigns supreme. Once when presenting some of the themes in this book to an academic 'research group', I was told I had cherry-picked too many bad examples, as if my colleagues were all paragons of balanced argument and nothing short of watertight pseudo-objectivity could be tolerated: in my view this itself is an example of silencing the DR nihilism that threatens an uncritically 'life is good' assumption. A dilemma facing anyone who hopes to capture the essence of depressive realism – and the *parrhesia* within it – concerns the style in which to write and the assumptions and allusions to make. Universities seem barely fit for purpose any longer, or their purpose is unclear and some have predicted their demise (Readings, 1997; Evans, 2005). This should not surprise us – on the contrary, we should learn to expect such decline as an inescapable part of the entropy of human institutions – but it is a current aspect of our depressing social landscape.

I have only partly followed the academic convention of obsessively citing evidence and precise sources of evidence. In some cases, where no references are given, my figures and examples derive from unattributed multiple internet sources; I do not necessarily make any claims to authority or accuracy, and the reader should check on sources if he or she has such a need. In many instances I use terms such 'many people believe', which might irritate conventional social scientists. I also use anecdote, opinion and naturalistic observations fairly freely. Academic discourse is, I think, very similar to the 'rhetoric' exposed by Michelstaedter (2004), in contrast with the persuasion of personally earned insights and authentic observation, as Kierkegaard too would have recommended.

A confession. What appears above is what is expected of a writer, a logical outline, a promise of reading pleasures to come and of finding and offering

8 Introduction

meaning even in the teeth of meaninglessness (a trick accomplished by the sophistry of Critchley [1997], among other academic prestidigitators). As I moved from the publisher's acceptance of my proposal to the task of actual composition I began to wonder if I could in fact do it. 'Let's do this thing' is a common American expression of committed and energetic project initiation. As befits a text on depressive realism, the author is bedevilled by doubt: more of a Beckettian 'is this thing even worth beginning?' The topic is so massive that one is suffocated on all sides by the weight of precedents and related information, the beckoning nuances, the normative opposition to it and the hubris of attempting it. I anguished over the possibility of a subtitle, something like 'perspectives on pointlessness', that might convey a mixture of nihilism and humour. Such are our needs for and struggles with sublimation, and our neophilia, that it is tempting not to bother. However, here it is.

References

Alloy, L.B. & Abramson, L.Y. (1979) Judgement of contingency in depressed and non-depressed students: Sadder but wiser? *Journal of Experimental Psychology: General,* 108, 441–485.
APA (2013) *Diagnostic and Statistical Manual of Mental Disorders (5th edn.).* Washington, DC: American Psychiatric Publishing.
Benatar, D. (2006) *Better Never to Have Been.* Oxford: Oxford University Press.
Bowring, J. (2008) *A Field Guide to Melancholy.* Harpenden: Oldcastle Books.
Breeze, J.M. (2014) *Beyond the Kinship of Pessimism: Beckett's Schopenhauer.* Unpublished PhD thesis, University of East Anglia.
Carson, R.C., Hollon, S.D. & Shelton, R.C. (2010) Depressive realism and clinical depression. *Behaviour Research and Therapy,* 48 (4), 257–265.
Critchley, S. (1997) *Very Little . . . Almost Nothing: Death, Philosophy, Literature.* London: Routledge.
Daniel, D. (2013) *The Melancholy Assemblage: Affect and Epistemology in the English Renaissance.* New York: Fordham University Press.
Dawkins, R. (2001) *River Out of Eden: A Darwinian View of Life.* London: Phoenix.
DeCasseres, B. (2013) *Anathema! Litanies of Negation.* Baltimore, MA: Underworld Amusements.
Dienstag, J.F. (2006) *Pessimism: Philosophy, Ethics, Spirit.* Princeton, NJ: Princeton University Press.
Evans, M. (2005) *Killing Thinking: The Death of the Universities.* London: Continuum.
Feld, A.N. (2011) *Melancholy and the Otherness of God: A Study of the Hermeneutics of Depression.* Lanham, MA: Lexington.
Frances, A. (2014) *Saving Normal: An Insider's Revolt against Out-of-Control Psychiatric Diagnosis, DSM-5, Big Pharma, and the Medicalization of Ordinary Life.* New York: Harper Collins.
Jeffreys, B. (2011) *Anti-Matter: Michel Houellebecq and Depressive Realism.* Winchester: Zero Books.
Kushlev, K., Dunn, E.W. & Lucas, R.E. (2015) Higher income is associated with less daily sadness but not more daily happiness. *Social Psychological and Personality Science.* Doi: 10.1177/ 194855061.
Ligotti, T. (2010) *The Conspiracy Against the Human Race.* New York: Hippocampus Press.
Michelstaedter, C. (2004) *Persuasion and Rhetoric.* New Haven, CT: Yale University Press.

Perry, S. (2014) *Every Cradle Is a Grave: Rethinking the Ethics of Birth and Suicide.* Charleston, WV: Nine-Banded Books.

Readings, B. (1997) *The University in Ruins.* Cambridge, MA: Harvard University Press.

Sloterdijk, P. (1987) *Critique of Cynical Reason.* Minneapolis, MN: University of Minnesota Press.

Sokal, A. (2009) *Beyond the Hoax: Science, Philosophy and Culture.* Oxford: Oxford University Press.

Weller, S. (2011) *Modernism and Nihilism.* Houndmills: Palgrave Macmillan.

Chapter 1

Big history, anthropathology and depressive realism

Can we say there is something intrinsically fantastic (unlikely), admirable (beautifully complex) and simultaneously tragic (entropically doomed from the outset) about the universe? And about ourselves, the only self-conscious part of the universe as far as we know, struggling to make sense of our own existence, busily constructing and hoping for explanations even as we sail individually and collectively into oblivion? Was the *being* or something that came out of nothing ever a good thing (a random assertion of will in Schopenhauerian terms), a good thing for a while that then deteriorated, a good thing that has its ups and downs but will endure or a good thing that must sooner or later end? Or perhaps neither good nor bad? Depressive realism looks not only to the distant future but into the deepest past, interpreting it as ultimately negatively toned.

It is quite possible and indeed common practice for depressive realists and others to explicate their accounts without recourse to history. It appears that much contemporary academic discourse, certainly in the social sciences, is tacitly structured abiologically and ahistorically, as if in spite of scientific accounts we have not yet accepted any more than creationists that we are blindly evolved and evolving beings. In other words, in spite of much hand-wringing, many maintain a resignedly agnogenic position as regards the origins of the human malaise: *we do not and may never know the causes.* But we have not appeared from nowhere, we are not self-creating or God-created, we were not born as a species a few hundred or a few thousand years ago, we are not in any deep sense merely Plato's heirs. Neither Marxist dialectical materialism nor Engels' dialectics of nature capture the sheer temporal depth of evolution and its ultimate cosmogony (Shubin, 2014). Existence, beyond the animal drive to survive, is ateleological and unpromising. Religious and romantic teleologies largely avoid examination of our material roots and probable limits. From a certain DR perspective it is not only the future that has a dismal hue; an analysis of the deep past also yields much sorry material.

My preference is to begin with certain historical and materialist questions. The reasoning behind this is that (a) we have accounts of and claims to explain the existence of life as once benign but having become at some stage corrupt; (b) we might find new, compelling explanations for the negative pathways taken by humanity; (c) recorded observations of human tragedy that can be loosely called depressive realism are found in some of the earliest literature; (d) this procedure helps us to compare large scale and long-term DR propositions with relevant micro-phenomena and transient patterns. This anchorage in deep history does not necessarily imply a materialist reductionism to follow but it tends, I believe, to show a ceaselessly adaptive, evolutionarily iterative process and entropic trajectory via complexity.

The emerging disciplines of deep and big history challenge the arbitrary starting points, divisions and events of traditional history by going back to the earliest known of cosmic and non-human events, charting any discernible patterns and drawing tentative conclusions. Spier (2011) offers an excellent condensed account of this kind, but we probably need to add as a reinforcer the argument from Kraus (2012) that *something from nothing* is not only possible but inevitable and explicable by scientific laws. Indeed, it is necessary to begin here as a way of further eroding theistic claims that want to start with God and thereby insist on God's (illusory) continuing sustenance and guiding purpose. It is not the *creatio ex nihilo* of the mythological, pre-scientific God, the omnipotent being who brought forth the universe from chaos that any longer helps us to understand our world, but modern science. We do not know definitively how we evolved, but we have convincing enough causal threads at our disposal. Here I intend to sift through those of most interest in exploring the question of why our world has become such a depressing place.

We are animals but apparently higher animals, so far evolved beyond even our nearest relatives that some regard human beings as of another order of nature altogether. Given the millennia of religious belief that shaped our picture of ourselves, the Darwinian revolution even today is not accepted by all. Even some scientists who purport to accept the standard evolutionary account do not seem to accept our residual animal nature emotionally (Tallis, 2011). But it is important to begin by asking about the life of wild animals. They must defend themselves against predators by hiding or fighting, and they must eat by grazing, scavenging or predation; they must reproduce and where necessary protect their young. Many animals spend a great deal of their time asleep, and some play. Social animals cultivate their groups by hunting together, communicating or grooming. Some animals protect their territory, build nests or rudimentary homes and a few make primitive tools; some migrate, and some maintain hierarchical structures. Most animals live relatively short lives, live with constant risk and are vigilant.

However it happened, human beings differ from animals in having developed a consciousness linked with tool-making, language and massive, highly structured societies that have taken us within millennia into today's complex, earth-spanning and nature-dominating civilisation. Wild animals certainly suffer – contrary to idyllic fantasies of a harmonious nature – but their suffering is mostly acute, resulting from injury, hunger and predation, and their lives are not extended beyond their natural ability to survive. Our ingenuity and

12 Big history, anthropathology and depressive realism

suffering are two sides of the same coin. Weapon-making and co-operation allowed us to rise above constant vulnerability to predators, but our lives are now often too safe, bland and boring, since we have forfeited the purpose of day-to-day survival. We have also benefited from becoming cleverer at the cost of loss of sensory acuity. Accordingly, and with painful paradox, we are driven to seek 'meaning' and we are gratuitously violent (Glover, 2001; White, 2012). Animals have no such problems.

How and when did our two-sided distinctiveness come about? In order to get at this topic we need to consider some fundamentals. The universe is thought to be probably 13.7 billion years old, the earth 4.5 billion years old and the origins of life lie 3.7 billion years ago. It is reckoned that five major extinction events have occurred since 440 million years ago (MYA), the most recent being 65 MYA in which large animals like dinosaurs perished. Another is sometimes predicted to occur within the present century. We live in a relatively hospitable interglacial period, but various ice ages have determined migrations with survival at stake and sometimes intergroup conflicts resulting in war and extermination.

The appearance of the great apes is dated to about 15 MYA and *Homo australopithecus* 5.8 to 3.5 MYA. Australopithecus is thought to have had a brain 35% the size of modern human brains, which average at about 1200–1400 cc; and human brain size has increased evolutionarily in relation to body size. The divergence of the human line from chimpanzees is usually put at 5 to 7 MYA. Use of tools may date from over 2.6 MYA, about the same time perhaps that a transition occurred from a mainly vegetarian to an omnivorous diet. The discovery and control of fire is sometimes dated to about 1.9 MYA, when primitive cooking may have begun, which in turn probably contributed significantly to our increased brain size and bodily changes (Wrangham, 2010). The exodus of *Homo erectus* from Africa may date from 1.8 MYA, but the exodus of modern humans is now often put at 75 KYA. Religion may date back to as early as 500,000 (500 KYA), but some put that figure at a mere 50 KYA. By some accounts both primitive speech and the opposable thumb date to about 400 KYA, but some place speech closer to 150 KYA. *Homo sapiens* can be traced to 200 KYA, about the same time as human settlements. Trade may date from about 150 KYA. Human burial originates from about 100 KYA. One disputed account estimates that schizophrenia may date from about 80 KYA (Horrobin, 2001). Another has it that artificial clothing dates to about 72 KYA. Forty-three KYA saw humans in Europe and 12 KYA the evolution of light skin in Europeans. From around 12 KYA we also see the move away from hunter-gatherer existence to the development of agriculture (domestication of plants and animals) and high levels of warfare. The origins of patriarchy are disputed but may date from between 12 to 6 KYA, if not much earlier. Picture writing comes from around 8.5 KYA and use of numbers and characters 5.2 KYA. The wheel is found from about 6 KYA. Precise dating and comprehensive evolutionary narrative is obviously not my aim here, nor is there anything like consensus among archaeologists. Indeed, Wade (2007) believes that 90% of human history is irretrievably lost to all efforts at rediscovery. But these few examples merely give some flavour of timescale and linearity and set the scene.

In Jaynes' (1976) unusual thesis, a bicameral mind existed prior to the subjective mind we know today, and it was characterised by a hallucinatory voice of God or gods commanding human beings. This bicamerality, mediated through the brain's right hemisphere, is a mere 3,000 years or so old, and we evolved obedient to its voice, living lives of a somewhat robotic quality. Somehow the earliest proto-language which partly distinguished us from animals was hijacked by a dominant brain function. Due to various historical catastrophes, the bicameral mind started to break down, religion gradually fragmenting, authority being lost and subjective judgement coming into prominence. Admittedly unlikely in its entirety, Jaynes's bicameral paradigm yet retains some explanatory power. It certainly helps to underline the enormous power religion still holds in an increasingly scientific, rational world, and why so many hanker for a higher authority. McGilchrist (2009), too, believes that the bilaterality of the brain is key to understanding human history and waywardness but regards Jaynes' account as untenable and back-to-front. To precis McGilchrist's view, it is 'left hemisphere bad, right hemisphere good,' or to be fairer it is a matter of both being necessary but the left hemisphere having become too dominant, and dangerously so. This latter account is very popular among anti-science arts and humanities observers and those who wish to see a 're-enchantment of the world'.

Anthropathology

Among the main explanatory candidates for what I call anthropathology, or human sickness, fallenness or waywardness, are the following: (1) the view that distinctive human consciousness arose gradually from perhaps about 2 MYA, with the double-edged features of accelerating creativity and cleverness, and tribal aggression, territoriality, deceptiveness and alienation. Tattersall (2004), however, argues that changes in consciousness have been rare and episodic, with the contrast between Neanderthals and Cro-Magnons about 30 to 40 KYA being the most significant critical threshold and constituting an 'incidental exaptation' towards symbolic consciousness. (2) A proposed 'Fall' or major, disastrous climatic and historical event that changed everything for the worse about 10 KYA. (3) An era of intensive agricultural settlement coupled with the advent of social hierarchies, formal religions, symbolic regulation and so on. The most compelling of these to my mind is number (1). I originally considered (2) and (3) very likely (Feltham, 2007) but I have never subscribed to either of two further views, that is (4) the modern, industrial era and capitalism as the culprits, or (5) our woes being minimal, temporary and soon to be rectified. Broadly then, I believe that Zapffe (1933) was right to name surplus consciousness (however so dated) as culpable. We tragically evolved beyond the point that it was useful and harmonious for us to evolve; paradoxically we 'know too much' and at the

14 Big history, anthropathology and depressive realism

same time we practise repression and lack wisdom. Currently, we cannot shake off ancient habits of violence, illusion, deception and greed; and our dysfunctionality may doom us, for example, via anthropogenic climate change and our unwillingness to face up to it.

Varki and Brower (2014) propose an unusual thesis regarding anthropogeny. Rather than beginning with the question of why humans have such an advanced consciousness, we might ask why other animals have not come anywhere near this threshold. Using 'theory of mind' (ToM) instead of consciousness as their guiding concept, the authors suggest first that a ToM is required in order to appreciate that others have minds like oneself and vice versa, and secondly that witnessing the deaths or corpses of others shocks one into realising that this is also one's own fate. But in evolutionary terms this devastating insight cannot be afforded since its depressing impact would rob any creature of the imperative to survive and would undermine natural selection. Accordingly, death awareness could not have arisen, claim the authors, without a corresponding cognitive mechanism to override it. This is, of course, self-deception, the faculty that has allowed us to survive, multiply and prosper. Although Varki and Brower do not use this term, we might conceive of human progress as hysterical in its grandiose expanse: indeed, these authors regard optimism as self-deceptive. Self-deception, lying and cheating, which partly characterise humanity, help to explain too why in large societies we will always have some level of crime and mental illness, and why we are bedevilled by religious denial of reality.

After bipedalism, our opposable thumbs, Swiss Army knife-style hands (Tallis, 2003) and fine hand-eye co-ordination, our large brain and ability to innovate, all made us more-than-animal and able gradually to transform the earth, to dominate it (Taylor, 2010). Fagan (2015) argues somewhat similarly that our dominance of animals has both advanced and shaped us; and Rowdon (2008) and Masson (2015) remind us that we are far more gratuitously cruel and violent than animals. But our actions also progressively and reciprocally shaped our brains so that we could only move in this 'artificial' or 'unnatural' direction. To this gradual development we might add evolutionary mismatch theory: living as hunter-gatherers in small populations worked quite well for thousands of years, but some combination of factors probably forced us out of the open savannah into dense communities and highly organised, symbolic cultures that have exacted a heavy toll across the last 10,000 years (Gluckman & Hanson, 2008; Wells, 2010). It is this overall irreversible push towards a humanity dominated by myth, thought and technology that has brought us to our current problematic state. While outgrowing religious myths, we nevertheless reflect something like Christian original sin in our stubborn and destructive mental and behavioural traits. Perhaps our consciousness may be wired like a Möbius strip, with creativity and self-deceptive destructiveness thoroughly entwined.

The novelist Kurt Vonnegut (1994) depicts a defunct human species a million years ago that perished due to its troublesome big brains. A variety of brain-blaming theories names the left brain, runaway brain, social brain and big brain (Lynch & Granger, 2008) as responsible for our ills. Brain size accounts for our advanced cognitive capacities but also indicates that individual development after birth crucially relies on dependency and nurture well through childhood, and the brain is probably not fully formed until the mid-20s. This means that human birth is highly susceptible to accidents and that human beings are especially vulnerable in adolescence. Since most human societies protect their young and vulnerable members, developmental problems do not result in death and elimination from the gene pool to the extent they would in the wild. But another view of the brain is the evolutionary tripartite one of MacLean (1990), which posits reptilian, limbic and neocortical components. Although not largely in favour today, affective neuroscience uses this tripartite model to focus on the emotional functions of humans that cognitive neuroscience tends to downplay. One of its key suggestions is that evolutionarily earlier aspects of arousal survive within us that retain the power to reassert themselves, particularly under stress. An ongoing battle exists, too, between proponents of the idea that our ignorance or denial of brain mechanisms is responsible for many of our woes (Churchland, 2013) versus the idea that we are rational free agents (Tallis, 2011).

Perhaps emotionally, many of us remain unconsciously suspended somewhere between attachment to religious teleological myths and to the assumption that science is definitively taking care of everything. We may concede that life can seem accidental and chaotic, yet we are addicted to, indeed wired for, the principle of patternicity, an illusion of durable order. Marcus's (2009) concept of the *kluge*, the makeshift engineering mechanisms that evolution produces to facilitate survival, suggests that kluge-like adaptations stay with us even when they have no further adaptive value and can become hindrances. In other words, we cannot simply shed those parts of our mind and behaviour that become obstacles. Often, we override them but sometimes they retain or seize control. We like to regard ourselves as agent-selves with free will, but we are probably more like composite kluge-units stumbling through life as well as possible. Arguably, however, life (inwardly and outwardly) has become so complex and contradictory that our brains cannot cope well and the result is epidemic confusion, desperately clinging to past knowledge and struggling to keep up with, assess and adapt to new information. Tainter (1988) analyses several past societies for clues to the components of their collapse, but it remains possible that our assumption that we are above the bad luck or poor decisions of Minoans, Mayans, Chacoans, Romans and others will prove disastrously incorrect.

Recent and impending human development and evolution

Cochran and Harpending (2009) and Wade (2014) have both argued against assumptions that evolution has stopped ('evolutionary stasis') or slowed down dramatically. Indeed, in the first text, the anthropologist authors argue that the 'great leap forward' of about 50,000 years ago has been superseded by a rate of

16   Big history, anthropathology and depressive realism

evolution 60 times faster than the average rate of evolution characterising our species' past. Drawing on parallels with domesticated plants and animals, they suggest that accelerated human genetic changes are highly significant. Increases in height and longevity and decrease of age of menarche are just three well-known examples, and in all cases causes are disputed. The interaction between evolution and culture is not easy to pin down. One of their examples, also picked up by Wade, is the apparent intellectual superiority and influence of Ashkenazi Jews, whose IQs are said to average around 112–115 (compared with an overall average IQ of 100) and is underpinned not only by historical obstacles to many forms of employment and a longstanding cultural emphasis on literacy but also by a prohibition on marriage to outsiders. Wade argues that the academically favoured condemnation of the concept of race is untenable, and that one can see as well as measure significant racial and behavioural differences worldwide. Original and continuing genetic explanations partly explain why, in Wade's terms, the West has been so scientifically and technically successful, as well as environmentally rapacious. The Jewish contribution to the West's progress seems in fact positively disproportionate to its population and certainly completely at odds with Nazi myths of Nordic superiority.

Such accounts are contentious, highly emotive and often decried, but they raise topics that are hard to ignore. Many social analysts seek to overcome intergroup or tribalistic problems by insisting that beneath them universal human equality and decency reigns, or will soon reign supreme given the right democratic conditions. In the meantime, the very idea that any group might be superior to another is considered racist anathema, particularly by social scientists who regard their own methodologies as superior to others'. But no-one outside laboratories can control what genes (or spontaneous cultural trends) do, and it is possible that the divisions between groups will *increase* and bring a conflicted and more hierarchical future. Contrary to the view that there are only economic and political barriers to worldwide equality and co-operation, it is quite possible that genetic and accidental forces may take humanity into an ever more divided future. This is already on the cards in the tension between attitudes towards mass migration and Islamic religion, and in threatened depletion of essential resources. But we see it too in the posthumanist challenge, suggesting an enhanced group of humans at one end of the scale, and Luddite rejectors or rejects at the other end (Garreau, 2005). Right-wing dogma will insist on its own version of this possibility, based on mere prejudice. But few are able to predict the outcome of the combined forces of genes, economics, climate change, migration, religio-cultural influences and international conflicts. The maxim 'life is what happens while you're busy making other plans' applies as much at the macro-level as at the individual level. Intellectual conflicts between academics abound. For example, Jared Diamond's geo-determinism is reviled by some; Diamond, like most other academics, utterly rejects the concept of race; Wade, a science writer, is pronounced racist by some, and so on. But these conflicts have little actual effect

Big history, anthropathology and depressive realism   17

on brute events. Productive scholarly disagreement (e.g. Downes & Machery, 2013) arising from open debate is quite different from unconscious tribal conflicts expressed intellectually.

Twenty-first century collective Western human consciousness remains haunted by Nazism and the Holocaust. Even more than the horrors of the First World War (about 37 million deaths); total Second World War casualties (1939–45) 50 to 80 million; Hiroshima (up to 129,000); Stalin's genocide and other atrocities (about 15 to 20 million); Mao's Great Leap Forward (1958–62) is estimated to have killed 45 to 60 million; but the Holocaust probably figures largest and exerts a huge influence. This is attributed to its systematic, industrial-scale, sadistic and racist nature, and also to the history of the Jews as a chronically persecuted people. Comparative, estimated tallies give the Congo Free State genocide (1885–1908) as responsible for between 5 and 22 million deaths; the Holocaust (1933–45) 5 or 6 million; Japanese War Crimes (1937–45) 3 to 10 million; the Red Terror in Ethiopia (1977–78) 30,000 to 500,000; Iraq and Afghanistan War (2001–14) 350,000; and so on. The Transatlantic African slave trade (16th to 19th centuries, up to 10 million or more deaths) is abhorred but also has a lower profile. The relative recency of the Holocaust is one reason for its continuing hyper-moral claim, and probably also its proximity if we are taking a Eurocentric approach. Its effects have included the rightful demonisation of racism, the promotion of human rights and alertness to any signs of dehumanising ethnic or other oppressed and powerless groups. Anti-Semitism is *the* emblematic charge of mass immorality.

Beyond its Jewish core, the Holocaust exerts a massive moral and symbolic pull towards the concept of human rights and their enshrinement in international law. Not only national and ethnic groups but minority groups of gay, lesbian, bisexual and transgender people, the disabled, religious minorities and women, unconsciously gain moral traction from implied associations with Nazi persecution, eugenics and threatened extermination. The language of racism, homophobia, misogyny and Islamophobia is accompanied by an ongoing inquisitorial scrutiny of the words and actions of public figures, on the grounds that demeaning labelling and name-calling is not only appalling in its own right but the first step on the slippery slope towards the next, history-repeating totalitarian nightmare. Such vigilance has an understandable character but also unintended consequences. One of the related trends here is the implicit misandry of much militant feminism, the one-sided critical deconstruction of patriarchy and the idealisation of the future as female (e.g. Konner, 2015). The eugenics terror of the early 20th century may be seen as having swung to its opposite (a phenomenon Jung named *enantiodromia*): older parenting, homosexual parenting via surrogates, international sperm markets, the rise of autism and other problematic conditions and significant changes in population genetics that are as yet not understood. In 2015, for example, a 65-year-old single German woman with 13 children, who had received *in vitro* fertilisation in Ukraine, had quadruplets by caesarean section at six-and-a-half months.

The Holocaust's traumatic and moral aftermath has extended from vigilant protection of Jews to numerous groups (many homosexuals, disabled and mentally ill people and others were, of course, killed in the gas chambers) and to the central discourses and practices of academia, politics, legislation and the media. Quite rightly, attention has focused on actual racism, equal employment opportunities and education regarding respect for differences. But arguably, this trend has taken us to the point where all strong power and unchecked enquiry is suspect, outspokenness on sensitive topics is dangerous and freedom of speech is sometimes compromised by laws of hate speech and anachronistic charges of blasphemy. Vigorous debate is almost impossible and nuances of argument are lost. Opposition to mass (northward and westward) migration, for example, or recommendations for some degree of worldwide population control, are seized upon as racism and the spectre of the Holocaust is invoked. Perhaps this represented a necessary corrective but as with most such correctives it does not recognise when it goes too far (Goldberg, 2009). It works both ways, however, so that opposition to gross capitalist inequalities and scientific hubris can also be easily silenced. It is depressing, or so I assert here, that we are unable to transcend our dualistic antagonisms, so that no alternative exists to the 'I am right and you are wrong' template. Arguably, it is not only depressing but *maddening* that our world is so complex, yet ostensibly analysable in facile bipolar terms, and presided over by intellectuals and politicians who *know* what is right, and that all individuals should know where they stand in our epistemological minefield. I have referred to this elsewhere as 'the dizziness of the choice-drunk thinker' (Feltham, 2015). A problem facing us is whether only an algorithmic future based on artificial intelligence can overcome our current cognitive behaviour of nuance-denying extremism.

This is not merely about Western preoccupation with a valid human rights agenda but a comment upon our moment in history. Democracy, for example, has become an unassailable American (and much wider) perceived moral and political good. But the anti-dictatorial roots of democracy may take us towards a populace of warring interest groups presided over by mediocre, cynical, vote-chasing career politicians. A traumatically sickening historical event, the Holocaust, becomes a justificatory and paranoid back-drop with which to silence many ideas and groups. Soviet communism, its atrocities and its fall, has been exploited by the political right to mock Marxist aspirations and render capitalism unassailable, yet already we see excessive free market capitalism itself rightly coming under fire following recent banking crises and ongoing collusion in excessive carbon emissions. This lurching from one fantasised total solution to another, from right-wing to left-wing moral high ground and utopian ideologies signifies a central problem today. Underpinning the volatile mix of agnosticism, passionate intensity, paralysis and enfeeblement is the sheer size of the human population and its interconnectedness, or rather its irreversible entanglement and profound tribal ancestry (Ehrlich & Ehrlich, 2005). Unrecognised intergenerational trauma dispersed through large group pathologies sows the

Big history, anthropathology and depressive realism   19

seeds of both right-wing and left-wing totalitarianism. And however recent, dramatic and affecting all such events and movements, even these are transient and insignificant against large scale imminent threats to humanity and the earth; and in the entropic long run they mean nothing whatsoever. Indeed none of our Western geopolitical anxieties and predictions means anything in the long run (Spengler, 1991; Gray, 2007), just as none of our anthropocentric agonising significantly affects the earth itself (Lovelock, 2010).

Summary

A tentative and simplified three-point summary schema may help. Whatever collection of factors happened to propel our distinctive human trajectory, we inherited a double-edged species character. First, our ingenuity is twinned with aggressive tribalism, with probable roots in distant mammalian and patriarchal ancestry (Wrangham & Peterson, 1996). Secondly, our deceptive linguistic symbolism is rooted somewhere in the switch from instinctive and sensory-dominated behaviour to language, between co-operative tool-making, dense communities, agriculture and reason (Zerzan, 2002, 2015). Thirdly, our greed, runaway consumerism and capitalist damage, the most recent significant development, stem from the industrial revolution. But all these are nested within each other. We *may* have partially escaped some of our aggressive tribalism (Pinker, 2012) but that level of maturity looks very fragile. We *may* transcend the follies of runaway exploitation and consumerism. But the stubbornest aspect of our species character is our addiction to the complex of ego, thought, symbolism and deception (Bohm, 1994; Trivers, 2011). No reform or revolution will radically change anything while we continue with this. Our persistent woes are not due to the latest right-wing government, nor to late modernity, capitalism, patriarchy or post hunter-gatherer existence: these are merely the consequences of our long-term evolution and the signs of our probable demise.

The importance of a big history account of anthropathology, or cumulative negativity, lies in attempting to explain to ourselves why we encounter the intransigent woes we do. If many of us today feel that life is absurd, futile, boring, damaging, it is unnecessary and I believe unintelligent to persist in the assumption that this is simply, mysteriously, the way it is. We now have a rather compelling hypothesis for the apparent meaninglessness of contemporary life. Human inventiveness has fostered a cumulative complexity that individuals can barely cope with. For all the progress we have made, the flip side also grows exponentially. The further we distance ourselves from raw nature and its threats, the more we also intuit that the cost-benefit ratio is not convincing.

Spier (2011) broadly categorises the development of big states (6,000 years ago); globalisation through geographical exploration (500 years ago); industrialisation (250 years ago); and the information explosion (60 years ago). Across these advances is threaded the rise and fall of empires, brutal wars and genocides, colonisation and slavery, runaway capitalism, fossil fuel use and pollution and

20 Big history, anthropathology and depressive realism

information overload. Blair (2010) demonstrates convincingly that our problem with information growth can be traced back at least 500 years. Indeed, since the Gutenberg printing press in 1440 we have garnered more and more of our information from flat oblong objects in the form of books, television and computer screens. In the Anthropocene we have created, human population and lifespan expands, nuclear annihilation remains a perpetual possibility, biodiversity suffers and anthropogenic climate change threatens devastating upheaval. Well over seven billion individuals struggle to understand their place in this vast interconnected yet alienating world. Some regard us as poised between collectively trashing the earth, being vulnerable to disasters and needing to escape into space towards other planets (e.g., Hawking, 2008). Many deny or ignore most of the above negative assessment, preferring religious explanations for our origins and passive hopes for our salvation, or are simply too overstretched already with infobesity and the competing demands of everyday life and self-maintenance.

Depressive realism can be seen as the beginning of an enquiry, albeit a 'sorrowful investigation', rather than as a state of chronically flattened affect: life is a terrible affliction, but *why* is it so? An evolutionary-historical account gives us a persuasive probabilistic narrative for our current state of affairs. Darwin's pivotal *On the Origin of Species* appeared in 1859, shattering complacent religious assumptions and confronting us with the randomness of natural selection. The Big Bang theory first emerged between the 1920s and 1940s (but is currently challenged by theories of rainbow gravity and a temporally infinite universe), and the structure of DNA was confirmed in 1953. Paleo-archaeological discoveries are still filling out the big picture of our collective past, and neuroscience does likewise with the brain. While we are generating a massive knowledge base and the potential for an objective new scientific trajectory, we are simultaneously undermined by our kluge-clogged past. The development and use of the atom bomb in 1945 attests to the duality of our inventiveness. A rather dismal anthropathological account provides no serviceable illusions or teleological inspiration, but if we could accept these likely reasons for our current plight we might construe our future very differently. Even if this account, along with big data with accurate predictive power, were to demonstrate that we are on an unavoidable path of destruction, we could argue that such a grounded negative prognosis is better than illusory alternatives.

We may choose to see ourselves as a glorious species with infinite potential, or as a species heavily skewed by evolution but on a 'freely chosen' moral path to awareness and change (Miles, 2003), or a cancer on the earth or a species under sentence of death. Diamond (2011) attributes to civilisations some sort of intentionality implying the possibility of wisdom. Let me end this chapter provocatively, however, with Cioran's words, echoing Zapffe's sentiments and those of many other DRs: 'We should have abided by our larval condition, dispensed with evolution, remained incomplete, delighting in the elemental siesta and calmly consuming ourselves in embryonic ecstasy' (1998, p. 108). This scenario also implies a choice that we never had. But here is a rejoinder: that this post-larval existence of ours has been and still is an interesting adventure, if painful and confusing. As we contemplate the loss of biodiversity we are causing, we are probably also the first species to intuit its own long-term non-viability and inevitable extinction. Against this probability is the slim possibility that we are poised to alter our nature and prospects dramatically and positively (see Chapter 8), but the pessimistic default DR position recommends not holding your breath.

References

Blair, A.M. (2010) *Too Much to Know: Managing Scholarly Information before the Modern Age*. New Haven, CT: Yale University Press.

Bohm, D. (1994) *Thought as a System*. London: Routledge.

Churchland, P.S. (2013) *Touching a Nerve: Our Brains, Ourselves*. New York: Norton.

Cioran, E.M. (1998) *The Trouble with Being Born*. New York: Arcade.

Cochran, G. & Harpending, H. (2009) *The 10,000 Year Explosion: How Civilization Accelerated Human Evolution*. New York: Basic Books.

Diamond, J. (2011) *Collapse: How Societies Choose to Survive or Fail*. London: Penguin.

Downes, S.M. & Machery, E. (eds) (2013) *Arguing about Human Nature: Contemporary Debates*. New York: Routledge.

Ehrlich, P. & Ehrlich, A. (2005) *One with Nineveh: Politics, Consumption, and the Human Future*. Washington, DC: Island Press.

Fagan, B. (2015) *The Intimate Bond: How Animals Shaped Human History*. New York: Bloomsbury.

Feltham, C. (2007) *What's Wrong with Us? The Anthropathology Thesis*. Chichester: Wiley.

Feltham, C. (2015) *Keeping Ourselves in the Dark*. Charleston, WV: Nine-Banded Books.

Garreau, J. (2005) *Radical Evolution*. New York: Broadway.

Glover, J. (2001) *Humanity: A Moral History of the 20th Century*. London: Pimlico.

Gluckman, P. & Hanson, M. (2008) *Mismatch: The Lifestyle Diseases Timebomb*. Oxford: Oxford University Press.

Goldberg, J. (2009) *Liberal Fascism: The Secret History of the Left from Mussolini to the Politics of Meaning*. London: Penguin.

Gray, J. (2007) *Black Mass: Apocalyptic Religion and the Death of Utopia*. London: Penguin.

Hawking, S. (2008) *Why We Should Go into Space*. NASA Lecture Series, Los Angeles, 21 April.

Horrobin, D. (2001) *The Madness of Adam and Eve: How Schizophrenia Shaped Humanity*. London: Bantam.

Jaynes, J. (1976) *The Origin of Consciousness in the Breakdown of the Bicameral Mind*. Boston, MA: Houghton-Mifflin.

Konner, M. (2015) *Women after All: Sex, Evolution, and the End of Male Supremacy*. New York: Norton.

Kraus, L. (2012) *A Universe from Nothing: Why There Is Something Rather Than Nothing*. New York: Simon & Schuster.

Lovelock, J. (2010) *The Vanishing Face of Gaia: A Final Warning*. London: Penguin.

Lynch, G. & Granger, R. (2008) *Big Brain: The Origins and Future of Human Intelligence*. New York: Palgrave Macmillan.

MacLean, P.D. (1990) *The Triune Brain in Evolution: Role in Paleocerebral Functions*. New York: Springer.

Marcus, G. (2009) *Kluge: The Haphazard Evolution of the Human Mind*. London: Faber & Faber.

Masson, J.M. (2015) *Beasts: What Animals Can Teach Us about the Origins of Good and Evil.* New York: Bloomsbury.

McGilchrist, I. (2009) *The Master and His Emissary: The Divided Brain and the Making of the Western World.* New Haven, CT: Yale University Press.

Miles, J. (2003) *Born Cannibal: Evolution and the Paradox of Man.* London: IconoKlastic.

Pinker, S. (2012) *The Better Angels of Our Nature: A History of Violence and Humanity.* London: Penguin.

Rowdon, M. (2008) *The Ape of Sorrows: From Stranger to Destroyer: The Inside Story of Humans.* New York: iUniverse.

Shubin, N. (2014) *The Universe Within: A Scientific Adventure.* London: Penguin.

Spengler, O. (1991) *The Decline of the West.* Oxford: Oxford University Press.

Spier, F. (2011) *Big History and the Future of Humanity.* Chichester: Wiley-Blackwell.

Tainter, J. (1988) *The Collapse of Complex Societies.* Cambridge: Cambridge University Press.

Tallis, R. (2003) *The Hand: A Philosophical Inquiry into Human Being.* Edinburgh: Edinburgh University Press.

Tallis, R. (2011) *Aping Mankind: Neuromania, Darwinitis and the Misrepresentation of Humanity.* Durham: Acumen.

Tattersall, I. (2004) What happened in the origins of human consciousness? *The Anatomical Record (Part B: New Anatomy),* 276B: 19–26.

Taylor, T. (2010) *The Artificial Ape: How Technology Changed the Course of Human Evolution.* New York: Palgrave Macmillan.

Trivers, R. (2011) *Deceit and Self-Deception: Fooling Yourself the Better to Fool Others.* London: Allen Lane.

Varki, A. & Brower, D. (2014) *Denial: Self-Deception, False Beliefs and the Origins of the Human Mind.* New York: Twelve.

Vonnegut, K. (1994) *Galapágos.* London: Flamingo.

Wade, N. (2007) *Before the Dawn: Recovering the Lost History of Our Ancestors.* London: Duckworth.

Wade, N. (2014) *A Troublesome Inheritance: Genes, Race and Human History.* New York: Penguin.

Wells, S. (2010) *Pandora's Seed: Why the Hunter-Gatherer Holds the Key to Our Survival.* London: Penguin.

White, M. (2012) *Atrocitology: Humanity's Deadliest Achievements.* Edinburgh: Canongate.

Wrangham, R. (2010) *Catching Fire: How Cooking Made Us Human.* London: Profile.

Wrangham, R. & Peterson, D. (1996) *Demonic Males: Apes and the Origins of Human Violence.* Boston, MA: Houghton-Mifflin.

Zapffe, P.W. (1933/2004) The last messiah. *Philosophy Now,* March/April. Transl. G. Tangenes.

Zerzan, J. (2002) *Running on Emptiness: The Pathology of Civilization.* Los Angeles, CA: Feral House.

Zerzan, J. (2015) *Why Hope? The Stand against Civilization.* Los Angeles, CA: Feral House.

Chapter 2

Religion, spirituality and depressive realism

Although based here on a transparent and forceful atheism, depressive realism does not *require* disbelief in God and is even partially informed by some religious concepts. For example, a number of theologians subscribe to the death of God or theo-thanatology movement, interpreting God as in one way or another beyond being or no longer present, and some avowedly DR writers have been considered not quite fully atheistic. In the arena of godless religions like Buddhism, pessimists like Schopenhauer, Cioran and Beckett were famously sympathetic. Even a bitter judge of existence like Houellebecq has been considered a significantly religious thinker (Betty, 2016) and an arch-figurehead of absurdity like Beckett, too, (Calder, 2012). Mulhall (2005) regards the philosophies of Nietzsche, Heidegger as Wittgenstein, while claiming no religious anchorage, as secular representations of the Christian concept of fallenness. Unamuno (1921/1954), for all his immersion in the tragic, cannot extricate himself from a romantic and religious anthropology.

Areas in which the present DR account parallels religious themes include the original sin of Christianity and the *dukkha* and *maya* of Buddhism and many prophetic and eschatological concerns. These are, of course, complex concepts that I can only hope to partly explicate in this book. It is possible to discuss DR without much reference to religion, but DR has probably intensified enormously since the quantitative undermining of belief in God associated with the Enlightenment project from the 17th century. Philosophical and scientific rationalism began a process of erosion of religious assumptions that Schopenhauer, Darwin, Nietzsche, Marx and Freud deepened. The so-called new atheism associated with Dawkins, Hitchens, Harris and others has most famously challenged the status of religion in the 21st century. It can be easy to forget, too, that the 'God exists-doesn't-exist' dichotomy is not shared by all, some – perhaps including some DRs – declaring that they do not care one way or the other about this debate; they are *apatheists*.

The Abrahamic religions

There is no agreement on when or why rudimentary religion as such began, some placing its origin as far back as 500,000 years, with evidence of burial

24 Religion, spirituality and depressive realism

rituals being placed at around 100,000 years ago and organised religion perhaps 10,000 years ago. Written records suggest that Judaism emanated about 3,500 years ago from Canaan and the surrounding area. Its ancient Israelites became its twelve tribes, who are said to have experienced much famine, slavery and exile. Yahweh, the God of 'ethical monotheism' led the Jews from Egypt and via Moses gave them the Ten Commandments. Archaeologists have not been able to confirm this narrative but some oral history presumably underpins it. From very early times the Jews kept holy scriptures and fostered scholastic academies. The Hebrew Bible features stories of persecution and exile, of a special relationship with God which made them his chosen people, guided by a series of famous prophets. Jewish history is marked by ritual, morality, patriarchy, learning and diaspora, as well as assimilation with Roman and Greek, and later Western cultures. The early Jewish history of persecution and exile finds its counterpart in contemporary anti-Semitism and diaspora. Orthodox Judaism keeps alive religious traditions that go back for centuries, reflecting an attachment to Yahweh and a determination to maintain purity and loyalty. Like all religions, Judaism is complex and fragmented, and it is not possible or necessary to go into doctrinal, social, ethnic or political detail here. What we might posit, however, is that Judaism is characterised to quite some extent by extreme adversity, group narrative, adaptability, philosophical humanism and intellectual and commercial success. As one of the smallest of the major religions by headcount, Judaism makes a disproportionate impression on world affairs.

Its scriptural and devotional traditions are entwined with the emotionally prized concept of a loving, personal God, the importance of human community, endurance of adversity and expectation of reaching the promised land. Original goodness, sin, evil, service to others, faith, awaiting the Messiah, understanding death, heaven and hell are all derived from ancient Jewish texts. We see in Judaism, from a modern critical perspective, the duality of positives and negatives in religion, in the advocacy of love on the one hand and the reality of unreason and tribal conflict on the other. In *Ecclesiastes* we read about the meaninglessness of life – the famous lines 'vanity, vanity, all is vanity' echo up to our own time – and the folly of attempting wisdom; and later interpreters have highlighted its profound pessimism (Sneed, 2012). Religion is not only about prophetic observations, however, but a source of superstition and conflict is rooted in Judaism, which in turn is, as I have argued in Chapter 1, rooted in our deep anthropathological past. Excessive Jewish religiosity resulting in obsessive compulsive disorder and other psychological problems has been commented upon by many Jews themselves (Ellis, 1980; Gerrie, 2011).

Religious conflicts in the Middle East were sharpened in the story of Jesus of Nazareth just over 2,000 years ago. We cannot be certain that Jesus actually existed and we have good reasons to doubt the recorded details of his life if he did, but the account agreed by Christians is that he was the Saviour promised in the Hebrew Bible. Not merely a good man, or a mystical genius, he was both fully human and the 'Son of God' who came to forgive human sin, to

Religion, spirituality and depressive realism   25

die for it and to offer renewed access to God. Jesus Christ is a tragic figure, misunderstood, betrayed by the Jews of his time and crucified by the Romans. But he is also the 'good news' that shows that this life of finiteness and suffering is merely a foretaste of the heaven to come. An alternative reading has also always been that Jesus 'brought back the now', the eternal, innocent present with our original sin washed clean. Christianity renews and expands ancient Judaic morality in the Sermon on the Mount and promises that individual death is not the end. Its morality is understood in most secular society today, if not practised in loving your enemy, resisting being angry, lustful, divorcing and being greedy and anxious. But its insistence on an omnipotent and personal God, and on survival after death, puts it at odds with everything we know from science and observation. Jewish and Christian observations of everyday suffering led to (necessarily pre-scientific) explanations and remedies. Sinful abuse of free will led to adversity, illness and death; prayer, repentance or the laying on of hands brought ease and health. The need for systems of morality has been universal and enduring but religious explanations for bewilderment or adversity relating to cosmology, geology, meteorology, neurology and medicine are now largely redundant and useless. But the problem of religion is deeper even than this. We can easily concede that religions have been necessary in a frightening, pre-scientific era, but their persistence now is an obstacle to understanding and a source of further suffering.

We should pause to remember that much of Christianity, certainly in the Old Testament and notably in the *Book of Revelations*, makes for grim reading. It is saturated with sin and evil and warnings of consequences for failure to obey God. *Psalm* 144/4 famously declares that 'Man is a mere breath [or vapour, or vanity]; his days are like a passing shadow'. The emptiness and transience of human existence, prominent in a DR account, is made very clear in the Bible. Nightmares to come are vividly portrayed for the unrepentant in *Revelations*. Meanwhile, we all forlornly exist in this *vale of tears*. Most religions agree that life contains a large portion of suffering and pain, mitigated by promises that if we engage in the right rituals and maintain faith, all shall be well eventually. Through conditioning, fear, intellectual inadequacy or longing for comfort, some are able to persuade themselves to believe such promises.

While Islam partly rests on Judaic scriptures and honouring Jewish prophets, it also partly rejects them. Muhammad, the last prophet, is said to have had the Qur'an revealed to him by the archangel Gabriel around the years 610–632 CE. Originally passed on orally, it was transcribed by Muhammad's faithful companions. More so than the Christian Bible, the Qur'an is designed for learning and recitation as well as giving copious ethical instruction and eschatological warnings. Reverence for Muhammad, study of the Qur'an and observation of religious traditions are Islam's cornerstones. Scholars, however, do offer conflicting interpretations – for example, as to the condonement of non-Islamic religions. Nevertheless, Islam contains strictures against 'contagion' from non-believers, which can breed pessimism. Pessimism, according to some Islamic

26 Religion, spirituality and depressive realism

interpretations, stems from 'pre-Islamic ignorance' (or *Jahiliyyah*), and good Muslims should avoid such contagion. Atheism is regarded as a sin in Islam (in the same way it still is in some Christian churches), and Muslim apostates may risk a serious backlash for lapsing into pessimism or atheism. Ayaan Hirsi Ali, for example, following her own deep, feminist and atheist critique and rejection of Islam (Ali, 2016) received many death threats, and has not been the only one.

Islam is centrally in the monotheistic tradition: 'no God but God'. But like all other movements it has its internal divisions. The rise of Islam in recent decades (it is said to be the world's second largest and fastest growing religion: PEW, 2015) may be explained by its relative recency as a major religion. Just when whole swathes of Western Christianity have yielded to atheistic secularism under the sway of science, rationality and respect for individual rights, Islam centring on the Middle East but influential in many parts of the world is flourishing and contrasts in many ways with Western capitalist hedonism, emancipation of women, relaxation of attitudes to sexuality and so on. From one point of view, Islam is the antidote to the wicked decadence and religious disobedience of the West. From the opposite viewpoint, Islam is a medieval, oppressive, patriarchal and ritualistic religion that has no place in the modern world. More charitable views declare that Islam is as diverse as its believers and that moderate Muslims like liberal Christians or non-religious Jews integrate well into Western societies (Esposito, 2010). The ambition of groups like Islamic State (ISIL/ISIS) to establish a worldwide caliphate by violent means represents but one aspect of fundamentalist Islam. We could suggest that this has a strange theoretical ally in contemporary American anarcho-primitivism which regards the modern world as 'no good' and in need of razing to the ground in order that a new order – or renewed, natural anarchism – be established.

Hinduism and Buddhism

Rooted in the Vedic religion of over 3,000 years ago, Hinduism is a highly pluralistic set of beliefs and practices from which Jainism and Buddhism emanated over 2,500 years ago. One way of looking at religious interpretations of human existence is to view them simplistically in east-west terms. Where Western civilisation can be regarded as roughly taking a trajectory from mythology through religion, to philosophy, science, exploration, appropriation and capitalism, we can argue that the Eastern arc developed much more slowly from pantheistic mythologies through godless spiritual practices, introversion, fatalism and only latterly towards a hunger for capitalism. Religious development may depend quite as much on geo-determinism as do outward practices. The East has 'always' focused on existence as suffering based on illusions and its response has often been fatalistic. The West, however, has taken the Abrahamic and Greco-Roman route which led to reason and striving. One reading of Western civilisation is that it has been slower to discover inner realities. Consider the following point on entropy offered by Rifkin: 'There will be those who find the Entropy Law utterly depressing. This is indeed strange since it is merely a physical law. When Copernicus announced that the universe does not revolve around the earth, many people were similarly depressed, but humanity somehow managed to adjust to reality' (1985, p. 281). Rifkin also argues that the entropic argument is neither optimistic nor pessimistic, neither good nor evil. This point certainly chimes with a Buddhist emphasis on the nothingness at the core of life.

The Buddha is said to have asserted that he taught only about suffering (*dukkha*) and the cessation of suffering (Harvey, 2015). Buddhist outlines of the nature of suffering resonate with much of what is depicted in this book. Yet three core differences pertain. The first is that Buddhism shows no interest in what we might call the material 'archaeology of suffering' (anthropathogenesis), or the analysis of its roots in history, adhering instead to the mythology of *karma*. The second is that the assurances of a methodical end to suffering via meditation, accompanied by an ethics of skilful living, derived from the Buddha's own purported enlightenment, is doubted by the DR who sees no extensive evidence for these claims. The third is that while Buddhism avers an avoidance of both pessimism and optimism about these matters, the DR largely leans towards the pessimistic.

For Buddhists and for much 'eastern fatalism' there isn't the same negative surprise and depression as experienced in the West. It is as if, after the long search through the physical and objectivist world, only now is the West facing the crumbling of its progressivist assumptions, while the East is belatedly waking up to the advantages of technologically delivered good health and hedonism. No colonialist overtones are intended here: my suggestion is simply that one part of humanity has focused somewhat more on inner and another on outer reality, and both have missed out in different ways. Each has its strengths, too, yet ultimately both remain mired in their respective illusions. Only a relative minority of Westerners live the best of the promised good, materialist life, and only a tiny minority of Easterners enjoy spiritual transcendence of painful illusions. If we in the West are increasingly depressed (and seeking relief in, among other mindfulness techniques, eastern meditation), it may be because we have wearied of having too much, while the East wearies of poverty and looks from Gandhi to Gates. Some may see hope in East-West rapprochement, but in all likelihood both will be disappointed.

Let me take another perspective on this. The majority of us are immersed in everyday banalities. This psychic state has been referred to by some humanistic psychologists as the 'psychopathology of the average' or the 'banal script'. And the gerontologist Aubrey de Grey argues that we are in a 'death trance', in which we keep our heads down and avoid any contemplation of the terminal prospects, dully accepting their distal inevitability. Some of us immerse ourselves in projects requiring hyper-commitment, whether these are fundamentalist religion, entrepreneurialism or romantic passion. We feel 'truly alive' and keenly purposeful. The mystically magnified 'now' of Eckhart Tolle and others differs from the now of the hyper-committed, suggesting slower, somewhat countercultural

28 Religion, spirituality and depressive realism

lifestyles. In one form of mystical Hinduism, Aghori sadhus who are follow-ers of Shiva dedicate their lives to an ascetic monastic existence in which they renounce the mundane, confront taboos, shun aversion to death and avoid false emotional solutions. They are considered disgusting by many for their practices, but they resemble Diogenes and his spurning of conventional lifestyles. Con-trast all this, however, with U.G. Krishnamurti's claims that he had no conflicts with contemporary society, considered money-making better than spirituality and used the term 'spiritual materialism' for self-deceived seekers who wish to transcend this world. In other words, or so I suggest, there are no escapes, only different responses to the same fundamental human condition.

Let us anticipate here a little of the lineage of DR travelling from ancient oriental religion through to modern Western intellectual pessimism and nihil-ism. Morrison reminds us that it was quite specifically in Leipzig in 1864 that Nietzsche came across Schopenhauer's *The World as Will and Representation*. As Morrison summarises this intellectual passage: 'In addition to finding his true vocation in life through reading Schopenhauer, it was undoubtedly Schopen-hauer who first introduced him to Buddhism and Indian thought in general. Schopenhauer saw in the Buddhist view of existence an early Indian parallel to his own: life was unconditionally unsatisfactory; it could never offer man true and lasting happiness or fulfilment but only endless disappointment and sorrow' (1997, p. 3). Although Nietzsche later changed the direction of his thinking, we can see a chain of influence from eastern to so-called western Buddhism via Schopenhauer, challenging Christian hegemony, pushing nihilism and colour-ing the thought of writers from Tolstoy to Hardy, Freud and Beckett.

Spirituality

I am firmly of the view that religion is an *interesting* aspect of intellectual, moral and cultural history. I am bound to assert, however, the hardline atheist position that God does not and never did exist, and it follows from this that we have a problem in accounting for continuing belief in God. 'If God did not exist, it would be necessary to invent Him,' said Voltaire, protesting in a poem to an anonymous author. I imagine that we did indeed *need* to invent God long ago in order to soothe our primitive anxieties, but now we are challenged to acknowl-edge and let go of that fiction (Stenger, 2008). Less of a problem exists, I think, in understanding the enduring interest in higher or different states of conscious-ness. We could argue in shorthand fashion that false religion is a corruption of genuine 'spiritual' experience, and many follow this line, but spirituality, or the pursuit of higher states of consciousness and ultimate enlightenment, looks very much like another set of false claims and doomed aspirations. Many Catholics and Jews unite in declaring spirituality a narcissistic retreat from the values of religious community life. Almost perversely, some atheists attempt to embrace a new spirituality (Comte-Sponville, 2009) and even the ultra-sceptical Sam Har-ris (2015) allows for realisation of a 'non-self' as key to enlightenment.

Buddha surely ranks as *the* idealised enlightened human being, and we have many examples of beloved mystics and saints who may have transcended common human bondage. We also have some recent examples of those perceived as either fully genuine or partially fake, such as Jiddu Krishnamurti (1895–1986), and living examples such as Eckhart Tolle. Most of these appear to have had fortuitous spiritual experiences, often after painful crises that took them out of normal anthropathological consciousness into a state of mind free from striving and illusion. But the two most damning observations that cannot be avoided here are (1) that we can never verify such claims but only have faith, and (2) that this post-anthropathological state of mind has rarely been transmitted to others by any teaching or practice, despite much longing for it. Bunge (2012) offers a relevant perspective on the personal effort to overcome acedia or despondency within a spiritual discipline, drawing from the writings of Evagrius Ponticus, a 4th century Desert Father. In this account an effort of will or soul is required to deepen the spiritual life, leading beyond sinful doubt. It is implied that many have anonymously and non-dramatically followed such a spiritual path to fulfilment but we will never know.

Religion as a negative

'Religion, or certain religions, are wholly good and true' remains a strongly held view. Atheism is growing but not yet catching up. But alongside these we must factor in the observation that religions have many negative features. These include the propagation of untrue explanations, the conservative opposition to social progress, brainwashing, guilt-induction, jihad, war and many absurdities besides. Catholic priests' paedophilic abuse, nuns' cruel treatment of pregnant teenage girls in Ireland, some Muslims' practice of female genital mutilation, indeed most religions' sexually repressive traditions – all these are now well known. Weber's writings on the Protestant ethic show how religion can be used to drive and justify capitalist practices, and many Americans today perversely equate wealth with religious virtue. Among the few who have put religion behind them and admitted why, Kahl (1971), as an ex-pastor, lists many varieties of religious hypocrisy – accusations of heresy, actual punishments and threats of punishment in hell; persecution of outsiders, notably Jews; aggressive crusades and missions; oppression of women, markedly in witch-hunts; censorship, mythologisation and artful demythologisation. Crawford (2010) tells us that it was on his emergence from a Christian cult that he came to see the fact that religion was a lie and life was mostly built on painful illusions. Many other stories of cult survivors are available. One can also see in the lives of many psychotherapists, for example, Carl Rogers, a rejection of religion leading to the formation of a 'new' psychology and therapy which unconsciously smuggles in much of the rejected religion.

The accusation of religion as superstition is one we have lived with for some time now. More unusual but increasing in modern times are outbreaks of religious intolerance and terrorism, which include the bombing of abortion clinics by some Christians, and bombing, shooting and decapitation by some Muslims. The assumption that secular humanism, reinforced by democratic and consumerist benefits, will assuredly erode religious superstition has been severely dented by such recent atrocities. We cannot say that all religions are inherently intolerant but many contain strictures so dogmatic that they must always lend themselves to potential violence. Opposition by religious creationists to evolutionary science may seem simply ridiculous, but also contains potentially regressive elements. Many fundamental religious tenets of altruism and community support are hard to fault but not confined to the religious, who sometimes use these arguments to shore up their declining fortunes.

Atheism

As a corrective to the view that religion is universal and primary, Whitmarsh (2016) presents evidence of atheism from the ancient world, showing that Diagoras of Melos, Democritus, Epicurus and others engaged unashamedly with atheist views. Since then religion has been either overwhelmingly dominant or at war with disbelief. The interface and mutual antagonism between religion and atheism grew to weary proportions with the so-called new atheism of the 2000s, and itself in large part a reaction to Islamist resurgence and militancy. Many scientists and philosophers have made explicit atheist statements, and strong theological defences and counterattacks have been advanced in turn. Although I would like to declare my own position a mature post-theistic indifference, I cannot quite stop shaking my head in disbelief. The sadness in this state of affairs is about humanity's entrenched, perennial need for beliefs and battles between beliefs that have no basis in physical reality, biological satisfaction or conviviality. The battles of ideas, faiths or whatever we name them, are not only ugly and irresolvable but pointless. We quarrel, sometimes to the death, over a bone that doesn't exist. We are ridiculous animals. Not content with building and clinging to egos that have no core reality, we also arm ourselves with cultural fantasies that divide us from others and from raw reality.

Watson (2014) asks whether we are going through a period of 'spiritual recession' from which we will emerge sooner or later; we might extend this metaphor to spiritual depression, a long-term collective slough of despond. Many antiatheist writers are now confidently predicting the end of the short-lived, premature atheist triumph. Humanistic and transpersonal psychologists who reject mainstream religions proclaim a spiritually informed re-enchantment agenda. Even the markedly DR writer John Gray expects the re-emergence of Islam to present serious competition to other ideologies in the years to come (Gray, 2004, 2007), and he refers approvingly to a 'godless mysticism' (Gray, 2014). My own assumption has been that reason and science are progressively eroding religion, which must surely die eventually. But this is a linear assumption which can be challenged by circular or other concepts of history. No atheist, however certain of the non-existence of God, can be sure that religion will wither and reason and science will triumph, and it is possible that faith in science will also wither as its flaws and catastrophes become apparent (see Chapter 8).

Many religious people have close brushes with atheism. Perhaps the sincerest Christians are those most self-searching, who confront their own doubts. Søren Kierkegaard lived with the anxiety of being an individual who took no succour from the church of his time. His works are famously full of references to existential sickness and 'silent daily anxiety' (Ferguson, 1995). He grew up with a religiously obsessive father and the early deaths of his mother and siblings. He knew, even cultivated, an outsider identity. But finally, he stuck with God and his gravestone declares that he expected to spend eternity conversing with Jesus. Leo Tolstoy went through a period of depression, of psychological agony in which he felt it would have been better never to have been born (Tolstoy, 1882/1987). He even came up with a four-point explanation for how human beings escape from despair, anticipating later existentialist schemas like that of Zapffe. 'Can it be that only Schopenhauer and I have been intelligent enough to understand the senselessness and evil of life?' he asks himself (p. 47). Tolstoy lived through his doubts, making heroic attempts to create a new Christian community based on shunning property ownership, on non-violence and rejection of state religion.

Paradoxically, while DR is probably always atheistic, on occasion the more vociferous and disinhibited DR may find himself proclaiming the dark insights of his so-called negative faith to people who react with horror. The disinhibited DR may resemble a high street Christian preacher declaring an imminent end of the world and the foolishness of typically superficial worldviews, all of which echo themes of original sin and divine punishment. This may earn him jibes, ostracism or worse. He will come across as eccentric, antisocial, an upsetter of youthful dreams, as a figure of disgust who traumatises the vulnerable or even as 'evil'.

Religions as worldviews among others

It is not axiomatically clear why religions have a legally protected status and why they should command respect from anyone not involved in them. It is not even clear what constitutes a religion, since some like Buddhism have no God, and some have either one or many gods; some have a saviour and others do not. Scientology has the legal status of a religion, so religion is not defined by historical pedigree. Religious status is not defined by the number of followers: worldwide according to the Wikipedia entry for *List of Religious Populations* there are approximately 2.2 billion Christians, 1.8 billion Muslims, 1 billion Hindus, 376 million Buddhists, 14 million Jews, 600,000 Rastafarians, possibly 40,000 Scientologists and so on. It is understandable that something may have to protect religious believers from persecution, but many religions are inherently persecutory of disbelievers or those from other faiths. It is not exactly clear what the definitional or legal lines are between religious belief and belief in Marxism, say, psychoanalysis, existentialism, humanism and other worldviews and ideologies. All utopian ideologies, not only religious, contain recipes for disaster (Gray, 2007). What is it, if anything, we can ask, that elevates religion above any other worldview?

For Marx and Freud religion was an obstacle to human progress and truth, deserving of the epithets 'opium of the people' and 'oceanic feeling' respectively. Religion impedes social justice by falsely promising a better posthumous existence or higher consciousness. It fails to stand up to rational tests as demanded by atheists. It frequently disappoints its own believers. Most glaringly, religious believers are in conflict with each other, even within the Abrahamic tradition, and even within singular religions. Religious wars testify to the intolerance here, but simple pronouncements also make this stand-off clear. Cardinal Ratzinger (later Pope Benedict XVI) famously said of Buddhism in March 1997 that it is 'spiritually self-indulgent' and 'autoerotic spirituality'. Even the harmless, spiritually generous Eckhart Tolle has come under fire from an evangelical Christian re-asserting a 'correct' version of Christian teaching (Abanes, 2008). Religion is as tribal as all worldviews.

If DR is a worldview among others, albeit a minority worldview, how should it rank among the techniques of transcendence? It has the sincerity of secular humanism but no programme to promulgate. It shares the Christian view of sin (understood as anthropathology) and the Buddhist view of *maya*, but sees no real prospect of any comfort or resolution. DR is existentialism without the illusion of freedom and choice. But we could also say, perhaps we must also say, that any DR that makes a pessimistic worldview out of itself chooses this position and creates its own illusion. Any dogmatic DR refuses to entertain the nuances of experience. Perhaps only a deeply felt depressive realism, which includes truthful attention to the mechanisms of one's own trouble-making, thinking ego, can rival suicide as a serious response to suffering. Cioran was aware of his own self-deceptive nihilistic tendencies. Some Beckett scholars have pronounced him a 'post-Christian mystic', as Zen-like (Foster, 1989) or as deeply influenced by gnosticism, Geulincz, existentialism and other systems of thought (Calder, 2012).

The world after god

Belief in God will not be substantially destroyed by atheists but by events. Rubenstein (1992) in his so-called Holocaust theology has been one of many Jews to reject the kind of God who could not or would not prevent the Holocaust. While the stock theodical response to human suffering is to emphasise humans' wicked choices in the context of free will, this does not satisfy Rubenstein and similar profound thinkers. No justificatory contortion can be considered either convincing or even minimally tasteful in the face of such immense suffering, and there can be only one conclusion, despite many attempts to redefine

God or artfully craft new meanings-of-life from such devastation. Hence, post-traumatic disillusionment from within (some) religion meets vigorous atheism from without.

The most poignant legacy of religious faith will be its vacuum. If, as many expect, belief in God continues to diminish without long-term hope of resuscitation, we face an interesting future. Religion has been a universal component in human cultures, basically in order to offer explanations where none was available and to provide comfort and morale-boosting. When it is finally accepted that science answers most of our former questions, we are only left with the problem of sustaining morale. If we succeed in refusal to re-create religious fantasies, we have to first see if we can proceed without creating substitute fantasies, and then see how we can adapt our minds to living in a godless universe. It has always, in fact, been godless but when we truly realise this beyond shadow boxing, we face a period of extended grieving. I imagine, too, that we will relatively soon have to face up to living without political and associated fantasies. All that is left is to see if a purposeless collective life is tenable, and when I use the term purposeless I mean without purposes other than survival, conviviality and exploration. Our collective reactive depression at the loss of God will lessen in time but a huge adaptation is required to negotiate the world thereafter. On gradually and painfully withdrawing from our ancient fantasies, our religious addictions, conflictual tribalism, absurd social institutions and egoic illusions, a new kind of human will have to emerge. This is, of course, presupposing that neither rational antinatalism nor accidental disasters decimate us before then. It is also to believe that we do not have an eternal and irreversible need for religious faith. Like many near-nihilists, Critchley (2014) sadly attempts to re-create a politico-theological 'faith', drawn partly from the experience of Oscar Wilde in *De Profundis* and requiring 'suffering alone', so that 'one becomes the smithy of one's soul' (p. 4). I do not envisage a kind of faith by sophistry, an anatheism or a renewed pantheism but a chastened mind, sober after millennia of religious inebriation. Posterity will surely look on the history of religions with bemusement at our doctrinal absurdities. Grim stoicism, mundane goals and ample distractions are all that is required to endure in this life, even if some love and humour sweeten the experience.

References

Abanes, R. (2008) *A New Earth and an Old Deception: Awakening to the Dangers of Eckhart Tolle's #1 Bestseller*. Minneapolis, MN: Bethany House.

Ali, A.H. (2016) *Heretic: Why Islam Needs a Reformation*. New York: Harper.

Betty, L. (2016) *Without God: Michel Houellebecq and Materialist Horror*. University Park, PA: Penn State University Press.

Bunge, G. (2012) *Despondency: The Spiritual Teaching of Evagrius Ponticus on Acedia*. New York: St Vladimir's Seminary Press.

Calder, J. (2012) *The Theology of Samuel Beckett*. London: Calder.

Comte-Sponville, A. (2009) *The Book of Atheist Spirituality*. London: Transworld.

34 Religion, spirituality and depressive realism

Crawford, J. (2010) *Confessions of an Antinatalist*. Charleston, WV: Nine-Banded Books.

Critchley, S. (2014) *The Faith of the Faithless: Experiments on Political Theology*. London: Verso.

Ellis, A. (1980) *The Case against Religion: A Psychotherapist's View and the Case against Religiosity*. New York: American Atheist Press.

Esposito, J.L. (2010) *The Future of Islam*. New York: Oxford University Press.

Ferguson, H. (1995) *Melancholy and the Critique of Modernity: Søren Kierkegaard's Religious Psychology*. London: Routledge.

Foster, P. (1989) *Beckett and Zen*. London: Wisdom Publications.

Gerrie, A. (2011) OCD really is the Jewish disease. *The Jewish Chronicle Online*, 28 February.

Gray, J. (2004) *Heresies: Against Progress and Other Illusions*. London: Granta.

Gray, J. (2007) *Black Mass: Apocalyptic Religion and the Death of Utopia*. London: Penguin.

Gray, J. (2014) *The Silence of Animals: On Progress and Other Modern Myths*. London: Penguin.

Harris, S. (2015) *Waking Up: Searching for Spirituality without Religion*. London: Transworld.

Harvey, P. (2015) Dukkha, non-self, and the teaching of the four "noble truths". In S.M. Emmanuel (ed). *A Companion to Buddhist Philosophy*. Chichester: Wiley.

Kahl, J. (1971) *The Misery of Christianity*. Harmondsworth: Pelican.

Morrison, R.G. (1997) *Nietzsche and Buddhism: A Study in Nihilism and Ironic Affinities*. Oxford: Oxford University Press.

Mulhall, S. (2005) *Philosophical Myths of the Fall*. Princeton, NJ: Princeton University Press.

PEW (2015) *The Future of World Religions: Population Growth Projections, 2010–2050*. Washington, DC: Pew Research Center.

Rifkin, J. (1985) *Entropy: A New World View*. London: Paladin.

Rubenstein, R.L. (1992) *After Auschwitz: History, Theology, and Contemporary Judaism (2nd edn.)*. Baltimore, MA: Johns Hopkins University Press.

Sneed, M.R. (2012) *The Politics of Pessimism in Ecclesiastes*. Atlanta, GA: Society of Biblical Literature.

Stenger, V. (2008) *God: The Failed Hypothesis*. Amherst, NY: Prometheus.

Tolstoy, L. (1882/1987) *A Confession and Other Religious Writings*. London: Penguin.

Unamuno, de M. (1921/1954) *Tragic Sense of Life*. New York: Dover.

Watson, P. (2014) *The Age of Nothing*. London: Weidenfeld & Nicolson.

Whitmarsh, T. (2016) *Battling the Gods: Atheism in the Ancient World*. London: Faber & Faber.

Chapter 3

Philosophy and depressive realism

As with theology, one does not have to be a philosopher or believe philosophy useful to subscribe to DR or make one's DR worldview explicit. One of the fiercest of such statements, for example, is that made by the horror writer Thomas Ligotti (2010), and many novelists and poets with no philosophical training espouse similar DR views. The Italian poet Leopardi wrote about investigating *l'acerbo vero* (the bitter truth) in his philosophical poems. Peter Heinegg, an ex-priest, offers one of the most concise yet comprehensive accounts of DR, pitched as pessimism, in Heinegg (2005). Beckett once claimed (not altogether honestly) that he did not read philosophy because he did not understand it. However, some philosophers have been or are explicit DRs (in my sense of the term) and most DR themes raise enormous metaphysical questions, moral issues and topics found in existentialism, philosophy of mind and mental health. 'Concerning life, the wisest men of all ages have judged alike: *it is no good*', pronounced Nietzsche (1971), a sentiment echoed by Benatar (2016). In some cases philosophy rightly challenges the sweeping and unsupported statements of DR, and in many instances DR finds philosophy part of the problem in its over-cognitivisation, obsessive attention to detail and general obfuscation. For all its intellectual weightiness and sheer pomp, philosophy may find posterity judging it to have been a monumentally misdirected effort.

Truth

The concept of truth is unfashionable yet persistent. Heidegger speaks tortuously of 'the possibility of correctness' or *aletheia* against its concealment, and of man as 'always astray in errancy', which 'belongs to the inner constitution of the Da-sein into which historical man is admitted'. There is a 'primordial essence of truth' (2008, p. 78). I believe the fundamental DR position is partly constituted by an angry incredulity about what passes among the majority (Heidegger's the *they*) as truth. Where the clinically depressed person may see his immediate environment as psychotically distorted into mockingly meaningless shapes, the average DR is inclined to experience the *social world* as 'unreal' and based on absurd untruths to which he is entreated to subscribe. The Kantian stress on

36 Philosophy and depressive realism

truthfulness rather than abstract truth sits well with the DR. And truthfulness so often leads inexorably to the ugly truth about human beings and their existence.

Let us begin with Diogenes of Sinope as the proto-truth-teller or anti-philosopher. Here it is useful to employ Sloterdijk's (1987) distinction between *kynicism* (Diogenes' and other Cynics' usage) and our contemporary cynicism, or 'cynical reason'. Depressive realism for all its nihilistic pull does contain a large element of kynical parrhesia. The outlook of the DR has an acidic quality that cannot accept false claims. DR is a *via negativa* and resembles the Hindu, or Vedic *neti neti* or 'not this, not this', approach to enquiry characterised by stripping away all that is not truth (*Anatman*) in order to approach *Atman* (ultimate reality). In colloquial terms it is also synonymous with the concept of bullshit detection (Frankfurt, 2005). I suspect that just as some people with a mental illness or affliction cannot control their asocial outbursts (Tourettes comes to mind, of course), DRs may inwardly experience hyper-veridicality (the 'fatal perspicacity' of Cioran), especially in insomnia but at other times too.

However, a commitment to truthfulness almost certainly undermines any DR claim to absolute truth. The claim that life is no good suggests that no redeeming features at all can ever be found in it. 'Life is mostly no good' can be more easily defended. Think of the term 'life affirming' for the positive view and ask whether DR can really defend a position of *life disconfirming*. It certainly seems true that for some people life holds no positive value that prevents their suicide. It may be true that for those people, in terms of personality dependent realism, life is no good. Or, more accurately, for some people at the darkest of times, life is subjectively no good and indeed painfully negative. But the proposition that life is no good for anyone, ever, is much harder and probably impossible to defend. 'My life has been a complete joy,' on the other hand, is not a statement with the ring of truth. It may be that a search for truth as to an absolute, all-embracing statement on the ultimate value of life is doomed, indeed futile. And yet the likely half-way acceptance of a platitudinous 'life is a mixture of good and bad' also feels unsatisfactory. Benatar (2006) argues that an asymmetry exists in such evaluations (see below), and the view that life is much more bad than good justifies the moral stance to desist from reproduction. But the subject is more nuanced than most such arguments. If truthfulness has to be our guide, then we have to say that we don't know just how good or bad future lives will be, but we have to agree that some lives have been so bad that some individuals have killed themselves and probably many endure with little pleasure. Even the positive term *life affirming* implies that doubt exists as to life's goodness and we therefore need to be reminded of it. Depressive realism doesn't demand suicide or antinatalism. It respects the rights of those who make such choices but may well also question dogmatic negativity.

But we should also reckon with the problem of language and reason. We have elevated logic above feelings (and faith), but we cannot presume that logic, or rational posturing, is always or forever correct. Philosophy strives to operate above visceral and emotional levels, and philosophers are forever correcting each other's limitations; indeed, the profession of academic philosophy is founded on infinite nit-picking. Alfred North Whitehead's well-known characterisation of European philosophy as being mere footnotes to Plato attests to this. But the possibility also remains that a visceral-emotional insight into the value of life is more 'truthful' than rational excavations. It is problematic to open this possibility, of course, since it appears to also open the door to religious faith as arguably more truthful than human reason. It is also possible, and I think probable, that our insights from whatever source are always flawed, subject to limited information, bias and mood; and this includes philosophers. Perhaps ultimately it does come back to faith, but personal faith in one's own judgement. There may be no final or absolute truth but we can claim, for example, that the theory of evolution by natural selection is more aligned with truth than the theory of intelligent design, that death regarded as final is a more truthful view than death as a gateway to heaven and so on.

In the last chapter I made it clear that my own position rests on what many (e.g., Tallis, 2011) pejoratively call a materialist-determinist base. Increasingly, some philosophers (e.g. Sterelny, 2003) have based their work on similar foundations rather than employing an ahistorical rationality as the instrument of enquiry. Sommers and Rosenberg (2002) are among those philosophers of biology who adhere to the view that Darwinism conclusively demonstrates the meaninglessness of life. Just as we were not created a few thousand years ago, neither have we wholly sundered ourselves from our animal inheritance. We are part animal, but also in what we boast of as our rationality, we may concede that human cognition is flawed and limited. Philosophy as the exercise of formal logic and analysis may in some cases rise above flawed informal thought (e.g. folk psychology, commonsense, etc.) but is itself also flawed and limited. Many have argued for the poverty of philosophy, including Jackson (2013) who advocates an anthropological take that incorporates some Heideggerian principles.

It often goes without saying (or contrarily, is emphasised *ad nauseam* by psychiatrists) that a depressive view is a distorted one, that is, a marked departure from consensual perception and agreed nomenclature. But we should consider the proposition that in depression one sees social phenomena for what they really are, even if direct perception is a possibility denied by most Western philosophers and psychologists. And since 'social reality' ultimately includes everything linguistic, perhaps in depression one sees natural phenomena for what they really are, stripped of their cognitive veil. If depression results from a transient state of involuntary de-conditioning, it can be regarded as a rude and distressing awakening of forgotten or suppressed pristine reality. Among others, Marsilio Ficino, the 15th century philosopher, argued that melancholy is not an illness but akin to a state of grace. We know that sudden negative life events such as bereavement, divorce, unemployment, threats to health and involvement in traumatic incidents, or the effects of certain drugs, can plunge almost anyone into unfamiliar psychological states. We even acknowledge that such negative experiences sometimes lead to an acute new appreciation of the positive value of life. But we do not appear to take this very seriously, or dwell on it, in philosophical terms.

Stripped of our usual perceptual filters, ingrained in us across millennia, we may with genuine mystics see through artificial constructs to the ground of pre-linguistic reality. This can entail seeing through common social traditions and personal habits, and renouncing them, but also, more profoundly, seeing through concepts of duty, religion, political schemas, even time itself. It can certainly entail the transient dissolution of (Hegel's) unhappy and (Engels') false consciousness. In severe depression one may experience 'psychotic' disturbances of normal consciousness that render the physical world distasteful, disgusting and painfully purposeless. Is this a distorted perception or inference, a pathological reaction or a valid realisation of an ultimate truth? Western philosophers tend to be self-selectively intellectually-oriented, highly analytical and unlikely to be sympathetic to accounts of valid affective or mystical perception. Likewise, most psychologists adhere to a scientific identity. Theologians on the other hand must always gravitate back towards a God-oriented view of reality, even when a challenging new concept of God is invented. It remains possible, however, that at least some kinds of depressive experience suggest a gateway to a non-consensual reality, perhaps via a neurological accident, even if this experience is unpleasant.

The Buddha (approximately 500–420 BCE) is said to have established the four noble truths: (1) that we are born, we age, suffer and die; (2) that we desire, including the primary desire for sex which begets future generations of suffering; (3) that there is an end to or fading of suffering; (4) that a path exists by which to exit from this suffering. The first of these might be called the primary canon of DR, and the second of antinatalism. None of these are cheerful truths and all are open to dispute. Ageing and suffering are receiving scientific attention. Procreation is in principle achievable without sex or sexual desire, although the desire for procreation remains a desire. DRs may vigorously dispute the final two, pointing out that little or no evidence exists for extensive nirvana, or indeed for nirvana at all; and even some of those allegedly enlightened, like Jiddu Krishnamurti, denied – especially in his famous 1929 'truth is a pathless land' speech – that there was any systematic route to nirvana. But my point here is that while Westerners agonise over the question of truth, we usually ignore longstanding Eastern insights.

Philosophy of mind and mental illness

Philosophy of mind examines the problems of how mind relates to brain, body and world, broadly dividing into dualist and monist camps but having developed into a highly complex subdiscipline. Its importance here, of course, is in the epistemological questions of where DR derives its worldview from and how accurate or otherwise this derivation is. Philosophy of mind overlaps with philosophy of mental health and illness in asking how we decide what is mentally healthy or ill, and how either state is related to brain functions, the body and the external world.

The philosopher of mind Graham (2010) gives short shrift to the DR view, which he refers to as a 'set of suppositions together with various observations about human psychology and the circumstances that allegedly back them up' (p. 211). Taking a polarised view of 'sadder but wiser' versus 'positive illusions' (Taylor, 1991), Graham acknowledges that the positive illusions argument is at odds with philosophy's truth-seeking mission but wants to stress the ambiguous nature of this world, and adds that hopefulness is not necessarily based on illusions. Comparing DRs with paranoiacs who may obsessively notice details accurately but unhelpfully, he argues that 'even if it should turn out that depressed people are more accurate in certain observations than normal non-depressives, it does not follow that they are in superior contact with cognitive reality' (p. 214). He is in a favour of 'maintaining a moderately positive image of things, . . . as pragmatically sensible and evidentially sound as purpose and circumstances permit' (p. 214).

He goes on to condemn the 'deep and dark pessimism' of philosophers who make unwarranted inferences from dark eras (including Bertrand Russell), and cosmic endtime scenarios (implicitly, Brassier, 2006), instead commending the 'immediate or smaller dimensions of life' (p. 214). DRs are, in his view, working against their own best interests, which would be better served by adopting a 'moderate optimism'. For a philosopher who fashionably challenges psychiatric assumptions of what is or isn't mental disorder, neurological disorder or just existential despair and problems in living, who devotes an approving chapter to Kierkegaardian notions of despair and who cites John Stuart Mill's own stubborn depression, Graham hangs on to a romantic American, optimistic philosophy of hope (not gung-ho, but merely *moderately positive* for an American). With some inconsistency he speaks above of 'normal non-depressives' in contrast with (presumably not-normal and therefore perhaps unreliable) depressives. Nowhere does he reckon with the assertion that philosophy itself can be regarded as a sad part of the spectrum of human psychological and cultural sickness, although he does concede that we all 'carry a mixed and discordant bag of attributes' (p. 265). There is a DR position of 'things are wholly bad and unimprovable' but a nuanced DR worldview can also claim that things are much worse and more absurd than Graham believes, and they certainly implicate status quo academics and psychotherapists, without descending into total bitter nihilism.

What is depressing about philosophy

The most devastating critique of philosophy concerns its sheer irrelevance. Philosophers' work is a mixture of sincere truth-seeking, personality-dependent obsessiveness, business-as-usual intra-disciplinary discourse and academic careerism. It makes little impact on any general public, even in its moral applications. Its language is mostly dense, obfuscatory, self-referential and exclusive. Even in

40 Philosophy and depressive realism

sheer numbers of personnel and texts the business of philosophy ranks very modestly. Popular philosophy and 'smart thinking' may be enjoying a small spike of book sales and conference exposure, but this is still targeted on a small section of the intelligentsia. Marx's famous admonition regarding philosophy's merely interpretative role remains apt, and even Marxist philosophy no longer has much impact. Indeed, one overarching, nihilistic critique of philosophy is that in the historical-entropic scheme of things, it superseded mythology and religious thought but has in turn been largely superseded by science, and we wait to see what will yet supersede science.

We might distinguish between philosophy's many forms and contexts, for example, between independent critical thought and academically-throttled thought. As Land (1992) puts it: 'Pessimism, or the philosophy of desire, has a marked allergy to academic encompassment. Schopenhauer, Nietzsche, and Freud all wrote the vast bulk of their works from a space inaccessible to the sweaty clutches of state pedagogy' (p. 10). To put this differently, the desire many feel for authentic attempts at explanations for existence is disappointed by philosophy. The more philosophy one reads, the further away from visceral engagement one gets; philosophers themselves appear to become ever more immersed in sophist detail and render academics ever more secure in their employment.

Arthur Schopenhauer

Schopenhauer (1788–1860) is probably the best known pessimistic philosopher, basing his philosophical system on the principle of will. All things in nature assert themselves, notably in humans via sex (anticipating our contemporary joke: 'life is a sexually transmitted disease'), and this in turn leads to suffering which can only be borne stoically, or perhaps Buddhistically. His reputation peaked around the same time as Darwin's and he influenced many writers. For Saltus (1885/2014) he was the 'high priest of pessimism' and Sim (2015) refers to Schopenhauer's worldview as 'inveterate pessimism'. But he was surely wrong to declare ours the *worst* of all possible worlds, since it takes only a little imagination to construct far worse. Nevertheless, we can say that ours is far from perfect and is a mixture of good and bad. Optimists want to declare that it is slowly but surely moving towards a state of minimal suffering and optimal happiness, while pessimists see no reason to support such hopes. Schopenhauer is distinguished by his unflinching adherence to the bleakest position which either resonates with or has influenced Leopardi, Kierkegaard, Nietzsche, Michelstaedter, Saltus, Zapffe, Cioran, Gray, Benatar and many others. Rather than examining all these in detail, I focus on a small selection below.

Schalkx and Bergsma (2008) compared Schopenhauer's written guidance on life and how to endure it with the supposedly objective findings of modern psychological research, only to find, fairly predictably, that Schopenhauer was, at least by today's standards, a poor psychologist peddling bad advice. They concede that his recommendations for stoicism, control of desires, spurning wealth

Philosophy and depressive realism 41

and status match modern findings. But they do not hesitate to add Schopenhauer's bleak worldview to his sad life events and facets of his personality – his father probably committed suicide; he got on badly with his mother; he was competitive, notoriously and unsuccessfully with Hegel; he was ill-tempered, vain, pessimistic, a 'depressing know-it-all', a hypochondriac, a loner, neurotic, apparently paranoid, misanthropic. He was wrong, say these authors, to commend solitude (indeed anti-marriage), anti-optimism and low expectations. Empirical happiness research – which they take to be synonymous with truth – shows that interacting, being married and having goals are all, contra Schopenhauer, positive. This kind of anti-Schopenhauerian position is defended by the philosophers Michael and Caldwell (2010), who argue that reason-based optimistic consolation can be found in Stoical beliefs.

Peter Wessel Zapffe

Peter Wessel Zapffe (1899–1990) was a Norwegian philosopher whose major work *Om det Tragiske* has yet to be fully translated into English. It is remarkable then that his influence still rests on a short essay *The Last Messiah* (Zapffe, 1933) best made known by Ligotti (2010). Zapffe is known as a pessimistic philosopher influenced by Schopenhauer and Nietzsche, who advocated antinatalism and championed environmental awareness and protection, or biosophy.

The main thrust of Zapffe's philosophical anthropology revolved around the concept of surplus consciousness. Our troubles are driven by a mistaken demand for meaning in life that just does not exist, something many modern philosophers seemingly find impossible to take on board (Wolf, 2010). We seek meaning because evolutionary circumstances have accidentally endowed us with the ability to think well beyond what it is useful for us to think. This consciousness works against us and constitutes our tragedy. What we seek to know, and somehow to overcome, are the facts of our origins, existence and death. Animals cannot wonder about the nature of the universe, their inevitable death and their purpose or destiny within it. But we cannot do otherwise. Faced with the bleak realisation that existence is accidental and has no purpose, that we suffer and die, we also have no choice but to defend ourselves against this anxiety. Zapffe names four universal defence mechanisms.

Isolation is the repressive mental process whereby we avoid distressing awareness of our predicament by sequestering it, that is, by denial. *Anchoring* refers to the mechanisms we attach ourselves to that offer psychological security, for example, religion, politics, cultural norms, institutional affiliations and more immediate personal goals. *Distraction* is the category of things we call on to help ourselves not to think about what is distressing, that is, our death and ultimate futility. *Sublimation* refers to the conversion of our tragic awareness into art, literature, philosophy and other aesthetic forms; this is not quite avoidance. The work of Samuel Beckett is, I think, an excellent example of sublimation. Zapffe's is a simple but compelling schema.

42   Philosophy and depressive realism

We might extend Zapffe's schema a little. Distraction covers a multitude of sins at every level of society. Trivial recreational distractions are easily identified, and contemporary compulsive novelty-seeking such as tattooing is pertinent here. But we want to believe that some of our activities are loftier than others. For example, academics consider their preoccupations to belong to an altogether serious realm of intellectual enquiry far above popular media, but from a DR perspective they look very similar, merely distractional horses for courses. Indeed, much of academia and intellectual culture is an artful blend of anchoring and distraction, giving a sense of purpose to those prone to overthinking, who might become depressed without the opportunity to profit from their own thoughts and their dissemination. Much here is class-related, too, as a majority depends on sports, recreation and pulp fiction while the intelligentsia derive reputational and financial goods from specialist micro-focused interests. We can also argue that something like the absurd Beckett industry is a curious mix of anchoring, distraction and sublimation. Or we might simply collapse all Zapffean categories into one, that of sheer defensive avoidance, or denial: we all know what a terrible existence this is and we chronically collude in order 'not to know'. I do not mean here a partial denial (Becker, 1973; Cohen, 2010) but denial of *all* uncomfortable and distressing aspects of existence. This remains true even when 'amusing' commercial house decorations appear bearing DR slogans like '*Don't take life too seriously, nobody gets out alive anyway*' or when fridge magnets carry 'deep' Beckettian one-liners about failure and futility.

It is hardly necessary to point out that Zapffe's is not a unique philosophy, having much in common with existentialism generally (see, e.g. Fremstedal, 2012) and advancing anthropathological concepts that have since been better explicated. Zapffe is, however, admirable for his conciseness and unshakeability. If we are nonplussed at the meaninglessness of life but at the same time by the absurdities of civilisation, of religion, tribalism, war and so on, we do not have to look any further. We go on when we can't go on, with Beckett, because we are biological beings, but we suffer disproportionately from dread, hope, regret, anxiety. Like Beckett, Zapffe and other DRs, many of us 'write of melancholy by being busy to avoid melancholy' (Burton, 1621/2001).

John Gray

Gray was Professor of European Thought at the London School of Economics before retiring. His identity sits within political philosophy, particularly as an admirer of Isaiah Berlin, but he is best known for his short aphoristic book *Straw Dogs* (2002), which reads as a highly Schopenhauerian, counter-Enlightenment tract. In this and other publications Gray has made the point strongly that human beings are rapacious animals who wrongly consider themselves to be above nature. We are also inveterate believers in progress, regarding history as moving in a straight line towards some utopian future that we ourselves command. As Gray starkly puts it: ' "Humanity" does not exist. There are only humans, driven

Philosophy and depressive realism 43

by conflicting needs and illusions, and subject to every kind of infirmity of will and judgement' (p. 12). We are 'not obviously worth preserving' (p. 151). He sees inevitable doom in the climate change scenario, in weapons of mass destruction, naïve delusions in religion, 'green humanism' and fundamentalist science. He attacks the illusions of the self and free will. Existence, he asserts like Zapffe, has no purpose, yet we persist in looking for one.

In *The Silence of Animals* Gray (2013) continues his theme of taking the animal perspective and mocking the grandiose human self-view. In *The Soul of the Marionette* (Gray, 2015) he focuses sharply on free will as perhaps our grandest illusion, and in doing so aligns himself somewhat with Ligotti (2010) and other DRs – and not only DRs – who are making similar points. Whether Tallis (2011), among others, is right to mock Gray in turn for failing to accept the distinctiveness of humanity is another matter. We are, certainly, partly animals and only superior to animals by our own judgement; whether puppet metaphors are suitable references for our limited freedom can also be questioned.

Benatar and antinatalism

Perhaps the hardest-hitting moral philosophy related to DR is the antinatalist kind, most prominently advocated by Benatar (2006). 'The quality of even the best lives is very bad' (p. vi), one of Benatar's opening lines, makes it clear that an evaluative stand is taken on the value of life with which many disagree. His stance automatically puts Benatar against the vast majority of religious people but also against the overall majority, as well as against many philosophers. But the nub of this argument cannot be brushed aside: *if* life is so bad, so full of suffering and ends for every one of us in death, which is universally feared, we should at least pause to weigh up the morality of bringing new lives into existence. Actually Benatar is already persuaded that life's negatives merit a complete antinatalist case, and that, therefore, the only truly moral course is abstinence from all further conceptions. He doesn't advocate suicide, distinguishing already existing from coming into existence. Thus, abortion can be regarded as a merciful avoidance of suffering for the human being denied existence.

Resistance to thinking hard about (and against) reproduction comes from many sources. Religion is probably the chief of these, driven by pronatalist scriptures and cultural admonitions. Sheer biological imperative always comes into play, with sex itself being for the majority life's greatest free pleasure. A majority of women seek the experience of pregnancy and motherhood, even if fertility measured by births has dropped over the past 200 years (Perry, 2016) and a relatively small number now opt for childlessness. Only recently have some women become more ambivalent than men about having children. But infertility is often regarded as one of life's saddest blights. China's single child policy, while instigated for good reasons, was criticised for totalitarian control and also for familial and psychological damage. But the Nazi Holocaust is probably a major factor in resistance to any de-population programme or philosophy.

44 Philosophy and depressive realism

Reproduction and population are hugely emotive topics. And the prospect of a falling world population with ever fewer delightful babies and fewer adults to work, pay tax and support pensions is most unwelcome, constituting a bleak vision of the future. The philosopher Samuel Scheffler (2013), in an intriguing thesis, takes this further to ask if species survival is even more important to us than our own individual deaths: without the prospect of a human future we might surely lose morale entirely.

Strong pronatalist views exist among philosophers on logical grounds as well as the general public on emotional and commonsense grounds. (And not only pronatalist but prolongevist, e.g. Overall, 2003.) Perhaps the best case is put by posthumanists who want to acknowledge the extent of human suffering but believe it can be overcome technologically. 'Life is so bad that it is morally right to desist from bringing new lives into existence' has some compelling charge to it but demands to be supported by evidence that life really is so bad, and such undisputed evidence is hard to come by. 'Life is extremely bad for most people right now but the means of effectively addressing and overcoming the volume of badness are at hand' is a different moral case. Benatar concedes that if his case were taken so seriously that large numbers of people actually stopped reproducing, suffering would probably *increase* significantly before world population reached zero, but this is nevertheless the desirable end state. While this is a shocking, counterintuitive and even immoral position as far as some are concerned, Benatar argues his case tightly. It is, after all, one thing to pause before conceiving if the future human being might experience grave genetic problems and existential misfortunes (which we usually cannot know in advance), but can one really say that every life is destined for significant misfortune? Benatar argues that the negatives are always underplayed in our assessments of life satisfaction, life does contain suffering for even the luckiest and the risks involved in creating new life outweigh alleged satisfaction. Many, perhaps most people conceal or lie about the extent of their actual distress (Benatar & Wasserman, 2015).

The case for voluntary human extinction is taken further by those sometimes dubbed efilists (life spelled backwards), whose view is that all sentient life suffers and this state of affairs should be ended. A significant minority of philosophical misanthropists make the case that humanity is terminally bad but the animal world is innocent, and humans should become extinct in order to restore nature to its pre-human beauty and balance. But an argument can be made, of course, that nature contains as much 'evil' and suffering as anything created by humans (Drees, 2003). Wild animals suffer tremendously. Unstable geological formations necessarily entail periodic disasters. Equally, even given the scenario of a world cleansed of humans, there is little reason to believe that something human-like could not eventually evolve again. Benatar does not go this far at all, and we should recognise that nature has no conscious awareness and choice, as we do.

Support for the philosophical case for antinatalism comes from those who, contrary to popular intuition, feel that a world population of well over seven billion is quite sufficient. Given the availability of effective contraception and freedom from religious coercion, individuals are now free to choose, and part of their moral assessment should include:'for whose sake am I making this baby, its own, or for mine?' All such matters are now receiving extensive attention (Crawford, 2010; Coates, 2014; Perry, 2014; Conly, 2016). A child-free life is sometimes promoted as simply an alternative lifestyle devoted to the greater pleasure of those who exist rather than making sacrifices. To some extent this is reflected in the Japanese phenomenon of *mendokusai*, of people in their 20s and 30s avoiding relational commitments and pregnancies in an already over-crowded and too-competitive society. Falling birth rates in some countries can also be interpreted as instinctive moral choices, although *smaller* families are not what Benatar has in mind. And although sections of the gay community have sought the right and the means to have or adopt babies, others such as Edelman (2004) emphasise the freedom to maximise pleasure, or *jouissance*, and to avoid the complications and responsibilities of conception and childcare.

Interestingly, no credible study linking these philosophical concerns to psychological experience has been made, to my knowledge. In other words, if we put the question to a large sample of people – 'If life is as bad as this, do you ever wish you had never been born?' – what would we find? We can assume that those who have killed themselves, were they able to be represented, would probably answer affirmatively. One must say 'probably' here because even lives that end in suicide triggered by acute distress may have had generally good times in them, when non-existence was not wished for. But the question is complicated by the probability that many people would lie, either consciously suppressing dismal thoughts or having chronically dismissed any conscious wish for non-existence: the cultural norm is overwhelmingly a pro-life view. We might also factor in the likelihood that many are poor judges of the hedonic-agonic balance. In an acute sense, this is where depressive realism in its original meaning is tested – are DRs better judges than others of life's hedonic-agonic balance? It is difficult to imagine a team of psychologists objective enough and a psychology experiment subtle and rigorous enough to capture such data.

Suicide and assisted dying

The desperate, sometimes barely premeditated suicide of the young, acutely depressed person may be different from that of the elderly person who has endured years of physical pain and other forms of suffering and seeks a merciful exit. But they share the concept of human rights. Any individual who finds his or her life so burdensome surely has the right to end it. Indeed, we may brush aside the question of rights, since most people can find the means to end their lives if they so wish, legally or not. Human rights are also, we might add, merely a rhetorical device that can be brushed aside by any determinedly brute act. Philosophers make the assumption that philosophical logic is compelling but psychological irrationality and physical strength and action tend to

46 Philosophy and depressive realism

trump deliberation: brutalism is usually ignored altogether by social science and philosophy academics, or it is assumed to have inferior status to thought since philosophers are thinkers.

Famously, Camus (1955/2005) declared that suicide is the only really serious philosophical problem: why do we persist when life is often so difficult, painful, repetitive and absurd? He comes to the conclusion that being and staying alive must be valued even amid dire struggles; we owe it to our future selves to remain alive. But such impassioned and/or logical pro- and anti-suicide arguments mean little to the person whose constitution is depressive, whose life experiences are grim and whose prospects look bleak. As the playwright Sarah Kane put it in her 1998 play *Crave*, which was partly modelled on T.S. Eliot's *The Wasteland*:

'She ceases to continue with the day to day farce of getting through the next few hours in an attempt to ward off the fact that she doesn't know how to get through the next forty years' (Kane, 2006, p. 183).

Kane hanged herself the following year. ('I'm not ill, I just know that life is not worth living' says character C on p. 188 of Kane's play *Crave*.) Philosophers can create all sorts of counter-arguments, as I have said, and psychotherapists in their habit of psychological reductionism create myriad theories and sell associated remedies. But these have no power over the acutely, viscerally despairing and decisive suicidal person, not even over the suicidal psychotherapist who 'should know better'. The suicide knows that the-entity-that-I-am is not viable; only occasionally does she or he articulate motives for suicide that go beyond personal despair into a negative worldview statement.

Arguably, the greatest moral pull against suicide is put by those close to those who commit suicide and who are devastated by it (Hecht, 2013; Wertheimer, 2014). Jennifer Michael Hecht wrote her book after her friends Sarah Hannah and Rachel Wetzsteon killed themselves; they had both been successful poets. Hecht's final, rather more emotional than philosophical admonition is to find 'the courage to stay.' She fully acknowledges the despair driving the suicidal impulse but promotes the counter-arguments, among which are the moral claims of one's future self, the effects on those bereaved and also the (unconvincing, I believe) objection that suicide solves nothing (although it's true that the suicidal person doesn't get to relish the solution). A converse ethical argument is put by those who are 'tired of living' with or without medical problems, who wish to die without stigma and whose physician might consider helping them, at least in some countries (Bolt et al., 2015).

What is rarely confronted philosophically or existentially is the problem of so-called copycat or cluster suicides, or the powerful ripple effects. It is well known that this phenomenon occurs. Rezső Seress's song *Gloomy Sunday* (the 'Hungarian suicide song') was written in 1933 and appeared to be associated with many subsequent suicides in Hungary, the United States and elsewhere, resulting in bans on the song being played. Seress, a Holocaust survivor, killed himself in 1968. I knew a middle-aged woman who hanged herself quite soon after her adult daughter committed suicide. Apart from the psychological explanations for this ('I should have known, I should have done more, I can't live with myself without that person, I must follow her to the other side'), we can pose the problem of completed suicide normalising suicidal action: suicide may then be considered morally wrong both because it induces immense sadness in loved-ones and because it appears to open the door to de-stigmatisation. The moral argument 'You should not kill yourself because it makes some others want to do it' is a curious one which almost confirms the DR case that life is bad, and many live their lives in chronic denial until something as negatively dramatic as this occurs which gives them permission to think and do likewise.

Suicides attributable to shame and honour, poverty, impulse, realistic fear of impending rape and murder, clinical depression and other forms of mental illness, group pressure (think of the mass suicide in Jonestown in 1978), release from pain and rational choice, are by no means identical. Suicides are recorded from ancient times and in different cultures with differing motives (Minois, 1999; Colluci & Lester, 2012). But there is a universal sadness attached to suicide and an implicit recognition that open discussion of the subject is distasteful. Yet it being pushed underground may be a factor contributing to it happening, and if Camus is right that it is such a serious philosophical problem, we should expect to see more open and robust discussion (Perry, 2014; Critchley, 2015). Is suicide a phenomenon related only to a minority of pathologically unbalanced individuals, or can it be regarded as a statement of philosophical pessimism and rejectionism? Is it always selfish and cowardly, or is it sometimes noble and brave and a sign of integrity that is lacking in those afraid to do likewise? Should it be seen as weird, exceptional and based on a wholly unacceptable worldview? Why do a significant number of human beings (not animals) kill themselves? These may be unpleasant challenges but they remain unsatisfactorily addressed.

How should we live?

Digby Tantam, in a text examining the concept of emotional well-being and drawing on a wide range of classical philosophical, psychological, health and psychotherapeutic sources, comes to the conclusion that trying to live well is the only thing that makes life worth living at all (Tantam, 2014). He fully recognises the objections to and nuances of this position. Yet this view implies that we really have a choice as to whether to live. Arguably, most of us carry on living not in order to live well but because the alternative, death, is extremely frightening. We live because we are biological beings programmed to do so, life has its norms and charms and also because we are locked into social systems that make it very difficult for us to opt out. There may be a slither of freedom and nobility in our minds and actions but much of our behaviour operates according to and resembles the billiard ball analogy, one thing simply causing or leading to another. One is born in certain circumstances, into a certain class, and the combination of educational, career and other pressures shapes a professional life. Anyone might with apparent free will opt out and follow a world-saving calling of some kind but few do, and about those who do we cannot confidently say they 'did well' or made a significant difference. We all say we 'did our best' and yet such phrases mean very little.

Whether to conceive and give birth and whether to commit suicide are perhaps the two most acute moral questions. However, the question of how best to live our lives once we have been conceived, born and grown up and decided not to kill ourselves, is probably the more pressing: it is the age-old question of the good life. This is a far from easy question – do we mean the good life as portrayed in religious scriptures, in philosophical history; the ideal good life; the tolerably good life or what? It is here we need sharper thinking, whether from philosophers or other specialists. I suspect that philosophy as narrowly conceived – as an academic enterprise characterised by intellectual genealogy, neurotic argumentation and practical irrelevance – will have to give way to philosophies of politics, science and technology to help guide us through the future.

We should expect to see the death of traditional, ritualistic philosophy follow the slow death of religion, if the laws of entropy follow through chronologically. First Middle East-generated myth loses its credulity (its bicameral pull), and then Greek-spawned abstract reason gradually loses its power. These have little if any further necessity. If humanity survives its current round of crises, its challenges are likely to be of a kind requiring hard-nosed practical reasoning. Kahneman has contrasted System 1 (fast, instinctive, intuitive) thinking with System 2 (slow, deliberative, logical, algorithmic) thinking, but even this model already looks dated. Philosophy like fashion generates infinite new products that beguile, anchor and keep the producers in employment. Philosophy has as its 'god' the chimera of omnipotent and impersonal logic applied to inexhaustible new intellectual quarries. One of its chief myths is the idea that it is essential to everyday and civilizational moral problem-solving. Dearden (2005), acknowledging the problem that philosophers frequently accuse each other of writing nonsense, examines a number of 'illusions of meaning' before concluding that philosophy should be chastened but not impeded in its endless quest. The Aristotelian quest for the answer to the problem of what the good life is has gone on since the *Nicomachean Ethics* and may go on forever. A downbeat, DR-adjusted calculation of the good life is given in a chapter titled *Eking out meaning and morale on miraginous uplands* (Feltham, 2015).

Personality dependent realism

Just as long-running tribal differences continue to divide us, so also individual differences of opinion seem never to fade. Not only must we concede that we cannot perceive things in themselves but only know our perceptions, but perhaps we also have to concede that any ideal of consensual human reality is troubled by both tribalism and personality dependent realism. The world appears this way, x, to you, but y to me and z to another. The world is not simply divided into believers and atheists or left and right-wing supporters but into an impossibly kaleidoscopic multiplicity of views. Long-married couples do not see eye to eye on everything, and often the differences in perception and belief lead to unresolvable conflict. No two philosophers, while paying lip service to objective logic, seem to agree on even the smallest of matters. Scientists may largely agree, at least provisionally, on proven physical laws but this does not necessarily unite them politically and philosophically. Evolution and history have bequeathed us deep-seated tribal differences and problems that are compounded by individual personality differences and problems. To some extent this makes the world a colourful, fascinating place: we can delight in cultural and individual differences characterised by ostensibly bio-epistemological variety. But the intransigence of views rooted in personality differences is problematic.

Human individuality and subjectivity are nested within cultural and species norms. There can be no truly independent free thinker. We value free thinking and indeed often elevate free thinkers to the vaunted status of genius. But an uneasy tension always exists between the conformist thinking of the *they* (variously dubbed the proletariat, bovine masses, bureautypes) and the rebellious or iconoclastic thinking of the outsider, the heretic. The gay community arguably over-estimates the importance of its cause in the greater scheme of things, exaggerating the extent of homosexuality and bisexuality. Estimates of gay identity vary but commonly centre on a figure of 1.5% to 5% of the population. Scientologists exaggerate their claims, and their perceptions of persecution. Likewise, depressive realists, another minority, may tend to see matters as worse than they are, and they may exaggerate the importance of what they have to say. And within all minority groups differences of opinion exist that are either silenced or lead to splinter groups. Against this scenario of irreconcilable differences, we hold the tacit ideal of logic, as if this God-like faculty will one day overrule all epistemological conflicts (Percival, 2012). However, it looks as if both cultural and personality dependent realisms – evolved, hardened, persistent, infra-rational – will always ultimately trump reason. The democratic-sounding cultural norm of 'everyone is entitled to their own opinion' is at odds with the probability that some are better epistemologists than others.

Kierkegaard wanted to combine radical individual moral responsibility with Christian faith. Ayn Rand's promotion of moral and economic individualism provides a curious bid for the status of rationality combined with a capitalist-based personality dependent realism. Quite differently, Michel Henry's radical phenomenology helps to justify individualism. Much psychotherapy theory rests on different notions of psychological truth serving individual, idiosyncratic and idiopathic ends. How we are to understand this bottomless quarrel between philosophies, philosophers and others? What is it that generates this ceaseless jostling for epistemological dominance, if not aeons of evolution embodied in the will of countless phenomena, including cultures and individuals, in relationships that are complex beyond human understanding? We can think of this question as depressing, untrue, poorly articulated, or as grounds for further thinking. We might see in it signs of ever-increasing entropic disorder.

Conclusions

What a terrible responsibility it is to live, to remain alive, to have children, to participate in and uphold complex social systems that we barely understand. What evasiveness it is to hand over serious questions to theologians, philosophers and other academics who then too often resort to dull repetition and fashionable obfuscation. As a lecturer I am sometimes acutely aware and ashamed of the superficiality of what I teach, the shallow theories passed down from year to year, from generation to generation: they have the appearance of weightiness but they do not engage with the seriousness of life. Svendsen (2005) admits that his own philosophy lectures must sometimes be boring and that he himself is often bored by them. As a parent I am ashamed of the casualness with which I have expected my children to accept and work within nonsensical social and economic systems (Jaeggi, 2014). I am ashamed that I allow to pass unchallenged the many disciplines like philosophy that pass as the best of deep thought about matters that concern us all. We sit beneath an awe-inspiring canopy of stars, alone in this weird universe, dogged by anthropathological millennia, sleepwalking into disaster and still produce mind-numbing philosophy. We reside in subjectivity and some of us strive for the objectivity promised by philosophy and science, yet most of us must surely flounder in the middle ground of prejudices, epistemic fog and social persuasion. We can surely do better or be more honest than philosophers. And into this appeal for seriousness we also have to inject the paradoxical futilitarian shrug that acknowledges the so-whatness of it all. After all the sound and fury of our learned efforts, so what?

References

Becker, E. (1973) *The Denial of Death*. New York: Free Press.

Benatar, D. (2006) *Better Never to Have Been: The Harm of Coming into Existence*. Oxford: Oxford University Press.

Benatar, D. (2016) Life is not good. In T.K. Shackelford & R.D. Hansen (eds). *The Evolution of Morality*. New York: Springer.

Benatar, D. & Wasserman, D. (2015) *Debating Procreation: Is It Wrong to Reproduce?* Oxford: Oxford University Press.

Bolt, E.E., Snijdwwind, M.C., Willems, D.L., van der Heide, A. & Onwuteaka-Philipsen, B.D. (2015) Can physicians conceive of performing euthanasia in case of psychiatric disease, dementia or being tired of living? *Journal of Medical Ethics*, 0, 1–7. Doi: 10.1136/medethics.2014–102150.

Brassier, R. (2006) *Nihil Unbound: Enlightenment and Extinction*. London: Palgrave.

Burton, R. (1621/2001) *The Anatomy of Melancholy*. New York: New York Review Books.

Coates, K. (2014) *Antinatalism: Rejectionist Philosophy from Buddhism to Benatar*. First Edition Design (Kindle). Sarasota, FL: Design Publishing.

Cohen, S. (2010) *States of Denial: Knowing about Atrocities and Suffering (2nd edn.)*. London: Polity.

Colluci, E. & Lester, D. (eds) (2012) *Suicide and Culture: Understanding the Context*. Cambridge, MA: Hogrefe.

Philosophy and depressive realism 51

Conly, S. (2016) *One Child: Do We Have a Right to More?* New York: Oxford University Press.

Crawford, J. (2010) *Confessions of an Antinatalist.* Charleston, WV: Nine-Banded Books.

Critchley, S. (2015) *Notes on Suicide.* London: Fitzcarraldo.

Dearden, I. (2005) *Do Philosophers Talk Nonsense? An Inquiry into the Possibility of Illusions of Meaning.* New Romney: Teller.

Drees, W.B. (ed) (2003) *Is Nature Ever Evil? Religion, Science and Value.* London: Routledge.

Edelman, L. (2004) *No Future: Queer Theory and the Death Drive.* Durham, NC: Duke University Press.

Feltham, C. (2015) *Keeping Ourselves in the Dark.* Charleston, WV: Nine-Banded Books.

Frankfurt, H. (2005) *On Bullshit.* Princeton, NJ: Princeton University Press.

Fremstedal, R. (2012) Peter Wessel Zapffe: Kierkegaard as a forerunner of pessimistic existentialism. In J. Stewart (ed). *Kierkegaard's Influence on Philosophy – German and Scandinavian Philosophy.* Farnham: Ashgate.

Graham, G. (2010) *The Disordered Mind: An Introduction to Philosophy of Mind and Mental Illness.* New York: Routledge.

Gray, J. (2002) *Straw Dogs: Thoughts on Humans and Other Animals.* London: Granta.

Gray, J. (2013) *The Silence of Animals: On Progress and Other Modern Myths.* London: Allen Lane.

Gray, J. (2015) *The Soul of the Marionette: A Short Inquiry into Human Freedom.* New York: Farrar, Straus & Giroux.

Hecht, J.M. (2013) *Stay: A History of Suicide and the Philosophies against It.* Newhaven, NJ: Yale University Press.

Heidegger, M. (2008) *Basic Writings (ed. D.F. Krell).* London: Routledge.

Heinegg, P. (2005) *Better Than Both: The Case for Pessimism.* Lanham, MD: Hamilton.

Jackson, M. (2013) *Essays in Existential Anthropology.* Chicago, IL: University of Chicago Press.

Jaeggi, R. (2014) *Alienation.* New York: Columbia University Press.

Kane, S. (2006) *Complete Plays.* London: Bloomsbury.

Land, N. (1992) *The Thirst for Annihilation: Georges Bataille and Virulent Nihilism.* London: Routledge.

Ligotti, T. (2010) *The Conspiracy against the Human Race.* New York: Hippocampus.

Michael, M. & Caldwell, P. (2010) The consolations of optimism. In D. Benatar (ed). *Life, Death, and Meaning: Key Philosophical Readings on the Big Questions (2nd edn.).* New York: Rowman & Littlefield.

Minois, G. (1999) *History of Suicide: Voluntary Death in Western Culture.* Baltimore, MA: Johns Hopkins University Press.

Nietzsche, F. (1971) Twilight of the idols. In W. Kaufmann (ed). *The Portable Nietzsche,* p 473. New York: Viking Press.

Overall, C. (2003) *Aging, Death, and Human Longevity: A Philosophical Inquiry.* Berkeley, CA: University of California Press.

Percival, R.S. (2012) *The Myth of the Closed Mind.* Chicago, IL: Open Court.

Perry, S. (2014) *Every Cradle Is a Grave: Rethinking the Ethics of Birth and Suicide.* Charleston, WV: Nine-Banded Books.

Perry, S. (2016) Fertility transition in the last 200 years. Unpublished presentation, Oakland University, Michigan, Conference on the Evolution of Psychopathology, 19 April.

Saltus, E. (1885/2014) *The Philosophical Writings of Edgar Saltus.* Underworld Amusements.

Schalkx, R. & Bergsma, A. (2008) Arthur's advice: Comparing Arthur Schopenhauer's advice on happiness with contemporary research. *Journal of Happiness Studies,* 9 (3), 379–395.

Scheffler, S. (2013) *Death and the Afterlife.* New York: Oxford University Press.

52 Philosophy and depressive realism

Sim, S. (2015) *A Philosophy of Pessimism*. London: Reaktion.

Sloterdijk, P. (1987) *Critique of Cynical Reason*. Minneapolis, MN: University of Minnesota Press.

Sommers, T. & Rosenberg, A. (2002) Darwin's nihilistic idea: Evolution and the meaninglessness of life. *Biology and Philosophy*, 18, 653–668.

Sterelny, K. (2003) *Thought in a Hostile World: The Evolution of Human Cognition*. Malden, MA: Blackwell.

Svendsen, L. (2005) *A Philosophy of Boredom*. London: Reaktion.

Tallis, R. (2011) *Aping Mankind: Neuromania, Darwinitis, and the Misrepresentation of Humanity*. Durham: Acumen.

Tantam, D. (2014) *Emotional Well-Being and Mental Health*. London: Sage.

Taylor, S.E. (1991) *Positive Illusions: Creative Self-Deception and the Healthy Mind*. New York: Basic Books.

Wertheimer, A. (2014) *A Special Scar: The Experiences of People Bereaved by Suicide*. London: Routledge.

Wolf, S. (2010) *Meaning in Life and Why It Matters*. Princeton, NJ: Princeton University Press.

Zapffe, P.W. (1933/2004) The last messiah. *Philosophy Now*, March/April. Transl. Gisle Tangenes.

Chapter 4

Literature, film and depressive realism

We face the intriguing but frustrating probability that we can never know when our species began to introspect, using words-made-thought, on the nature of existence. Nor can we know when and how our distant ancestors first communicated with each other about existential matters. All we have to go on regarding beginnings are scattered texts on moral instruction, notably from Sumerian and Egyptian sources dating from about 27th century BCE. The Mesopotamian *Epic of Gilgamesh* is probably the best known of ancient (approximately 18th century BCE) texts. Death, grief, the search for immortality, leadership and the good life, the relationship between the gods and mankind, are its main themes. It also features a proto-biblical flood and motifs later taken up by Homer. *The Egyptian Book of the Dead* probably also dates from the time of *Gilgamesh*. The Indian *Rigveda* may date from as early as 1700 BCE and contains stories about the origins of the world, hymns to the gods, ritual use of the consciousness-changing plant *soma*, death and marriage. If there is any merit in Jaynes's (1976) thesis, *Gilgamesh* and similar epics may represent the shift from what he refers to as the bicameral mind (in which the early gods spoke to mankind as aural hallucinations) to the subjective consciousness we possess today, which bears the marks of introspection, analysis and mortality salience among others.

How did we get here, how did anything get here, why must we suffer and die, how can we best live? These are the common themes and they have continued into the present day, although often now dissected more within philosophy and the sciences. Animals do not do any of this, lacking necessary consciousness, language and technology. Some animals use very rudimentary tools, and many human texts are about practical instructions, but it is a peculiarity of humans that we frequently write ponderously and in anguished and tragic terms. It is frequently noted that we are story-telling beings, that mythology and narrative are central to our self-understanding. Yet we analyse literature more often for its greatness than the sadness of its arguably regrettable necessity. We had to wait until 1964 for Marshall McLuhan to tell us the medium was the message, yet perhaps we have still not fully appreciated the sad coincidence of language and alienation both in our evolution and everyday life. In other words, language, thought and literature can be considered part of the *problem* of being human, a record of wrenching ourselves from so-called brute existence to an increasingly symbolic and self-alienated existence. Wilson (2008) argues that the large slice of melancholy to be found in literature is essential to its very identity. Compare this claim with the following: 'the real gloom, the sincere despair, is dumb and blind; it writes no books' (cited in Unamuno, 1921/1954). We have no direct literary record, no documented sublimation, from our profoundly DR ancestors.

Poetry and drama

Humans have lamented their existence and struggled to articulate means of overcoming problems for unknown millennia and struggled to convey this through language that is often inadequate for the task. About the same time as the Buddha proclaimed that all life is suffering, the Greek tragedian Aeschylus famously pronounced that 'death is easier than a wretched life; and better never to have been than to live and fare badly'. The Hindu *Mahabharata* from about 400 BCE is said to be the world's longest poem. Drama and poetry have been the natural forms of literary and philosophical expression for a very long time. As well as ancient Hindu and Greek texts, we have many epic poems that express humanity's most central concerns, from Homer's *Iliad* and *Odyssey* to Dante's *Divine Comedy* and Milton's *Paradise Lost*. Key themes of limited time have ranged from Marvel's 'wingèd chariot hurrying near' of the 17th century, to Ingeborg Bachman's 'I am the Continual-Thought-Of-Dying' in the mid-20th century.

The Italian writer Giacomo Leopardi (1798–1837) is often referred to as a poet but was also a philosopher and philologist, like Nietszche. His celebrated *Canti* (1831) contains poems on civilizational decay, on the disappointments of modernity, unrequited love, death, fate, solitude, illusion and the 'emptiness of everything' and have a generally pessimistic tone. 'Natural man' is contrasted with the troubled modern human whose passions are blunted (so-called historical pessimism), but according to Williams (1987), Leopardi had a deeper second phase of 'cosmic pessimism' in which he considered human life at all times and places essentially unhappy. Leopardi often expresses a preference for not being over existence, and voices some clearly antinatalist views. In his massive volume *Zibaldone* he presents a brilliant if rambling commentary on classical thinkers, on language and translation, aesthetics, animal life, history, politics, metaphysics, science and music. Like Robert Burton in his equally weighty *The Anatomy of Melancholy*, Leopardi shows encyclopaedic energy for and intriguing speculation on such depressing themes. Leopardi is surely an intuitive proto-psychologist and proto-anthropathologist. His work, much admired by Schopenhauer and Beckett among others, is filled with DR gems. 'It is against the constant laws that we can see observed by nature that the principal being cannot enjoy the perfection of its being, which is happiness, without which being itself, that is, existence, is burdensome' (1898/2015, p. 51). Confirming Zapffe's concept of sublimation, Leopardi wrote that for 'a great soul that finds itself in a state of extreme dejection, disenchantment, nothingness, boredom, and discouragement about life. . . . such works always bring consolation' (1898/2015, p. 177).

James Thomson, the Scottish poet who – like the Danish philosopher Søren Kierkegaard and the Norwegian artist Edvard Munch – experienced several deaths in his family as a youth, in his long, far from elegant but darkly pithy poem *The City of Dreadful Night* (1874) summarised and anticipated many classic DR themes:

As if a Being, God or Fiend, could reign
At once so wicked, foolish and insane,
As to produce men when He might refrain!

The world rolls forever like a mill;
It grinds out death and life and good and ill;
It has no purpose, heart or mind or will.

Man might know one thing were his sight less dim;
That it whirls not to suit his petty whim,
That it is quite indifferent to him.

It is paradoxical that so many poets like T.S. Eliot have enjoyed relative popularity and a Nobel Prize, when their work has been so gloom-laden. Philip Larkin managed to hold the status of Poet Laureate while 'terms such as "philistine", "parochial", "suburban" or more sympathetically "wistful", "sad" and "circumspect" would follow him to the grave' (Bradford, 2005, p. 13). Far worse was said about him, including references to his weariness with religion, cynicism, nationalism, racism, misogyny, infidelity, fondness for alcohol and utter gloom. Yet Larkin's one pithy line 'They fuck you up, your Mum and Dad' is now well lodged in popular consciousness, and his preoccupations with transience and death abound in lines like 'the sure extinction that we travel to' and 'death is no different whined at than withstood' in *Aubade*. In the collection *The Less Deceived* we encounter many poems that earn Larkin his reputation for grimness. In the poem *Deceptions* Larkin considers the publicised plight of a girl who has been raped, hence 'deceived' in one sense, while contrasting this with the self-deception of the rapist who imagined his act would bring some sort of fulfilment.

Many poets are noted as illustrating the link between creativity and mental illness. Gerard Manley Hopkins experienced much depression mixed with religiosity ('I wake and feel the fell of dark' being one of his famously melancholy lines), but he is only one among many writers and artists who struggled with dysphoric moods and worldviews (Fox, 2009). A number of suicidal female poets and novelists stand out – Emily Dickinson, Virginia Woolf, Sylvia Plath and Anne Sexton. Plath's preoccupation with dark themes, especially death, has been amply analysed by both literary critics and psychologists, with some agreement that she suffered from childhood grief, high intelligence, transgenerational or endogenous depression, situational stressors and inappropriate pharmaceutical treatment (Cooper, 2003). Yet Plath did not necessarily view all life for everyone as a grim affair. Plath's daughter Frieda Hughes, who was not yet three years

56 Literature, film and depressive realism

old when Sylvia gassed herself (with Frieda and her younger brother in another, sealed room in the house), subsequently had to endure the suicides of her father's next partner, Assia Guttman, with her child, and her own brother Nicholas later in life. Although she does not appear to have become a fully-fledged DR, ample death awareness is apparent in her own poetry. In *The Reason for Not Being*, for example (in Hughes, 2009, p. 69), we can detect antinatalist refrains from Hardy's Jude Fawley, and from Philip Larkin ('Man hands on misery to man/It deepens like a coastal shelf'):

> The six-year old daughter that I never had
> Sits on her bed-edge kicking her heels . . . . . .

In Macbeth we hear among other haunting judgements about life that it is (as well as a brief candle, a walking shadow, ending in dusty death, etc.) 'a tale told by an idiot, full of sound and fury, signifying nothing'. The remarkable quality of such lines, apart from their intrinsic artistry, is that they make such an impression as to become an accepted aspect of mainstream culture. Their DR and nihilistic message is blatant and yet apparently accepted without fuss. If you said anything to this effect in polite conversation today, you would probably be called cynical or depressed. In *Hamlet*, written around the same time (the dates are disputed but close to 1600), we see another revenge theme playing out, also surrounded by ideas of madness and existential doubt. Hamlet's 'what a piece of work is a man' and 'to be or not to be' have been subjected to repeated analysis by literary critics, philosophers and psychoanalysts, including Kant, Coleridge, Schopenhauer, Kierkegaard, Heidegger, T.S. Eliot, Freud and Lacan. The esteem in which Shakespeare is held seems paradoxical when his tragicomic outlook presumably does not match mainstream worldviews. Hamlet's celebrated melancholy and nihilism continue to exercise academics worldwide (Cutrofello, 2014), just as the play itself, like *Waiting for Godot*, is one of the most frequently performed and admired. Perhaps we might say that it illustrates the Zapffean defence of sublimation, drawing on the unconscious fascination with meaninglessness and non-being of both elite and ordinary people who would otherwise claim to be well-adjusted, optimistic individuals who do not overthink. If so, can we ask if the greatness of a work of literature lies in its ability to unlock its consumers' darkest fears? Perhaps not, after all, given the success of the genre of horror in popular literature and film; or perhaps the metric of greatness itself is simply another illusion we live by.

Novels

Novels appeared from about the medieval period and manifested in quite different genres, by no means all tragic. Cervantes' *Don Quixote* is often regarded as the first modern European novel (1605), which Dienstag (2006) summarises as 'pessimistic wisdom'. Goethe's *The Sorrows of Young Werther* (1774) depicted unrequited love resulting in suicide and led in real life to so-called copy-cat suicides. A book of the present kind could be amply illustrated by reference to Thomas Hardy alone. Both his poems and novels carry the heavy weight of social injustices, tragic biographies and an overarchingly indifferent universe, yet often mitigated by romance and rural charms (Rai, 1996; Avery, 2009). *Jude the Obscure*, first published in 1896, must stand as one of the all-time greats of the DR oeuvre, with its themes of unmet hopes, social absurdities, doomed romance, suicide and murder. Following a scene in which young Jude discusses with his step-mother the hardship they face as a family, he kills his two siblings and himself. The elder Jude is told by the doctor that 'there are such boys springing up amongst us . . . the outcome of new views on life. They seem to see all its terrors before they are old enough to have staying power to resist them' (Hardy, 1896/1985, p. 410). Hardy's work has long been linked with Schopenhauer (Garwood, 1911).

Horace McCoy's *They Shoot Horses Don't They?* (1935), describes the desperate participation of Gloria Beatty in a dance marathon during the Great Depression, and was dubbed by Simone de Beauvoir the first American existential novel. When Gloria, who perspicaciously observes that 'the big break is always coming tomorrow,' entreats Robert Syverton, her dance partner, to shoot her because she cannot do it herself, he obliges in the same way his grandfather had had to shoot a horse with practical compassion, and he is convicted of murder. The necessary historical situatedness of the above novels may belie their perennial DR themes. Philip Roth's slim but powerful novel *Everyman* dwells on a 20th century American life but calls upon the 15th century morality play of the same name to pose questions of ageing and death and how well one has lived.

In Sartre's (1938/1965) philosophical novel *Nausea* we read the observations of Antoine Roquentin on daily life. Amid the bare, mundane descriptions of his days are scattered phrases giving insight into Sartre's view of life. 'Then the Nausea seized me' (p. 33). 'The Nausea isn't inside me: I can feel it *over there* on the wall, on the braces, everywhere around me . . . it is I who am inside *it.*' 'It is I, *it is I* who pull myself from the nothingness . . . Hatred and disgust for existence are just so many ways of making me exist. (p. 145)'. What Sartre refers to as 'horrible ecstasy' (p. 188) is the negative revelation I refer to here. Clear though it may be to psychoanalysts that 'the Nausea' is unconsciously projected from within, we see that the Bible's words 'the whole creation groans' (Romans 8.22) posits sin as affecting the entire phenomenal world. Brennan's (2004) 'transmission of affect' speaks of pervasive reach; and the 'affective turn' calls attention to fashions in intellectuality giving way to feelings. The Japanese term *kanashii* refers to 'the melancholy which is embedded in objects' or the 'sadness of things' (Bowring, 2008, p. 127). Another Japanese term, *wabi sabi*, refers too to the melancholy within objects, the recognition of their ephemerality. Beckett's decaying landscapes (White, 2009) and Eliot's wasteland are forever lodged in the contemporary mind. Readers may have experienced both the *bookshop blues* feeling of being among thousands of new books one will never have time to read, and the counterpoint observation of so many sadly discarded, now unfashionable books sitting in charity shops. Human constructions stare back at us but nature, too, polluted and carved up by us, elicits more feelings than only aesthetic pleasure (Schwenger, 2006).

Cormac McCarthy's *The Road*, made famous by the film, begins and continues in deep bleakness, in an environment akin to nuclear winter that is thinly populated by desperate humans driven to brutality and cannibalism. The father's protectiveness and his son's love make for aching pathos. The novel can instantly recall many related texts, such as Eliot's *The Wasteland*, Beckett's *Malone Dies*, Thomas Glavinic's *Night Work* or David Vann's *Legend of a Suicide* that share desolate landscapes and near-hopelessness. But where Beckett uses an ageographical and absurdist narrative device, McCarthy places his figures in a vague but once real post-apocalyptic American landscape that we can easily envisage and even see as inevitable. His tale is not an argument from anthropathology to antinatalism but a tender recognition of affective bonds, perhaps even a fragile hope that love may after all conquer all. In P.D. James's novel *Children of Men* (and its 2006 film interpretation) a futuristic, wrecked and partly barren landscape is contrasted with an elite opulence, and human barrenness is punctuated only by the arrival after 18 years of civilisation's first new baby. But where female fertility and hope is projected in James's future, in McCarthy's novel the wife is absent, having been unable to bear the horrors of the future world and killed herself, with the father then carrying the role of protector, urging his son to 'carry the fire within'.

In the first few pages of *The Possibility of an Island* Michel Houellebecq packs in sufficient sexism, racism, ageism, barbed atheism and general misanthropy to feed his critics all they expect. The narrator Daniel1 is a comedian who provides mercilessly cynical commentary on everyday life, its superficiality, the deterioration of the body and waning of sexual desire and performance and the declining human population. A kind of immorality is provided by cloning and protection of the rich. Daniel's future clone Daniel24 has less bitterness and more melancholy. 'Horror at the unending calvary that is man's existence' (p. 43) is one of numerous asides in this book which earn Houellebecq his reputation.

In his most recent novel Houellebeq (2015) took as his theme the possibility of Islamic rule of France in 2022. In order to avoid a Front National political leadership, the French accept a moderate Muslim, Mohammed Ben Abbes, as President. The key character is a Sorbonne academic François, who finally decides to convert to Islam in order to secure his job and a pay increase, as well as warming to the prospect of polygamy. Houellebecq, given his previous, successful court battle against charges of racial hatred, was accused of sensationalism and the worst of Islamophobic motives but this novel can also be seen as prophetic in a DR vein. A naïve Left with fantasies of triumphant human goodness sleepwalks into a political and social disaster that turns back the very freedoms it cherishes. Fortuitously, the author appeared on the cover of the magazine *Charlie Hebdo* on the same day its cartoonists were massacred in January 2015 by radical Islamists, following which Houellebecq himself had to accept police protection Salman Rushdie-style. Houellebecq is no doubt mischievous and somewhat misanthropic but *Submission* accidentally brings together many of the absurdities of traditional religion, left-right politics, violence, ambition and other aspects of human folly. The central character embodies *accedie*, loses interest in sex, pontificates on his literary preoccupations and opines that 'the mere will to live' is no match for life's many adversities.

Samuel Beckett

Beckett – absurdist poet, dramatist and novelist – warrants his own section here at least. Indeed, we must remark that the 'Beckett industry' is now so vast that the allegedly minority status of DR should be called into question. How can we understand the reputation of a Nobel Prize winner like Beckett whose works are often barely intelligible and at best read as testaments to the meaninglessness, absurdity and suffering of life? How much more literary commentary can be added to an oeuvre that itself was merely an artful commentary on nuances of futility? The same can be said of many other artists and their admirers, of course, Francis Bacon having professed his sense of purpose within a purposeless existence (Lewis, 2014, p. 150/570) and his vision of the human as ultimately mere meat.

Beckett's *Happy Days* explores the absurdity of trying to insist on a contra-Sisyphean view of life when one is half-buried in sand, repeating clichés and talking to a man who barely replies, who is perhaps already dead. Although part of the genre of theatre of the absurd, the play plainly mocks the cultural norm of insistence on happiness in all circumstances. 'Another heavenly day . . . marvellous gift . . . so much to be thankful for . . . can't complain . . . great mercies' are some of Winnie's main platitudes, interspersed with inane actions including cleaning spectacles and filing nails and commenting on the weather. Yet 'sorrow keeps breaking in' and Winnie mysteriously possesses an unused revolver.

The novella *Worstward Ho* was published in 1983, when Beckett was 77. At first reading by anyone uninitiated it must seem gibberish, with its typically pared-down opening lines of 'On. Say on. Be said on. Somehow on. Till nohow on. Said nohow on' (p. 7). It can be read as the fragmented, demented thoughts of an old person, ruminating on the body, on Sisyphean routines, on everyday motivational micro-decisions, on approaching death and death itself. It can be read as any attempt to make sense of life, but particularly of the crumbling body. But over the entire novella surely hangs the anguish of the thinker who faces the slow inevitable end and tries to accept it: 'faintly vainly longing for the least of longing' and 'vain longing that vain longing go' (p. 36). Such hopes were characteristically dismissed by U.G. Krishnamurti as pointless, and clearly Beckett knew acutely their pointlessness, which he converted again and again into poetic rumination. Beckett made no claim to any personal enlightenment and had no mission to enlighten others, his work fitting squarely within the

Zapffean category of sublimation. Yet Calder (2012) interprets the voice in *Worstward Ho* as something like a Schopenhauerian will, the impersonal force that drives everything on, however much suffering it entails. The voice can also question itself and its own actions but it cannot stop the process. One can try not to play the game, but only the infinitesimal minority of the allegedly enlightened can sidestep it.

In the novel *Watt*, Beckett remarks that 'Some see the flesh before the bones, and some see the bones before the flesh, and some never see the bones at all, and some never see the flesh at all' (Beckett, 2009, p. 60). We can interpret this straightforwardly as viviocentricity and optimism vying with mortality salience and pessimism. We could interpret it as a trite comment on individual differences, and we can certainly take sides, placing the one attitude in the healthy camp and the other in the pathological. Indeed, there is no final agreement on whether Beckett is the pessimist he seems to be (Shobeiri & Shobeiri, 2014).

It is as if, along the royal road of integrity to total meaninglessness some meet a diversion which carries them into the Village of Beckett Studies. On reading Beckett, an artist of observation of the absurd, some are enchanted and become dedicated Beckett scholars. Beckett himself had decades ago become enchanted by the writings of Arnold Geulincx and had made notes on them. Today, I am reading Tucker (2012) on Beckett's interest in Geulincx. To some small extent I am interested but also weary. How is it that on my travels towards total meaninglessness I was diverted towards Beckett, and then into various hamlets housing Beckett Studies? How is it that an obscure 17th century religious philosopher like Geulincx pondered the tremendously distal nature of God and his indifference to, possibly even his ignorance of human existence, and the ethics of surrender that flow from that? That this was picked up by Beckett who resonated with it, and later by Beckett-lovers? Are they, or we, all ironically straining off erudite midges of micro-meaning in a meaningless universe, and thinking it all means something? Much as I admire Beckett's work, I sometimes wonder if he along with other essentially early 20th century writers belong to a post-religious but pre-Darwinian tradition, deeply attached to abstract notions that have been superseded by more satisfying scientific explanations.

Depressive and absurdist themes have long filled many novels, plays and poetry, with a disproportionate number of pessimistic authors gaining reputations and winning prizes. (The position of Dante, Shakespeare, Milton, Goethe and all who have historically depicted life in classical good-and-evil or tragicomic terms is a slightly different matter.) However, we have to remind ourselves that in sales terms the romantic, historical, crime, mystery, science fiction, fantasy and spirituality genres easily outsell the kinds of texts we are discussing here. It is the intellectual critics, not the general public, who have a special love of erudite, gloomy and difficult literature. Dystopian novels like *1984* have proved very 'popular', as also, if for different reasons, J.G. Ballard's novels, and occasional gems like Ann Sterzinger's *The Talkative Corpse*. But the modernist-blaming dystopian does not equate to the perennial depressive realist. We can ask whether the literature of (Zapffean) distraction necessarily overshadows that of elitist sublimation, and clearly fiction sales always put non-fiction sales (especially those of DR-oriented works) in the shade.

A fitting way to end this section on novels is to consider an interview with the British novelist Howard Jacobson on the publication of his post-apocalyptic novel *J* (Thorpe, 2014). Jacobson emerges as a 'natural pessimist' whose novel is 'determinedly bleak'. Jacobson says provocatively that he has 'never met an intelligent optimist', an offhand remark that unintentionally plays into the stereotype of the clever but depressive Jew. *J* depicts a dystopian future based on an unnamed 'thing that happened [like McCarthy's *The Road*], if it happened' which implicitly recalls the Holocaust and contains many characters with ironically Jewish names. 'I am a catastrophist, perhaps like all Jews,' says Jacobson. In the novel he has for once desisted from being funny and from being explicitly Jewish in his focus. But the most telling aspect of this interview, to my mind, is Jacobson's declared pleasure in finally, at 72, receiving and being nominated for prestigious literary prizes and being established as a 'man of letters' rather than an 'under-rated British humorist'. Thorpe describes him as 'driven by a fear of obscurity that he feels masks a fear of death'. The sad reality here is that Jacobson remains a minor novelist, that he must die soon enough and he and his novels will quickly be forgotten like all of us; the unknown masses, minor celebrities and enduringly famous are all annihilated by death. And not only that, but given enough time the Holocaust too, in spite of repeated 'lest we forget' warnings, will eventually be forgotten or at least will fade into the history books and into dark legend. The thing that happened (everything) will in a distant future be as if it never happened (Brassier, 2010).

Film

We are unlikely to agree on choice of most depressing films, definition and taste presenting serious obstacles. *Cries and Whispers, The Swimmer, Threads, Magnolia, Schindler's List, Requiem for a Dream, The Road, Melancholia, Love Lisa, 21 Grams* – everyone has their negative favourite. It is worth remembering too that DR appears not only in depressing and tragic genres but also comedy, for example. The character of Boris Yelnikoff in Woody Allen's *Whatever Works* is a classic DR whose misanthropic pronouncements and sense of intellectual superiority are slightly tempered by his ability to bend with the winds of chance. The laughter evoked by Yelnikoff is in proportion to his ridiculously omniscient and outsider status amid the relative affluence and hedonism of New York. His gloomy talk of entropy and meaninglessness is situationally incongruous.

The 1975 film *One Flew Over the Cuckoo's Nest*, based on Ken Kesey's (1962) novel, 'saved' me personally even more than had *Jude the Obscure*. In what is much more than an anti-psychiatric film, when Chief smothers McMurphy it is an act of respect for his already extinguished exuberance. When he puts his arms around the water fountain and rips it from its fitting, then throws it through the hospital window, jumps out and runs to freedom, this has little to do with psychiatry specifically, escape from any one social context, or even the prospects of actually being able to escape. It is the archetypal gesture of furious contempt for unjustified and absurd constraints and the assertion of one's insight and freedom. After years of conformity, trying to adapt to an insanely organised world, finally one can take it no longer. It is the moment when depressed resignation to oppressive social norms breaks open and one is (sadly only briefly) determined to be oneself at all costs. It is the acute individual negation of chronic social negation. It is the vindication of McMurphy's life-affirming spirit, and not essentially different from the reaction of the early apostles of Jesus – an abrupt emotional freedom. But pause to consider whether brief cathartic reprieves actually constitute the 'powerful transformative potential' that Ambrose (2013) and others believe in.

The 2000 film *Requiem for a Dream* is undeniably depressing. At face value it is mainly about three addicted characters. A widow, Sara, sits in her apartment, deeply lonely, and her spirits pick up when she receives notification that she may appear on a television show. On trying to lose weight to fit into her favourite old red dress, her failures lead her to use prescribed amphetamines. Alongside this her son Harry gets involved in heroin pushing with his friend Tyrone. Harry and his beautiful girlfriend Marion are in love and believe they can make enough money to set themselves up with a better lifestyle. Sara ends up psychotic and receiving electroconvulsive therapy, Harry is addicted and has to have his badly infected arm amputated, Tyrone is imprisoned, and Marion is so addicted and impoverished that she resorts to paid sex which escalates to the most degraded form of exhibitionist group sex for money and heroin. The film depicts things going relentlessly from bad to worse. While it is in the drug film genre, *Requiem* is also a comment on the American Dream affecting all generations, all of us having some sort of miserable addiction to unattainable goals. It isn't only about personal weakness of will and street pushers, but about systemic exploitation by corrupt doctors and profiteering pharmaceutical companies. It isn't only about amphetamines and heroin but about alcohol, nicotine, sugar, junk food, television and other taken for granted addictions.

In the acclaimed television series *True Detective* Rust Cohle is a deeply jaded detective from Texas whose lifestyle and opinions render him a loner. The character and the plot throw up relevant questions for our purposes here. The context of their work in Louisiana presents us with gory, ritual serial murder, poverty and prostitution; other police officers are cynical and often corrupt; Cohle's work partner Marty Hart is ostensibly a 'normal' family man but is having an affair. Cohle had a young daughter who died in an accident (he comments that her death at least spared her from later suffering); he is divorced, alcoholic, takes drugs and his apartment is sparsely and indifferently furnished. But it is his personality and observations that are remarkable for their mainstream media attention, including Zapffean or Ligottian asides on the evolutionary misfortune of human consciousness. Hart asks him not to talk 'that odd shit'. Contrary to the image of DR as an unpopular minority view, some reviewers described the show as the best thing on television and as symbolising American deterioration. But while Willie Loman in *Death of a Salesman* is something of a naïve victim of the mid-20th century American dream and Woody Allen's Boris Yelnikoff is a comically unbelievable DR, Cohle's nihilistic views come across as much more threateningly thoughtful. We cannot tell if *True Detective* is merely the latest dark fashion in TV drama, cashing in on the genre of modern horror writing or a sign of DR-predicted acute social entropy.

Film, like music, carries us along, sucks us in on a tide of sensuality. In the case of film we have powerful narrative, visual and aural cues directing us towards certain inferences and emotional states. When we watch *American Beauty*, how do we respond to its final words? Lester Burnham, played by Kevin Spacey, while newly dead from a shooting, provides the voiceover: 'There's so much beauty in the world . . . I can't feel anything but gratitude for every single moment of my stupid little life', while the camera pans across rooftops and music lifts the spirits. I, at least, am inclined to stop and wonder if my life has been too cynical and too ungrateful. Perhaps Melanie Klein was right about the depressive position and some of us are tragically stuck there for a lifetime, angry about what we never had instead of grateful for existence itself. Perhaps Lester reminds us of what we do have to be grateful for, and perhaps all of us may get that dying moment of retrospective grace or neuro-mystically delivered sense of completion. But remember, we are on the receiving end of the film-maker's art and technology, manipulated into certain thoughts and feelings. The sense that I the viewer have a profound insight is facilitated by a set of illusions, and my insight may be no more than another illusion. Should we be depressed at the possibility that film is just another distraction, or allow that it is one among many possible portals to higher consciousness?

The 2011 film *Detachment* shows a slice of American high school life, packed with the negativity of disaffected and violent students, depressed teachers, politicking school governors and aggressive parents. The lead character Henry Barthes is portrayed as an alternating mixture of cynical detachment and great compassion. He refers to Camus. He attempts to save a young prostitute, empathises with an overweight girl who subsequently kills herself and advocates angrily for his dying grandfather in a poorly staffed home. Hopelessness dances with engagement, the film's atmosphere shifting from bleakness to tenderness. Contemporary urban alienation (think, too, of *Falling Down*) is interspersed with flashbacks of Barthes' traumatised childhood, finding his mother having killed herself, and growing up uncertain whether she had been sexually abused by her father. The adult Barthes (sadder but wiser) laments the betrayal of the young, not by wishing that antinatalism had spared them their existence, but observing how uncared for they are. Everyone agrees they have felt 'the weight pressing down on' them. At the end of the film Barthes is teaching his students about Edgar Allen Poe's *The Fall of the House of Usher* and cites Poe's lines: 'a sense of insufferable gloom', 'utter depression of soul' and 'sickening of the heart'. But

64 Literature, film and depressive realism

like most films, *Detachment* offers some slender hope that life need not be like this, things could be different.

Compare two films that both comment on tragic human estrangement from nature: *Walkabout* (1971) and *Into the Wild* (2007); both of them can just about be categorised as belonging in the survival genre. In the first of these, set mainly in the Australian outback, a businessman on a picnic with his children appears to go mad, shoots at the children, sets fire to his car, and then shoots himself. The teenage daughter and younger son walk away into the desert and become progressively dehydrated and sunburnt in this hostile environment. A wandering young Aborigine man discovers them after some days and accompanies and feeds them. None of the characters are named. Much of the film comprises beautiful landscape shots, hunting scenes, flashbacks to 'civilised' behaviours and innocent play and swimming. But sexual tension is evident between the girl and the Aborigine boy, who engages in a ritual courtship dance that the girl cannot understand; unsuccessful, he kills himself. The sister and brother reach civilisation again but the last scene is a fastforward to the girl, now a young married woman, listening distractedly to her young husband talking superficially about office politics, while she remembers her vivid adventure in the outback. The message of innocence lost is clear, and motifs of alienation and tragic male choices are haunting.

Into the Wild is based on the true story of Chris McCandless who soon after graduating from university, rejects a law career and indeed any conventional path, goes on the road and after various adventures ends up solitary in the Alaskan wilderness. We are told little about his decision to turn his back on conventional civilised life (his parents' difficult marriage is mentioned, along with their money-oriented lifestyle), but it is clear that he has inwardly dedicated himself to a personal mission to embrace a radical return to nature. He hunts and fishes and lives in very simple conditions, reading Tolstoy. Unfortunately, in his ignorance he becomes cut off from the route back, attempts to live self-sufficiently, and eats a wild potato that turns out to be poisonous; he slowly dies of induced starvation. In flashbacks we see his family increasingly distraught at his unexplained disappearance, and finally his father falling to his knees in grief when he hears of his son's death at twenty-four. Like *Walkabout*, the heartbreaking film *Into the Wild* contains many shots of natural beauty and contrasts soulless modern life with the challenges of nature. I believe both reflect postlapsarian misery (in Biblical terms) or Zerzan's vision of loss of hunter-gatherer innocence; and in DR terms they speak to melancholic nostalgia and tragic irreversibility. We are better off materially but in many ways estranged, and there is no authentic way of going back, either individually or collectively.

Two films that challenge aspects of DR are Malick's *To The Wonder* and McDonagh's *Calvary*. Malick's typically music-borne film depicts much aching disconnect between lovers, set against vast prairies. Against the romantic ravages we see the hope of love enduring and spirituality edging back into credibility. The film uses angular and jumpy shots, beautiful landscapes, architectural

Literature, film and depressive realism 65

close-ups, international contrasts (from rural France and Paris to the American Midwest), seasonal extremes, flashbacks and sparse narrative to achieve an effect of immense pathos. 'Just to go a little of our way together' is the French heroine's expressed hope, yet we are reminded again of the ephemeral intensity of combined erotic and spiritual love. Barren affluence and male taciturnity and ambivalence meet European aesthetic and female longing. Broken faith and on-off relationships – need and betrayal, reflect contemporary alienation. The littleness of the human against the landscape is mismatched with the human impact on it. Father Quintana, a dry priest, strives to regain real faith through service of others however unlovely and sick they are. It is like Beckett with a little more colour, character, plot, emotion and meaning – perhaps midway between Beckett and Mike Leigh.

In the case of *Calvary* a Catholic priest, Father James, is the focus. Although troubled himself by drink, widowed and facing adversity on many fronts, he has great integrity and wisdom. He is threatened at the beginning of the film by an anonymous parishioner who is bitter about past abuse by a priest and seeks revenge by killing a good priest. The theme of forgiveness is prominent and despite dark elements and anti-ecclesiastical attacks the film carries a strong sense of residual religious value. The hills and coastline of western Ireland dramatise the story. Religion is dead, priests are mistrusted and love may be on its way out too, in DR terms, and yet a slender possibility of authentic spiritual love remains. Most of those wrapped in cynicism and ugly behaviour still recognise some better possibility. Father James adheres to his destiny, shot by the adult sexually abused as a child, and in the last scene the killer is visited in prison by James's daughter, who forgives him. In both cases film can sweep us away with beautiful landscapes and beautiful illusions of religion and love.

A less classy, more popular film like *Love Actually* is on the face of it a heartlifting romcom affirming the powers of love of erotic and other kinds. It is apparently for all ages and circumstances, a masterpiece of emotional manipulation that surely only the nastiest of cynics could resist. Yet its cast of mostly beautiful, middle class and affluent characters, unlikely scenarios and rosy snapshots shorn of heartache and long-term tedium give the game away. *Love Actually* does contain some nuggets of tenderness and mitigating realism (some bereavement, betrayal and mental illness), but overall hides the law that what goes up must come down: the 135 minutes of uplift, projected by this film and its feelgood genre siblings must end in the back-to-earth reality of love-rationing. Of course, we could equally accuse works like Beckett's *First Love* and Sarah Kane's brutal drama of being unlikely, exaggeratedly negative literature: nothing, or very little, is quite as good as feelgood film or as chronically awful as feelbad literature.

If there is a handful of DR film classics, *Melancholia* (2011) surely ranks among them. The opening scenes include Breughel's (1565) atmospheric *Hunters in the Snow* and Wagner's highly emotive *Tristan and Isolde*. A wedding celebration is taking place in which Justine is the central character. There are obligatory dances and speeches in an opulent setting, contrasting with tension between

66 Literature, film and depressive realism

the bride's divorced parents, her solicitous and anxious step-sister Claire and brother-in-law John. Justine tries hard to look happy on the officially happiest day of her life but gradually descends into her familiar clinical depression. Above the small human drama, a rogue planet Melancholia is in the news: it is coming close to Earth and Claire is worried but John, backed up by scientific instruments, assures her it is merely a 'fly by' or close encounter. While the horses display their disturbance, Justine in one scene lies naked on the grass as if sacrificing herself sexually to the planet Melancholia. 'The Earth is evil and we don't need to grieve for it,' she tells Claire. When the reality of imminent catastrophe becomes clear, John kills himself, and Claire, becoming panicky, tries to drive away with her young son. All this time Justine has emerged from her own depression. When the apocalyptic ending comes she is calm, making a flimsy symbolic shelter from the catastrophe to momentarily soothe Claire and her son.

The film contrasts typical optimistic expectations ('life is good, be happy') with severe depression (Justine at one point cannot get out of bed and says the meatloaf tastes like ashes); but this is reversed when we note the family conflicts involved, the lies and so on and when denial of Melancholia's apocalyptic impact meets terminal reality. 'Life is only on Earth, and not for long,' says Justine. She has known all along that the worst must come to pass, and her depression is vindicated. The DR knows that finally he is right, and when the end comes he is ready. Von Trier has said that he always expects the worst. The chances of an actual impact such as that portrayed in the film are very small but possible. But the emotional impact of the film is not concerned with planetary collision; it focuses on the collision between denial (isolation, in Zapffe's terms) and lucid revelation of how bad things can yet become. The DR as prophet.

In their application of terror management theory to film, Sullivan and Greenberg (2013) examine the copious use of themes of death. Music can and does transport us via its aural illusions to distinct emotional states, and it may be that DR has its own musical genre (Houghtaling, 2014). Yet all such media are built on manipulative illusions. Plato contrasted the search for truth with the illusory charms of poetry, and by extension all literature, film and other forms of entertainment whether television, sport or whatever, face Zapffe's charges of distraction and sublimation. Unlike the social sciences and philosophy, the arts do not usually purport to offer or refine truth, they may be transient and they are overall massively popular. However, visual art is often absurdly exploited by capitalism and all the arts are susceptible to claims of exaggerated importance. They often express the hard to articulate or perhaps the spiritually ineffable. They help us to pass the time. Avid book lovers must wonder what life would be like without books. Yet those who have ingested LSD will know that immediate experience can be, perhaps should be, far more absorbing than second hand literary experience. Beckett certainly appreciated the irony of feeling compelled to write even though bitterly aware of its futility.

References

Ambrose, D. (2013) *Film, Nihilism and the Restoration of Belief.* Winchester: Zero Books.

Avery, S. (2009) *Thomas Hardy: The Mayor of Casterbridge/Jude the Obscure: A Reader's Guide to Essential Criticism.* Houndmills: Palgrave Macmillan.

Beckett, S. (1983) *Worstward Ho.* London: Calder.

Beckett, S. (2009) *Watt.* London: Faber & Faber.

Bowring, J. (2008) *A Field Guide to Melancholy.* Harpenden: Oldcastle Books.

Bradford, R. (2005) *First Boredom, Then Fear: The Life of Philip Larkin.* London: Peter Owen.

Brassier, R. (2010) *Nihil Unbound: Enlightenment and Extinction.* London: Palgrave.

Brennan, T. (2004) *The Transmission of Affect.* Ithaca, NY: Cornell University Press.

Calder, J. (2012) *The Theology of Samuel Beckett.* London: Calder.

Cooper, B. (2003) Sylvia Plath and the depression continuum. *Journal of the Royal Society of Medicine,* 96 (6), 296–301.

Cutrofello, A. (2014) *All for Nothing: Hamlet's Negativity.* Cambridge, MA: MIT Press.

Dienstag, J.F. (2006) *Pessimism: Philosophy, Ethic, Spirit.* Princeton, NJ: Princeton University Press.

Fox, D. (2009) *Cold World: The Aesthetics of Dejection and the Politics of Militant Dysphoria.* Winchester: Zero Books.

Garwood, H. (1911) *Thomas Hardy: An Illustration of the Philosophy of Schopenhauer.* Philadelphia, PA: John C. Winston.

Hardy, T. (1896/1985) *Jude the Obscure.* London: Penguin.

Houellebecq, M. (2015) *Submission.* New York: Farrar, Strauss, and Giroux.

Houghtaling, A.B. (2014) *This Will End in Tears: The Miserabilist Guide to Music.* New York: It Books.

Hughes, F. (2009) *The Book of Mirrors.* Tarset: Bloodaxe.

Jaynes, J. (1976) *The Origin of Consciousness in the Breakdown of the Bicameral Mind.* Boston, MA: Houghton-Mifflin.

Leopardi, G. (1898/2015) *Zibaldone (Rev. edn., ed. M. Caesar, trans. K. Baldwin et al.),* New York: Farrar, Straus & Giroux.

Rai, G. (1996) *Thomas Hardy's Realism and Pessimism.* Delhi: Shipra.

Sartre, J.-P. (1938/1965) *Nausea.* Harmondsworth: Penguin.

Schwenger, P. (2006) *The Tears of Things: Melancholy and Physical Objects.* Minneapolis, MN: University of Minnesota Press.

Shobeiri, A. & Shobeiri, A. (2014) Samuel Beckett's absurdism: Pessimism or optimism? *International Journal of Humanities and Social Science,* 4 (11[1]).

Sullivan, D. & Greenberg, J. (2013) *Death in Classic and Contemporary Film: Fade to Black.* New York: Palgrave Macmillan.

Thorpe, V. (2014) Interview with Howard Jacobson. *The Observer,* 14 September, p. 33.

Tucker, D. (2012) *Samuel Beckett and Arnold Geulincx: Tracing a Literary Fantasia.* London: Bloomsbury.

Unamuno, de M. (1921/1954) *Tragic Sense of Life.* New York: Dover.

White, K. (2009) *Beckett and Decay.* London: Continuum.

Williams, P. (1987) *An Introduction to Leopardi's Canti.* Hull: University of Hull Press.

Wilson, E.G. (2008) *Against Happiness.* New York: Sarah Crichton Books.

Chapter 5

Psychology and depressive realism

Psychology may be said to have broken with philosophy as a study of the mind in the 1870s, arguably with long roots in the philosophy of the ancient Greeks[1]. It developed in different parts of the world and splintered soon enough into different schools of enquiry. At the end of the 19th century a would-be scientific behaviourism began to assert itself against a psychoanalytic psychology that relied on privately derived and non-verifiable case studies. It remains true today that Freudian psychology is suspect within academic departments of psychology. Behaviourism, however, especially in its originally classical insistence on there being no mind for science to study, had to give way to the cognitive dimension (there *is* a mind) and hence the broad discipline of cognitive science has arisen, which also includes information science and neuroscience. Like sociology, however, psychology is built on promises it never fulfils and is characterised by a weakness of purpose, nebulousness of scope and poor achievement when compared with the natural sciences.

The birth of depressive realism

Strictly speaking, psychology is the home of depressive realism, or the place from which the precise term originated. Although psychologists have studied a great deal of negative behaviour, they are obviously not the originators of the longstanding negative worldview. In Alloy and Abramson (1979) it was found that when comparing 144 depressed with 144 non-depressed undergraduates' performance on laboratory tests of judgement, the depressed participants were more accurate. Subsequent experiments have either questioned (Moore & Fresco, 2012) or confirmed the original DR hypothesis, but many now accept that DRs with so-called mild depression do appear to make more realistic judgements (Msetfi et al., 2012) and are better at detecting deception (Forgas & East, 2008), and perhaps also have other benefits (Forgas, 2013). This goes against the grain of the received wisdom that cognitive distortions are found more often in depressed individuals. What experiments in DR cannot do, or have not attempted to do, is to measure any differences between depressed and non-depressed individuals' long-term and global predictions; for example, are DRs better at estimating negative social trends and the frequency or scale of natural disasters? Longitudinal studies might take on such projects.

The DR hypothesis has exercised many psychologists since its inception. In one study Blanco et al. (2009) compared the responses of 'dysphoric and nondysphoric' participants in tests of illusions of control. As they put it, 'findings about depressive realism . . . clearly show that certain biases and illusions are part of a healthy, nondepressed, and well-adapted mind, and that the lack of these biases, even though it leads to realism and objectivity, is associated with depression and maladaptation' (p. 558). One of their recommendations is that therapists 'should sometimes encourage some degree of illusion . . . instead of pursuing an unbiased, objective way of thinking' (p. 559). Such tests are admittedly conducted with *mildly depressed* individuals doing trivial tasks in laboratory conditions and cannot tell us directly anything about how these people function in the everyday world (except that they are indeed functional). Psychologists continue to sound surprised and intrigued at such findings. But what they do not seem to do is generate alternative hypotheses or more ambitious experiments. If DRs were more objective, we might expect to find them in careers, for example, where objectivity is a key requirement (e.g. science, insurance, accountancy), and we would expect to find in their ranks fewer people subscribing to the more obvious illusions such as belief in homeopathy, astrology and having a significant chance of winning the lottery. Such variables could easily be measured. However, the most astonishing component of such findings (or recommendations) is that *illusions are healthy*. Furthermore, the seemingly uncritical acceptance of such a position is remarkable among academic psychologists who, one would expect, are part of the community of scholars who work to expose and reduce illusion.

Surprising, indirect confirmation of the tenets of DR came from a major review of bad events and phenomena conducted by a team of psychologists (Baumeister et al., 2001). Referring to an earlier study of research articles in psychology journals, they noted a 69%–31% bias in favour of bad to good negative issues. This was before Seligman and other positive psychologists set out to redress the imbalance. Baumeister and his colleagues trawled through publications on the domains of close relationships, emotions, learning, child development, information processing, memory, stereotypes, impression formation, self and health, and found that research confirmed a quite consistent negativity bias. 'Bad events have stronger and more lasting consequences than comparable good events' (p. 355), and 'the lack of a positive counterpart to the concept of trauma is itself a sign that single bad events often have more lasting and important effects than any results of single good events' (p. 355). Exceptions were hard to find. They call this a 'disappointingly relentless pattern' (p. 362). They speculate that pessimism has been adaptive, preparing humans for negative events and they argue, as is now fashionably accepted, that five times more good is needed to offset the bad. Remarkably honest as this paper is, the authors' attempt to conclude optimistically is rather lame: 'good can still

70 Psychology and depressive realism

triumph in the end by force of numbers' and 'many lives can be happy by virtue of having far more good than bad events' (p. 362). Rozin and Royzman (2001) outline similar concepts, adding that of contagion of positive or neutral states by stronger states.

One common assertion in all this is that sadder but wiser DRs are mildly depressed (using tests such as the Beck Depression Inventory), not clinically depressed, and even Beck appears to concede this. We could almost link this with Freud's assertion that psychoanalysis aims to replace hysterical misery with common unhappiness, except that this implies that the majority suffering with common unhappiness are mildly depressed and hence are relatively illusion-free DRs, which is plainly not the case. Either there is a smaller subgroup of unidentified mildly depressed individuals (neither severely depressed nor the unhappy but so-called well-adjusted majority), or something else is at work here. Some DRs may become more depressed at times; hardcore DRs would probably not take part in such experiments, which they might well deem absurd; and the objective ability to judge short times or exert personal control might not extend to making objective judgements about the existence of God, the likelihood of an afterlife or the hedonic calculus of the worthwhileness of living. Typically unremarked upon, too, is this train of logic – that if psychologists (their own levels of depression going undeclared) can seriously commend illusions as healthy, presumably they themselves hold and value illusions; and belief in the value of psychology itself may well be one of these illusions. If the discipline and practice of psychology is objective, it may not be healthy, and vice versa. I labour this point too much perhaps, but compare Sutherland's account of irrationality (2007) with Hutson (2012). It may simply be that the vast majority of us, or indeed *all of us* in one way or another, is prone to, if not hardwired for, illusion. As Hutson points out, even Richard Dawkins became irrationally moved by a preserved pigeon that had belonged to Darwin, as if it held some magical, transhistorical essence of Darwin himself.

We can, however, push our understanding of the origins in psychology of markedly positive and negative strands to the writings of William James, one of the pioneers who represents the split between philosophy and psychology and in some ways theology, too. In Alexander (1980) it is argued that James saw healthy-mindedness as optimal in terms of happiness while the sick or 'twice born' soul had a fuller understanding of human consciousness (James, 1902/1985). James included Augustine, Bunyan and Tolstoy in his examples of sick souls, all of whom passed through the sickness to vigorously re-embrace Christian faith. We may suspect that today's tension between positive psychology and depressive realism re-creates James's two categories, as well as the ancient Socratic claim that 'it is better to be a human being dissatisfied than a pig satisfied', objected to by John Stuart Mill's utilitarianism. James was no superficial advocate of happiness or life satisfaction, but one who wrestled with the two sides of the question, shown vividly in his 1895 lecture *Is Life Worth Living?* (James, 1895/2000).

Optimism bias

One of the conundrums of the psychology of the positive-negative debate is that while many positive psychologists argue that we are wired for pessimism, based on evolutionary pressures to vigilantly expect the worst, nevertheless certain pressures tilt us towards optimism. This field is closely linked with the study of egoic and other illusions. The field has moved across the 'Pollyanna hypothesis' to the 'negativity bias,' often coming down on one side or the other. Lewicka and Czapinsky (1992) summarise many of these problems. Sharot (2012), for example, outlines many of the brain mechanisms that make for optimism. Sharot et al. (2011) demonstrate that unrealistic 'optimism is tied to a selective update failure, and diminished neural coding, of undesirable information regarding the future' (p. 1457). They claim on the basis of neural scanning that the right frontal cortex processes and distorts these unrealistically optimistic judgements. The likely explanation for this, they aver, is that it makes sense for human beings (or some of them) to override cumulative negative information in order to remain open to necessary risk-taking. This does indeed make some kind of evolutionary sense in terms of spreading our bets group-wise, so that some of us are ready for risks and others caution that dangers outweigh risks.

Some of the most interesting thinking on affect in relation to happiness, depression and optimism recently has come not from psychology but from affect studies generated in literature departments. Berlant's (2011) analysis of the fashionable economics and psychology of optimism amounting to a 'cruel optimism' challenges the emphasis on these myths of positivity in a society that simply cannot deliver them. We might even say that she altogether overturns the implied morality of the positive psychologists and the agenda of happiness politics of Layard, even though that is not her specific target.

Evolutionary psychology

Evolutionary psychology takes its mission from the question of deep aetiology; in other words, what are the distant and entrenched roots of our behaviour, particularly our universal stubborn behaviours? This question is disliked both within traditional psychology and more generally in the world of liberal academia. Evolutionary hypotheses for current behaviours have to be highly speculative and cannot be tested in the laboratory, thus threatening psychology's longstanding scientific aspirations. But evolutionary psychology also leans towards determinism (hence its being often conflated with sociobiology), which invites a reflexive condemnation from left-wing academics with a positive view of human nature, insofar as they will admit to having any view of a suspiciously essentialist-sounding 'human nature' (Ashcroft, 2000). As I have explained in Chapter 1, I cannot see how we can ignore the effect that millions of years of evolution have had on our development, even if we believe these effects to be only residual now.

The attraction of evolutionary psychology (for me) is that it offers some explanation for those problematic behaviours for which we have no better account. These include tribal loyalties, intertribal conflicts, patriarchal social systems, mental illness and crime, gender differences and conflicts, sexual drives, family dynamics, damaging personal and cultural habits and the sheer difficulty of changing those behaviours we wish to change individually or socially. It is true that much of evolutionary psychology is speculative; in some varieties it appears to have intellectually totalitarian ambitions, some of it is almost certainly improbable, and a great deal of it may leave us feeling impotent. We do have to exercise some caution in selecting from its works. But as Buss (2005) has argued, evolutionary psychology emerged in the space left by traditional psychology's avoidance of the big questions and of our deep past, as if this has had no or minimal influence.

Depressing aspects of psychology

Rose (1999) among others has argued that the 20th century in particular was shaped by the discipline of psychology and all its applications. This charge is broadly about psychology and its products overreaching themselves and driving rather than studying some parts of society. Psychological reductionism trivialises socioeconomic factors, for example. I began with some account of what psychology tells us about depression and depressive realism before now focusing on what is depressing about psychology. Some argue that the 'depressing' in such sentences should read 'disappointing' so as to avoid conflation of attitudes but I disagree. The many disappointments one finds in academia and the professions are part of the aggregate DR, based on a DR instinct that bleak truth is always being disguised in cloaks of illusion.

Psychology has had longstanding pretensions to a scientific identity which simply do not hold up. Its well-known experiments on obedience and conformity, for example, are mildly interesting but cannot compare for weightiness or utility with anything in physics or medicine. Forensic and clinical psychologists often like to make pronouncements on why the perpetrators of school shootings acted as they did, but their observations are mundane, improve little on commonsense and have almost no predictive value. Perhaps the psychology establishment recognises this in the way in which new fields are always being added, so that the protected title of psychology can be endlessly prefixed by abnormal, developmental, educational, occupational, transpersonal, humanistic, feminist, positive, etc. Anachronistic aspects of psychology are quietly dropped in favour of the psychology *du jour*. Perhaps the most depressing aspect of psychology is that, contrary to its promise to help us understand, it really does no such thing. Instead of making any serious inroads into the human condition it becomes an academic and professional commodity. This is unsurprising when we remind ourselves that psychologists are like all of us victims and perpetrators of anthropathology.

Lies, frauds and the games some psychologists play

If we include Freud here (he was not technically a psychologist), recall that his life's work, psychoanalysis, has been called 'the biggest hoax of the 20th century' (Medawar, 1975). But look at the educational psychologist Sir Cyril Burt whose research on twins in the 1970s was widely believed to be fabricated and fraudulent. The Dutch academic psychologist Diederik Stapel was suspended in 2011 for extensive fabrication in his research. Many cases of plagiarism, malpractice and negligence among psychologists are on record. Recently, we have the example of embarrassments in the positive psychology field in the United States. First, consider the now infamous paper by Fredrickson and Losada (2005) which claimed to identify a 2.9013 ratio or tipping point from negativity towards happiness, also referred to by some as the 'mathematics of happiness' (a reminder of how the hubristic aping of science goes wrong). A paper by Brown et al. (2013), identifying its errors and hinting at fraud, forced a partial retraction. But Fredrickson denies any wrongdoing and has extended her ideas in various self-help books on happiness and love, including Fredrickson (2009). The point I wish to press here, however, is that even without outright fraud, it is difficult conclusively to invalidate research and inferences that may be technically legitimate but in other ways suspect, for example, based on poor methodology, unrepresentative samples, suffering from the airbrushing of inconvenient flaws, conducted by people with vested interests and so on. It is often suggested that psychology is among the weaker of the sciences, if a science at all, and that its research is almost always self-confirmatory (Fanelli, 2010).

Now, we briefly consider Martin Seligman, a past President of the American Psychological Association. Seligman is credited with being the founder of the contemporary positive psychology movement, after moving on from some fame as the creator of the concept of learned helplessness. He enthusiastically endorses Fredrickson's work. He reportedly commands $30,000-$50,000 for a commercial lecture. Barbara Ehrenreich (2009) has called Seligman a huckster and a canny commercial operator after interviewing him for her book. Seligman, who was influenced by Aaron Beck, advocates the study and practice of strengths and virtues, and presents models such as PERMA (positive emotion, engagement, relationships, meaning and achievement) and equations like H = S + C + V (enduring happiness = set range + life circumstances + voluntary control). Ehrenreich clearly ranks Seligman and other positive psychology academics alongside yesterday's positive thinking gurus like Norman Vincent Peale, something hotly denied by the former group, who regard themselves as serious scientists.

Finally, Lord Richard Layard, not a psychologist but an influential British health economist, has enthusiastically co-edited the *World Happiness Report* (Helliwell et al., 2013), endorsed the 'science of happiness', Fredrickson's books on flourishing, cognitive behaviour therapy (CBT); and he has been a champion of the UK's Increasing Access to Psychological Therapies (IAPT) project. Layard

74 Psychology and depressive realism

has fashionably argued that happiness depends less on having more money and possessions and more on there being greater equality in society. He himself had a father who was a prominent anthropologist and psychoanalyst who was analysed by and collaborated with Jung; and Richard Layard is an old Etonian and affluent man. However, he claimed that on the basis of research evidence the British government had every reason to spend a great deal on establishing IAPT centres offering mainly CBT, in large part in order to address the levels of depression that are associated with people being unemployed, but he also argued that cost would be covered by savings made by getting people back into work. The grave flaws in Layard's case are (a) that in endorsing CBT he largely ignores the economic arguments that depression and unemployment have some glaring systemic causes calling for better economic support for the poor rather than any form of psychotherapy; (b) that he ignores the rather obvious matter of many jobs being inherently depressing (contrary to CBT's location of depression in the individual's head and under their cognitive control); and (c) that both 'on the ground' and in some research CBT was predictably being shown, contrary to exaggerated claims, as a very limited success (Feltham, 2013).

There may be little doubt about the sincerity and integrity of someone like Layard, but it is depressing to see how a case like this can get so out of hand. Yet the rhetoric of happiness, well-being and flourishing is all part of a psychologically fashionable view from which many psychologists continue to profit and on which they can conduct endless research on optimism, forgiveness, curiosity, gratitude and hope (see, e.g. Hogan, 2009; Macaskill & Denovan, 2014). Layard's psychologist collaborator David King (Layard & King, 2014) pushes even further the case for CBT, IAPT and so-called evidence-based therapy. Perhaps betting shops might offer odds to DRs who predict that such flimsy fashions will have demonstrably collapsed within, say, 20 years, when their failures will be quietly filed away in the dim recesses of the history of psychology. Stress management and emotional intelligence, for example, were yesterday's big ideas. But this will not matter either, since the public hunger for explanations and myths acts perennially as the gullible counterpart to the pundits' relentless myth-making (Sigman, 1995). Coyne (2014) offers a good analysis and discussion of many of these points.

Consider the labyrinth of comparative statistics, associations and inferences. According to Myers (2000), across representative samples 90% of people report being happy or very happy. Even allowing for a time lag, we might ask what kind of increase in happiness the positive psychologists are hoping for: 90% looks pretty good. But on the other hand, we are repeatedly told that 25% of adults experience a mental health problem in the course of a year (but note that many of these may nevertheless be happy); and certainly a significant percentage die every year, perhaps happily. We are also told that 82% of Americans believe in God; 76% in miracles; 72% in angels; 61% in hell; 61% in the virgin birth; 42% in ghosts; 40% in creationism (Shermer, 2011, p. 3). Other sources regularly proclaim that psychotherapy has an 80% success rate (up from about 66% in the

1950s). Whether any meaningful correlation exists between all such figures is anyone's guess. Some, like the happiness and depression figures, appear at least partly to contradict each other. We are bound to question the research methodologies involved, not to mention the possibility that interviewees' responses to happiness surveys may represent an unreliable default self-image. It is an unpopular position to take, but we might also question the intelligence of those who believe in God, virgin birth and ghosts, along with the credibility of self-reports of happiness and improvements achieved by psychotherapy. As Trivers (2011) suggests, both individuals and groups, lay people and psychologists, are inclined to be immersed in self-deceptive strategies, and this includes Trivers, me and you. Nevertheless, we must ask if some are more self-deceived than others, and if some are indeed sadder but wiser than others.

Psychology is now largely predicated on a positive view of the world. The idea, therefore, that one could speak meaningfully of a negative worldview and attempt to value and understand it in psychological terms, is not taken very seriously on the whole. To give an example, *post traumatic growth* is part of a celebratory resilience-and-transcendence phenomenon: see how tough and resourceful we humans can be. However, consider the obverse, that of *negative revelation* (roughly equivalent to Tønnessen's (1966/67) 'inverted serendipity'). It is quite likely that some of us experience the sudden, or cumulative, realisation of just how awful life is, and perhaps this hits hardest among those who had previously assumed that life was wholly or mainly good. The shock of perceiving life as characterised by brutal negativity can be witnessed in some religious people who come to see the inferior value of worldly goods and the fleeting nature of pleasures. Like Sartre's character Roquentin in *Nausea*, Tolstoy's lead character in *The Death of Ivan Ilyich*, Prince Siddhartha Gautama discovering life beyond his father's palace or others experiencing profound disillusionment, the person subject to negative revelation may be flooded by bleak insights into the nature of illusion-shorn reality. Often this will be interpreted as clinical depression, especially in those unable to articulate the experience clearly. Psychology is constituted as an ameliorative enterprise and is largely unable to consider the possibility that negative revelation and a persistent negative worldview may have objective value. To some extent, terror management theory is an exception to this rule, but even terror management theory (TMT) cannot promulgate the view that life is hopeless.

An experiment in taste and meaning

Almost certainly, neither academic psychology nor depressive realist literature appeals to the majority of people. Let's accept that both are relatively minority status pursuits and that psychology (especially since it often leads to a well-paid profession) is much larger than DR. Still, it does not follow that either one of these proffers a 'true' account of the human condition. One day I was reading some Beckett (*Lessness*), which describes the deterioration of the human body,

76 Psychology and depressive realism

and by chance I then picked up a standard successful psychology textbook (Gross, 2012) and started reading Chapter 8, 'Fear of death and other 'facts' of life'. The contrast is striking. Beckett's style is much more to my taste (obviously), while academic psychology often strikes me as ridiculous, pretentious and irrelevant. I am not wholly anomalous here; many people claim to prefer learning about the human condition from novels than from formal psychology. Gross's writing on death advances various clichés, statistics, flow-charts and pseudo-certainties based on typically shallow, science-aping psychological discourse. Take a random sample sentence: 'self-esteem serves as a buffer against the negative effects of mortality salience' (p. 230). This is presented as a significant slice of actual knowledge, yet it is in my view neither weighty nor indisputable. Beckett's writing, however obtuse, by contrast has an honesty and visceral impact that is, arguably, entirely missing from Gross's, and indeed from most psychology. O'Hara (1997) tries to analyse Beckett's work in terms of a depth psychology that is truer to experience but would almost certainly not be endorsed by Beckett.

The experiment, then, is to do likewise, to pick up and compare two similarly contrasting accounts of death, and to study your own reactions to style and substance: does psychology live up to its portentous scientific claims? I think not. Another example might be the contrast between Faulks's (2006) novel *Human Traces*, which details a tragic search for the causes of madness and human suffering generally. Contrast this with almost any textbook on clinical psychology. Of course, the audiences and purposes are different, but my contention is that psychology long ago placed itself in the impossible position of claiming to analyse and categorise objectively human thought, feeling and behaviour. Humanistic psychology, honouring subjectivity, sometimes overcomes this problem, but like traditional academic psychology its focus hovers over the positive or status quo aspects of life.

A further variation on this experiment is to come up with almost any behavioural concept, say, promiscuous male sexuality, and subject it deliberately to jargonisation: for example, 'Infinigamy as unconsciously operationalised negentropic neophilia'. You might, following Sokal (1996), then write an article about this and submit to one or another academic journal and await the response. The phrase above once deciphered means something like a never-ending search for sexual novelty as a way of feeling more alive, but academia depends on a certain amount of obscurity for its existence. (Jungians might write in terms of a *puer complex*, say.) Why else would not only postmodernism-inspired publications but even the most sober of psychology journals couch their wares in impenetrable jargon?

Conclusions

Like its siblings in the social sciences, psychology has delivered disappointingly little in the way of genuinely new or useful knowledge. Nehemiah Jordan referred

Psychology and depressive realism   77

to it as 'the sterilest of the sterile' that 'has yielded precisely nothing' (see Cohen, 1977, p. 30). While splitting from philosophy to forge a would-be rigorous new discipline promising to analyse the human mind, it merely descended via rats, pigeons, statistics, schisms, and academic psychobabble into disappointment. It remains riven by epistemological conflicts, triviality of topics and findings and power-seeking. Psychologists themselves seem endlessly fascinated by artificial experiments that rarely demonstrate anything meaningful or exciting and are frequently inconclusive. It often simply confirms commonsense, for example, in the vaunted social psychology literature on obedience to authority. Even in its softer and more radical forms, such as humanistic and critical psychology (not to mention positive and pop psychology), it holds no answers to the problems of the human condition beyond rhetorical and romantic appeals. Psychology is often popular in academia because new students retain the naïve fantasy that it can explain the human psyche, soothe the troubled mind and elevate functioning; and many of its academics have the power to license clinical, counselling and related psychologists, and hence have secure employment. Research psychologists expand their territory indefinitely, for example, issuing ponderous works promising more nuanced accounts of the optimism-pessimism conundrum (Chang, 2002).

Psychology struggles to retain its forlorn attachment to scientific identity. In the vacuum left by religion and theology, psychology and its affiliated therapies fill some sort of need for explanation, for authorities and for illusory comfort. But thoroughgoing atheists may see in psychology many of the same features one finds in all religions, and psychology is eventually destined to meet the same fate of exposure and redundancy, particularly as greater genetic and neurological knowledge is opened up. The DR sees through the dismal hype of psychology's edifice but knows that it is here to stay – by the temporary grace of slow entropy – as part of the grand illusion separating the human majority from the terror of nihilism. The DR might propose an alternative, DR-informed psychology, for example, that is imaginatively open to the possibility that not only is normality dysfunctional but that clinical depression results from too much denied awareness that misery is ubiquitous.

Note

1 Following Western academic convention and the limits of my own knowledge, I here discuss Western psychology, which omits many of the valuable insights of, for example, Buddhist psychology (e.g. Trungpa, 2005).

References

Alexander, G.T. (1980) William James, the sick soul, and the negative dimensions of consciousness: A partial critique of transpersonal psychology. *Journal of the American Academy of Religion*, 48 (2), 191–206.

Alloy, L.B. & Abramson, L.Y. (1979) Judgement of contingency in depressed and non-depressed students: Sadder but wiser? *Journal of Experimental Psychology: General*, 108, 441–485.

78 Psychology and depressive realism

Ashcroft, P. (2000) *Psychology and 'Human Nature'*. Hove: Psychology Press.

Baumeister, R., Bratslavsky, E., Finkenauer, C. & Vohs, K.D. (2001) Bad is stronger than good. *Journal of General Psychology*, 5 (4), 323–370.

Berlant, L. (2011) *Cruel Optimism*. Durham, NC: Duke University Press.

Blanco, F., Matute, H. & Vadillo, M.A. (2009) Depressive realism: Wiser or quieter? *The Psychological Record*, 59, 551–562.

Brown, N., Sokal, A. & Friedman, H.L. (2013) The complex dynamics of wishful thinking: The critical positivity ratio. *American Psychologist*, 68 (9), 801–813.

Buss, D.M. (ed) (2005) *The Handbook of Evolutionary Psychology*. Hoboken, NJ: Wiley.

Chang, E.C. (ed) (2002) *Optimism & Pessimism: Implications or Theory, Research, and Practice*. Washington, DC: American Psychological Association.

Cohen, D. (1977) *Psychologists on Psychology*. New York: Taplinger.

Coyne, J. (2014) Will following positive psychology advice make you happier and healthier? *PLOS Blogs*, 18 December.

Ehrenreich, B. (2009) *Smile or Die: How Positive Thinking Fooled America and the World*. London: Granta.

Fanelli, D. (2010) 'Positive' results increase down the hierarchy of the sciences. *PLoS One*, 5 (4), e10068.

Faulks, S. (2006) *Human Traces*. London: Vintage.

Feltham, C. (2013) *Counselling and Counselling Psychology: A Critical Examination*. Ross-on-Wye: PCCS Books.

Forgas, J.P. (2013) Don't worry, be sad! On the cognitive, motivational, and interpersonal benefits of negative mood. *Current Directions in Psychological Science*, 22 (3), 225–232.

Forgas, J.P. & East, R. (2008) On being happy and gullible: Mood effects on scepticism and the detection of deception. *Journal of Experimental Social Psychology*, 44 (5), 1362–1367.

Fredrickson, B.L. (2009) *Positivity: Top-Notch Research Reveals the 3:1 Ratio That Will Change Your Life*. New York: Three Rivers Press.

Fredrickson, B.L. & Losada, M.F. (2005) Positive affect and the complex dynamics of human flourishing. *American Psychologist*, 60 (7), 678–686.

Gross, R. (2012) *Being Human: Psychological and Philosophical Perspectives*. London: Hodder.

Helliwell, F.J., Layard, R. & Sachs, J.D. (eds) (2013) *The World Happiness Report*. OECD.

Hogan, M. (2009) Enlightened happiness and pragmatic systems science and positive psychology meets Colin Feltham's anthropathology thesis. *Irish Journal of Psychology*, 35, 138–148.

Hutson, M. (2012) *The Seven Laws of Magical Thinking: How Irrationality Makes Us Happy, Healthy, and Sane*. London: Oneworld.

James, W. (1895/2000) *Pragmatism and Other Writings*. London: Penguin.

James, W. (1902/1985) *The Varieties of Religious Experience: A Study in Human Nature*. London: Penguin.

Layard, R. & King, D.M. (2014) *Thrive: The Power of Evidence-Based Psychological Therapies*. London: Allen Lane.

Lewicka, M. & Czapinsky, J. (1992) Positive-negative asymmetry or 'When the heart needs a reason'. *European Journal of Social Psychology*, 22, 425–434.

Macaskill, A. & Denovan, A. (2014) Assessing psychological health: The contribution of psychological strengths. *British Journal of Guidance and Counselling*, 42 (3), 320–337.

Medawar, P. (1975) Victims of psychiatry. *New York Review of Books*, 23 January, p. 21.

Moore, M.T. & Fresco, D.M. (2012) Depressive realism: A meta-analytic review. *Clinical Psychology Review*, 32 (6), 496–509.

Psychology and depressive realism 79

Msetfi, R.M., Murphy, R.A. & Kombrot, D.E. (2012) Dysphoric mood states are related to sensitivity to temporal changes in contingency. *Frontiers in Psychology*, 3 (368), 1–9.

Myers, D.G. (2000) The funds, friends and faith of happy people. *American Psychologist*, 55 (1), 56–67.

O'Hara, J.D. (1997) *Samuel Beckett's Hidden Drives: Structural Uses of Depth Psychology*. Gainesville, FL: University of Florida Press.

Rose, N. (1999) *Governing the Soul: The Shaping of the Private Self*. London: Routledge.

Rozin, P. & Royzman, E.B. (2001) Negativity bias, negativity dominance, and contagion. *Personality and Social Psychology Review*, 5 (4), 296–320.

Sharot, T. (2012) *The Optimism Bias: Why We're Wired to Look on the Bright Side*. London: Constable & Robinson.

Sharot, T., Korn, C.W. & Dolan, R.J. (2011) How unrealistic optimism is maintained in the face of reality. *Nature Neuroscience*, 14 (11), 1475–1479.

Shermer, M. (2011) *The Believing Brain: From Spiritual Faiths to Political Convictions*. London: Robinson.

Sigman, A. (1995) *New, Improved: Exposing the Misuse of Popular Psychology*. New York: Simon & Schuster.

Sokal, A. (1996) Transgressing the boundaries: Towards a transformative hermeneutics of quantum gravity. *Social Text*, 46/47, 217–252.

Sutherland, S. (2007) *Irrationality (Rev. 2nd edn.)*. London: Pinter & Martin.

Tønnessen, H. (1966/67) Happiness is for the pigs: Philosophy versus psychotherapy. *Journal of Existentialism*, 3 (26), 181–214.

Trivers, R. (2011) *Deceit and Self-Deception*. London: Allen Lane.

Trungpa, C. (2005) *The Sanity We Are Born With: A Buddhist Approach to Psychology*. Boston, MA: Shambhala.

Chapter 6

Psychotherapy and depressive realism

In the mental health field we face a number of overlapping and competing professions that rest on conflicting epistemologies. Psychiatry, for example, is a medically-oriented statutory profession with strong legal powers over individuals, while much counselling and psychotherapy is antagonistic towards the biomedical model and has no legal power over individuals. The mental health professions in the UK include psychiatry, mental health nursing, psychoanalysis, clinical and counselling psychology, psychotherapy and counselling, and it is not immediately clear where coaching and related complementary therapies fall. These psychological therapies are delivered by statutory professionals but also by therapists in the educational, corporate, voluntary and private practice sectors. Different but also similar professional pluralism operates in other countries, often causing confusion for referral pathways and consumer choices. This degree of professional complexity results not from necessity but simply from historical forces; and some faltering attention is given to integration in the field but with little success. We also need to factor into the mental health debate the variety of so-called psychiatric disorders or psychological problems, amounting to over 300 (up from an original 106), according to the famous American psychiatric Bible, the *DSM* (APA, 2013). Even acknowledging ongoing critiques of the *DSM* and psychodiagnosis generally, we may concede that myriad problematic conditions exist, which are themselves refracted via culture and personality.

But we must add to this the hundreds of competing theoretical models of therapy. Some defend this state of affairs as a richness of choice and the loose coalition of talking therapy professional bodies tends to mutely accept it, but it should probably be regarded as a scandalous waste of resources, an obstacle to far better mental health treatment and a deeply embarrassing epistemological problem. The chances are that if you become seriously depressed, you will be at the mercy of agencies and professionals that have no consensus, or at best an array of politically convenient documents, as to effective help. The UK's National Institute for Health and Clinical Excellence (NICE) draws on research that allegedly underlines the best evidence-based therapies to be utilised, but such research is itself deeply flawed and open to further interpretation (Feltham, 2013).

Psychotherapy is one of the major touted cures for mild, moderate and severe clinical depression. Many cavil at the word *cure* and some object to the term depression but most of the psychological therapies sometimes diagnose and always acknowledge depression or low mood and hold out hope of alleviating and reducing depression; some claim to work more effectively than others, and some are held out as hopes for ambitious social change. Many schools of therapy claim, or let it be believed, that psychotherapeutic theory explains individual depression, the social effects of depression and ideologies related to depression, such as depressive realism. Since some psychotherapeutic writers regard therapy as explaining religion and supplanting it, we also have to reckon with psychotherapy itself being regarded by some as a faith, a panacea, an ideology or a scientific advance towards an enduringly better world. In retrospect, it has been suggested, if psychotherapy had been available much earlier and more accessibly, perhaps we would have had no Hitler. In novel form, the psychotherapist Irvin Yalom (2012) has a fictional psychiatrist trying to engage the actual, leading Nazi Alfred Rosenberg in therapeutic work: if only psychotherapy could be administered retrospectively, so many evils could be averted. These naïve views are necessary background for this chapter, which examines the grandiose ambitions of therapy.

Against Yalom and psychotherapy generally, we can offer the voice of the Norwegian philosopher Herman Tønnessen[1]: 'Were (say) Frankl to attempt to cure (say) Zapffe from his "existential frustration," "ontological despair" or "metaphysic-melancholic clairvoyance," the chances are that Zapffe (rather than "cured") would be baffled by Frankl's sophomoric philosophizing' (Tennessen, 1966/67, p. 204). Tønnessen goes on to berate Frankl and other psychotherapists for posing as philosophers when they are, rather, 'prelatics', counselling psychologists or pastoral counsellors and only at best amateur philosophers. I believe Tønnessen is right to stress that therapists are not philosophers and therapy is not founded on reason, but (putting it in the strong case) on adaptation to the social status quo, expression of emotion and pro-life banalities, sometimes masquerading as evidence-based. Tønnessen refers to the 'tragicomic encounter of clinical psychology and existential philosophy' (1966/67, p. 183). Logically, if psychotherapists were to listen seriously to pessimistic (DR) philosophers like Tønnessen, they might be cured of their delusion that life is good.

On the bright pro-psychotherapy side, we can argue (and I support this idea from personal experience) that many therapists are nice middle class people with good intentions who have some natural warmth and empathy and who endeavour to listen non-judgementally to their clients' turmoil. Probably, in cases of severe suffering such as psychoses, some therapists can offer pragmatic, non-pretentious relief and some hope (e.g. Fuller, 2013). It is also the case that all therapists believe themselves to be offering understanding, relief and sometimes even cure. An indeterminate number of clients attest to the benefits received. Even the most anti-therapy pundits sometimes concede that in spite of its problems, therapy may be the only game in town, that is, the only hope and comfort

82 Psychotherapy and depressive realism

held out to individuals who suffer from a range of specific and non-specific psychological troubles. The world is now too big, busy and problematic for friends to understand and help each other. We could also argue that psychotherapy is part of a much larger morale-boosting social phenomenon that includes pop psychology and self-help literature, traditional and New Age spiritualities and distracting fiction and entertainment generally (Feltham, 2015). A few DRs like Cioran have admitted that their writing has been therapeutically motivated.

One common pro-therapy argument is that friends and family cannot be expected to offer ongoing and unbiased support to the depressed. According to this reasoning, significant others are too emotionally entangled with us, too naïve in their understanding, too lacking in subtle counselling skills and not bound by any obligation of confidentiality. The professionals have all necessary interpersonal attitudes, skills, knowledge, boundaries and codes, and will not confuse their own problems with yours. It is true that too much depressed behaviour or complaining can elicit typically naïve and dysempathic responses: 'pull yourself together, count your blessings, look on the bright side' and even occasionally the impatient 'why don't you kill yourself then?' Who might not, in these circumstances, have a go at therapy? But instead of calling in the supposedly skilled professionals, perhaps we should pause to reflect on the sheer facticity of depression and its prevalence, and the resigned way in which we take depression to be a mysterious inconvenience which, fortunately, kindly professionals have been trained to endure, understand, interpret and cure.

We have many problems, we experience many psychological aches and needs, as well as physical needs. Why should we not visit a prostitute or psychotherapist to relieve us bodily and sexually? Well, we may do so, but psychotherapy enjoys higher status than prostitution and often pays better. The comparison has been made before – psychotherapists are like prostitutes, simply asking money for something very personal that you don't get elsewhere – but therapists bristle indignantly at this downgrading of their status and argue that they offer a principled relationship aiming not to *indulge* you (to feed your inadequacies) but to facilitate serious insight and change. Well, some prostitutes offer long-term relationships paid sessionally, are unconditional, non-judgemental, unshockable and ready to respond to idiosyncratic needs. Most of us appear wired to need to feel that we matter to others, that even if we are not intensely loved we are cared about in this distressing world, and this craving for care can be partly satisfied by psychotherapy, religion, cults and prostitutes.

Psychoanalysis and depression

Dienstag aligns Freud somewhat with Schopenhauer when considering metaphysical pessimism. 'For both Freud and Schopenhauer the centrality of death is a defining feature of their philosophies, and refusal to acknowledge death is one of the chief weaknesses in the optimism to which they are opposed (2006, p. 101). Freud 'was no less pessimistic than Schopenhauer' (p. 100). Yet Freud laboured assiduously to develop a clinical practice of psychoanalysis, not a philosophy.

Not all psychoanalysts agree on the importance of psychodiagnostic categories such as depression, beyond acknowledging the universal difficulties of living. Ladan (2014) like many is much more interested in describing the analyst's sophisticated grasp of in-session ironic nuances. Our psychological malaise is fuelled or magnified by the illusions we carry about how life should be. This illusion-heavy experience is found in everyday life, particularly in crises, but also most intensely in the analytic relationship, the analyst too being prone to his own forms of illusion and disillusionment. The analyst, however, appears to have the trained nous to rise above all this. Hence, 'psychoanalysis and disillusion are inextricably connected. I am not referring to disillusion *with* analysis – which can also occur – but psychoanalysis as a psychology of disillusion' (Ladan, 2014, p. 17). The analyst here is portrayed as a wily disillusionist, not taken in by the traps of unconscious fantasy to which the uninitiated are prone. But why the italicised 'with' above? Psychoanalysis is not, as implied by Ladan, the end of illusions but just another illusion that happens to anchor a minority of psychoanalytic believers. Oddly too, Ladan cites the Freudian view that our individual lives must be seen as part of the social network, as a sign that 'we have fulfilled the first duty of all living beings, which is to tolerate life' (p. 112). Are we to believe with Ladan that the kind of psychoanalytic judo he subscribes to is a credible and enduring means of merely getting us to do our existential duty?

The novelist Houellebecq tears into psychoanalysts: 'Handsomely remunerated, pretentious and stupid, psychoanalysts reduce to zero any aptitude in their so-called patients for love' (2011, p. 102). Oddly, John Gray (2013) for all his generic iconoclasm is warm towards Freud, who he reads, I think, as a sophisticated modern Stoic expounding a gospel of resignation: humans are sick and there is no cure. In this reading Freudian psychoanalysis might be taken to be a highly convoluted form of CBT which aims only to take the edge off suffering at best. One pointed battleground between psychoanalytic psychotherapy and DR can be seen in Miller's (2013) account of Bion's therapy with Samuel Beckett in 1933–35. Beckett displays a 'fierce and sometimes attacking intellectualised defensiveness' (p. 60) in Miller's reconstruction of external events and internal states. In such an account, psychoanalysis can ultimately do no wrong and psychoanalytic writing is always a kind of triumphant, quasi-omniscient sophistry. Bion restored to Beckett an ability to live with some maturity, in Miller's view, partly by allowing Beckett to internalise Bion's 'constancy'. Others might see in Miller's orthodox view the usual, unverifiable jargon of mystifying expertise, and nothing if not an intellectualised defence of the untenable psychoanalytic worldview and profession.

Cognitive behaviour therapy and depression

Cognitive behaviour therapy (CBT) holds a central position in our consideration of depressive realism for three main reasons. First, it was the boast of early CBT that it specifically targeted and successfully treated depression (although it subsequently expanded to include most other diagnostic categories). Secondly, a principal part of its aetiology of mental ill health concerns *depressogenic thinking*. That is to say, we generate our own depression (and anxiety) by negative automatic thoughts which we project on to our self-view, view of the future and of the world. Thirdly, CBT explicitly takes on the concern with pessimism in a way other models do not (Pretzer & Walsh, 2002).

In order to grasp the core of CBT and its relation to ancient stoicism, let us look at the claim of Albert Ellis, founder of rational emotive behaviour therapy (REBT), an early form of CBT, as embodied in the title of one of his books: *How to Stubbornly Refuse to Make Yourself Miserable About Anything – Yes Anything!* (Ellis, 1996). Ellis did not deny that life could be challenging and unpleasant, or that we harbour some non-specific genetic tendency towards irrationality. He did, however, argue that we exaggerate the badness of our circumstances, we fail to see and utilise our own agency, we reason poorly and expect things to change for us with no or minimal effort. In REBT's core ABC model of psychological disturbance, A is the actualising event, the trigger that is commonly taken to cause our emotional upsets. B is what we believe about these events and their power over us. C is the emotional and behavioural consequences of our beliefs. Every event, past, present or anticipated, of whatever kind or scale, is mediated by our cognitions. It is in our irrational beliefs – like Beck's negative automatic thoughts – that we construe events as terrible, catastrophic, unchangeable and inevitably distressing. But when in REBT we begin to expose these beliefs to Socratic disputation, we realise the role that our own cognitions play, the power we have to change them to more rational beliefs, and it is then up to us how well and forcefully we employ new rational thinking and behaviour.

We can see here that *what goes on inside our heads* is primary. We choose which attitudes to take up in relation to events. We are free to suffer if that is our choice but if we wish to change, then we need to vigorously dispute with ourselves our cognitive errors and reinforce new beliefs with new behaviours. Ellis's '*yes anything*' can be applied to bereavement, divorce, lost employment, examination anxiety; personality traits like shyness; and clinical conditions such as post-traumatic stress disorder and obsessive compulsive disorder. We have to learn that some discomfort is probably inevitable but endurable, and where change is not forthcoming, self-acceptance is still possible and desirable. But we do not have to be miserable. It is in Ellis's assertion that REBT can change our responses to *anything*, and that *everyone* can do this, that we see a grandiosity that resists nuance and failure. Someone with a strong character and forceful will addressing a certain situation differs significantly from a person who is weak-willed or timid facing another situation. Losing your family in a house fire does not, and perhaps should not, lend itself readily to efficient therapeutic resolution. A person being tortured is unlikely to benefit much from a quick *in situ* recap of REBT principles. Ellis's book title is clearly misleading (as is Kabat-Zinn's [2013] *Full Catastrophe Living*). REBT was, however, a welcome corrective to prevailing psychoanalytic thinking that emphasised the necessity for accessing distant personal memories, insights and transference reactions over a long period of time.

Beck has conceded that those with mild to moderate depression may offer accurate views on the negative aspects of life but insists that sufferers from severe depression do not (Haaga & Beck, 1995). This may give the impression of humility, learning from experience and carefully calibrating the nuances of depression levels. However, it is commonplace in British health service settings where CBT is offered for tight assessment procedures to be administered, and it is not uncommon for some clients to be turned away (or referred for medication) due to their being considered 'too depressed' for CBT. One wonders how this adds up – those with mild depression may be among the sanest in an insane world; yet some of those with moderate to severe depression may be too damaged, not ready or not compliant enough for CBT. In spite of its origins lying in ancient philosophy (Nussbaum, 1994; Robertson, 2010), modern CBT makes little real use of philosophical logic.

In the turf wars between therapists a particular contempt is harboured for CBT, if usually masked by polite tolerance or even brotherly pseudo-inclusiveness. The contempt is directed mainly at CBT's perceived shallowness and brevity, and its mechanical tendency to reduce the client to a set of negative automatic thoughts awaiting the practitioner's corrective interventions. Given the ascendancy of CBT in recent years, it is further disliked due to its uptake and funding by governments based on positive research evidence and promotion by positive health psychologists and happiness economists such as Layard (2011). Layard and Clark (2014) have gone further still, bringing together various pro-CBT arguments. It is said to be scandalous that epidemic mental health problems in contrast with physical problems go untreated when the means to do so are at hand; the means are all contained in relatively short-term CBT, queen of the allegedly evidence-based therapies, which is being delivered successfully via IAPT projects. The costs will be more than covered by savings in unemployment benefits, and we need a 'better culture' to improve overall happiness. The charge that mental illness is regarded as less important than physical illness (when research shows that depression is more incapacitating than asthma, for example) is used as a lever of moral outrage here. The question of whether the authors' reputations may be more important to them than truth and others' benefit lies unasked in any explicit way, but both are passionately and chronically attached to these views, promoted as evidence-based.

Beck has kept to a fairly tight course of reasoning on the development and treatment of clinical problems, but he has also allowed himself to join fellow big name pundits such as Freud, Jung and Rogers, and pronounce on matters of global concern. In Beck (1999) the principles of cognitive therapy are applied to an understanding of the aggressive emotions and their influence in the spheres of crime, violence, genocide and war. In this text he recounts an incident where a man became aggressive towards him at a book-signing, calling Beck attention-seeking, a phony and attributing to him a sense of superiority (1999, pp. 4–6).

86 Psychotherapy and depressive realism

Later, at a distance, Beck interprets this man's behaviour as egocentric, as clearly irrational and illustrating 'mind-reading' (that is, the man appeared to know what Beck was thinking about him). No doubt this man had problems of envy and low self-esteem, but Beck failed to see that CBT partly rests on an assumption of mind-reading negative automatic thoughts, and a view of people 'stumbling blindly through life' (p. 5). Beck also fails here to attribute any place in this interchange to the very real social and economic chasm between a wealthy, world-famous professor of psychology and a 'nobody'. He also, presumably, has no interest in the possibility that CBT may indeed be phony, based on little more than exaggerated commonsense (see Purton, 2014) and that, therefore, its beneficiaries are in some real sense phony, and perhaps the man was entitled to feel angry.

All things must change and pass, and CBT has already seen the decline of classical behaviour therapy, rational emotive behaviour therapy (REBT) and Socratic disputation, and the rise of mindfulness-based modifications. CBT has also been manualised and computerised and served up as a statutory means of addressing unemployment and boosting happiness. It has been mildly critiqued and received some negative research publicity. So far, however, it has not been exposed to the kind of rigorous philosophical analysis to which a therapy claiming philosophical foundations should be exposed. This, however, is only a matter of time—CBT—remaining one of the relatively newer therapies.

Humanistic, existential therapy and depression

It would be too much of a caricature of humanistic therapy to say that within its discourse *there is no depression*. But broadly speaking, the insistence in humanistic therapy on the wholeness of the human being and refusal to resort to psychological dissection and labelling does mean that psychiatric disorders and diagnosis of symptoms are often played down or dismissed. This is no Pollyannaish dismissal of unhappiness but an appeal to the client's self-perception, her precise bodily and emotional nuances, instead of privileging medico-psychiatric certainty. But humanistic therapy in its many forms is also the most ambitious and optimistic of the therapies, certainly compared with psychoanalytic (Weatherill, 2004). It is, after all, part of the wider human potential movement with roots in 1960s California. Not only can depression, such as it is, be overcome, but the client, all of us, the entire world, can be re-enchanted. As a prime initiator of this movement, Maslow remains distinguished for his criticism of 'deficit values', 'grumble theory', and the view that European existentialists showed 'high IQ whimpering on a cosmic scale' (Maslow, 1968, p. 16).

As if many of us were not bullied enough in childhood by statements such as 'there's no such word as *can't*', in Gestalt therapy we could be asked to rephrase can't as *won't*, in order to rediscover our negative agency and change it to positive: nothing is impossible, I *choose* not to do certain things. This ostensibly hopeful accent on personal responsibility and agency resonates with the Christian

Science emphasis on sin as lack of faith: for humanistic therapy to succeed all that is needed is absolute faith and credulousness. Similarly, in person-centred therapy, there is an overall flavour of human beings as an essentially pro-social species, with the internal resources to use the 'actualising tendency' within to convert bothersome 'conditions of worth' – with therapists' help – into positive self-acceptance.

Viktor Frankl's *Man's Search for Meaning* (Frankl, 2004, originally published in Germany as *Saying Yes to Life in Spite of Everything: a Psychologist Experiences the Concentration Camp*) is a long-running bestseller. His authority rests on his having been an inmate of Auschwitz and other concentration camps, where his wife and other family members died. Subsequently Frankl launched an inspirational psychotherapy. Logotherapy and its theory do not have much of the professional respect accorded to CBT or even the mainstream of existential therapies, but Frankl is a big hit with the general public. Frankl undoubtedly captured the market in the need for meaning and in the belief that any adversity can be overcome. In spite of Ellis's equal and possibly stronger case for being able to overcome suffering, Frankl is better known to the public, almost certainly due to the meaning brand. 'Suffering itself has meaning' is the watchword here. From a DR perspective, logotherapy and the movement for therapeutic meaningfulness is embarrassingly thin on believable substance while heavy with exhortation. It is difficult to criticise Frankl the concentration camp survivor, and the one who asserts hope and meaning in any circumstances. But logotherapy in its combined philosophical and crypto-theological aspects belongs squarely within what Heinze (2004) has called 'Jewish psychological evangelism'. Its Holocaust roots are powerfully emotive but its avoidance of evolutionary data, deep history, and insistence on modern meaninglessness reveal its serious limitations (Frankl, 2010).

Ghaemi (2007) appears to believe that DR is a special category of chronic mild to moderate depression that is best treated with existential psychotherapy. He sees no role for either CBT or psychoanalysis here, since the former can only remove cognitive distortions and the latter can only strip away illusions and the DR has neither. Instead, he argues that the existential despair experienced by DR clients should be accepted as valid: the existential therapist will 'meet patients where they are, completely and wholeheartedly, . . . a pure encounter of two souls in the travails of life, rather than a treatment of a sick person by a healthy one' (p. 127). Existential psychotherapy is, in his view, 'the necessary corollary of the DR model' (p. 112). In his brief trawl of phenomenological therapists, no mention is made of the person-centred approach, which certainly accepts clients (not sick *patients*) wholeheartedly. And no real justification of existential psychotherapy is given, apart from citing its jargon of existential despair. However, Ghaemi suggests that 'many apparent morbidities may in fact represent existential despair' (p. 128) and in doing so appears to open the door to DR being considered a more widespread position that is usually thought. What he cannot concede is that any DR paying good money for existential psychotherapy may find himself both psychologically unchanged and economically short-changed.

The question of suicide

Suicide is perhaps the most distressing of human phenomena, first for the person who is so unhappy that he or she feels driven to self-annihilation, and secondly for those left behind (Wertheimer, 2014). Yet it is reckoned that worldwide between 800,000 to a million people kill themselves every year. Suicide has often been spoken of as 'the coward's way out' or 'the easy way out', which is both a curious and arguably disgusting argument. It is curious because suicide takes not cowardice but courage, or at least distress so enormous that killing one-self becomes the only solution; and it is disgusting because it seeks to blame the already distressed person. It is well-known that some nursing staff are unsympathetic to people who are in hospital after a failed suicide attempt, regarding their professional mission as saving lives, and being resentful of those whose self-destructive actions 'block beds' for the more needy.

Another way to think of suicide is as the lesser of two evils, the other being living. Since suicide is messy and upsetting, living miserably will have to do, and after all continuing to live leads to the same end result, death, if much more slowly. The term *the coward's way out* implies rather oddly that non-suicidal people understand at some level the pull of suicide – after all, it is a way out of what exactly? Presumably, the misery that we can all experience, but that the psychologically strong and dysempathic can somehow override. The strange logic of the dysempathic coward-denouncer is that in fact deep down we all feel suicidal at times, which if true is an ironically depressive endorsement. Now, quite probably the kind of person who makes such a statement is naturally stoical, or high on denial, and unlikely to be helpful to the suicidally inclined person.

This is where therapists come in. From the Samaritans comes the empathic ideal of listening non-judgementally to the suffering individual's distress in the hope of averting a suicide but without any reference to the argument of cowardice or any other moral judgement. However, the Samaritans are regarded as frontline amateur volunteers who are not up to the job of professional understanding and deeply skilled intervention. The distress that has led the person to consider suicide must consist of complex layers of suffering at unconscious as well as conscious levels that can only be safely unravelled by trained psychotherapists and counsellors. These practitioners do not always explicitly make this argument but, I suspect, they let it be believed. Suicidality is such a deep and complex process that it should be entrusted only to the professionals. And since many of us are *potentially* suicidal, this threat underpins all psychological problems; if things go wrong, if the client is not helped professionally, she or he may deteriorate and commit suicide.

Are therapists valiant suicide resistance fighters? Sometimes they do help clients to choose not to kill themselves. Occasionally, a client will nevertheless kill him- or herself, and this is the most feared of outcomes for therapists. It signals that no-one can really be prevented from such a decision if so inclined, but it also suggests ultimate professional powerlessness. Someone not killing himself, and even perhaps becoming slightly less unhappy, signifies therapeutic success. However, we must ask whether therapists themselves are immune from depression and suicide and the answer is plainly no. Although I know of no register of therapist suicides, one hears of them occasionally and some well-known therapists have killed themselves. These include Paul Federn (1871–1950), Bruno Bettelheim (1903–90), Charles Truax (d.1973), Nina Coltart (1927–97), Petruska Clarkson (1947–2006) and Michael J. Mahoney (1946–2006). Freud himself died by morphine overdose administered by agreement with his physician, in order to end his suffering from terminal cancer of the jaw; and the psychoanalyst Wilhelm Stekel also overdosed to end his suffering. These experiences leave some scars on the profession and surprisingly receive very little attention, presumably being a shameful testament to perceived failure. Nevertheless, they can be written off, or forgotten as anomalies, like abusive priests or corrupt politicians, for letting the side down. Therapist suicides reveal a chink in the fantasy of a profession that may be the only thing standing between common unhappiness and suicidality. They show that anchoring mechanisms can always break down when God, utopia or therapeutic nirvana are seen through as illusions, and one remains staring at inescapable bleakness. One of very few texts representing the honest insights of a survivor of attempted suicide, who is also critical of therapy and the mental health 'circus', is Webb (2010).

Psychotherapy and death

Most of the aetiological emphasis in therapy theories is on early development and current functioning. Some admission of the place of death and brutalism generally is found in psychoanalysis (Freud's death drive, Langs's (2007) adaptational theories, and so on), existential therapy (death as one of the 'givens of existence') and transpersonal therapy (death as symbolic or a gateway). Freud's view that the unconscious sees itself as immortal holds some meaning; our inner animal does not dwell on death. Most therapy is an activity for younger to middle-aged, relatively physically healthy clients; indeed much therapy was originally conceived as a life-changing activity for psychologically-minded people at around age 30. However, extensions in statutory psychological health provision and in the law regarding age discrimination mean that many counsellors, counselling and clinical psychologists will now be working with older clients, clients who are ill and sometimes terminally ill. Working hopefully to change feelings and behaviour is very different from working with clients with, for example, terminal cancer. Therapists (often in the NHS) whose caseload includes a wide range of clients, from healthy but experiencing mild to moderate transient anxiety to old and bereaved clients, and those who are unhealthy and have terminally ill conditions, have to rapidly switch their expectations from optimistic to negatively acceptant. The British Psychological Society (BPS) trend towards doctoral-level training of relatively young counselling and clinical psychologists also means that an increasing gap will appear between their ages and experiences and that of their older (and not to mention poorer, sicker and often more depressed) clients. It is tacitly accepted that the empathic skills of the psychological therapist will put them in touch, indeed equally so (and into relational depth) with *all* their clients. This seems unlikely, however, and greatly over-stretches the burden on idealised empathy (Feltham, 2010).

Few psychologists would be so bold or foolish as to claim to eradicate death or even forestall it, but some humanistic therapists such as Harvey Jackins and Will Schutz have intimated that the total discharge of accumulated distress patterns, or radical acceptance of responsibility for living and dying, points in this direction. According to Schutz (1979), 'every death is a suicide' (p. 53). Arthur Janov, too, suggested that primal therapy would potentially, in removing neurotic sickness from our systems, lead to far longer lives. In the existential therapy camp death is taken on in a low-level heroic way that leads to wisdom and overcoming (Josselson, 2008; Yalom, 2011). In the CBT tradition death anxiety is regarded as akin to health anxiety and seen as eminently treatable (Furer & Walker, 2008). While most acknowledge that fear of death is 'normal', many nevertheless want to calibrate and professionalise it (excessive death anxiety as pathological and a legitimate clinical target) and claim successful modification. Even at the humble level of generic bereavement counselling, while views on how long grieving should take have faded, the principle that those trained in death awareness can help you better confront death is a powerful belief today.

What is depressing about the talking therapies

Whatever they may say to the contrary, most therapists want their clients to adapt to the world the way it is. Psychotherapy is not politics, and certainly not radical politics, the wordy efforts of critical psychologists notwithstanding (Feltham & House, 2016). Most therapy is oriented towards improved individual functioning, psychological-mindedness, better problem-solving, greater happiness and deeper insight. Few therapists, if any, are likely to be open to the idea that the world is a miserable and fundamentally unchangeable place. Some may comfort clients that their problems stem from distal political causes and are not of their own making (Smail, 1993), and some encourage clients to feel empowered to engage in political activism unless this is interpreted as a 'flight from health'. Very few are open to clients discussing suicidal wishes without intervening. In principle, person-centred therapy should have this mission – to listen empathically to clients' own wishes and perceptions – but few therapists work in a context where they are uninfluenced by prevailing viviocentric values. Existential therapists, too, while respecting their clients' phenomenological position on suicide, are likely with Camus to exert at least a nudge towards choosing to live. Most therapists believe their clients have deeply hidden emotional hurts against which they defend themselves and that with their skilful attention clients will overcome these, provided the clients really want to. Ultimately, no therapist is free from his or her own susceptibility to disturbing visions and ideas, and clients who persist in discussing deeply depressive realism might well trouble their beliefs and their sense of competency.

A radical DR summary of psychotherapy might run as follows. Our civilisation is problematic and distressing for many reasons. Psychotherapy is a century-old endeavour claiming to understand and effectively address human psychological distress. In this endeavour its practitioners are partly sincere, partly thoughtful and partly ignorant, partly altruistic and partly self-interested. They are merely human, too, they suffer, and unintentionally propagate suffering, as much as everyone else (Adams, 2014). Therapists are by no means more intelligent or insightful than the average person but are simply people who have put themselves through a 'training' that contains highly disputable knowledge claims. Some of them secretly relish their guru-like status. Like all of us they are enmeshed in economies which force them to defend their livelihoods against threats. New models of therapy arise constantly but these are mere unproven, enthusiastic novelties rather than scientific advances. No consensus on the epistemology of mental health problems exists, and this is highly unlikely ever to happen, given the complexity of aetiology spanning biological, historical, socioeconomic and idiopathic factors. While it is sometimes conceded that a few bad apples exist in the therapy profession, the idea that psychotherapy itself might be a massive confidence trick — whether perpetuated consciously and collectively or more likely by a coalition of naïve beneficiaries — is dismissed by all but the fiercest of its critics.

In this practice melange, probably due mainly to placebo factors, it appears according to disputed research that about 80% of clients make some improvement. Indeed, one piece of research claims to identify the contributions of change ingredients within psychotherapy to placebo factors (15%); technical/ theoretical factors (15%); common factors such as the therapist's acceptance, warmth, interest (30%); extra-therapeutic factors such as social support, ego strength, etc. (40%) (Lambert, 1992). If true, this is fairly damning, suggesting that most therapeutic 'success' comes from the client and community, human warmth and belief rather than anything therapy-specific. (See Lilienfeld et al., 2014, for possible explanations of pseudo-effectiveness, although this article too is biased.) A growing number of consumers, however, comment on the inadequacies of therapists and the defensiveness of the therapy professions. Meanwhile, depression looks set to increase significantly in worldwide terms. Psychotherapy probably ameliorates a little of the worst distress for a minority of people. But as Beckett's character Hamm, in *Endgame* put it, 'You're on earth, there's no cure for that'. Psychotherapy, like religion and spirituality, shores up our morale in a meaningless universe, provides us with transient illusions of personal mastery and sometimes takes the edge off our painful awareness of lifelong struggles and social absurdities to be definitively punctuated only by death. It is, in Zapffean terms, one form among others of anchoring, something to believe in that keeps the wolf of nihilism from the door.

Psychotherapy is certainly part of the triumph of hope over experience. Centuries of psychiatric effort have not made dramatic inroads into the worst forms of psychological distress. The radical psychiatry, or anti-psychiatry, and psychotherapy of the 1960s died a death or re-emerged in various romantic packages, for instance, in hopeful claims of cures for schizophrenia in Northern Finland going back to 1969 but not replicated elsewhere (Whitaker, 2011). Indeed, the very proliferation of new therapies often claiming significant breakthroughs are always prey to the entropy of only moderately good outcomes. The entire profession appears to believe that endless research is constantly improving therapy and the lives of its patients/clients (see, e.g. Wampold & Imel, 2015), but little solid and enduring evidence of this can be seen. The profession *has* to believe that therapy works, just as most religion has to insist that God exists.

The ethics of depressive realism and psychotherapy

If it were true that a group of people, DRs, had a negative but compelling take on significant matters like personal distress and its origins and prognoses, we would have a case for listening to them seriously and applying their insights. Psychoanalysis has a certain take on significant matters of distress, it is over 100 years old and is practised in private (commercial) and state funded services. While not endorsed by any majority, psychoanalysis has captured the imagination of an influential minority who train in it, propagate its ideas and make money and reputations from it. It probably has a grain of truth in it. However, as we know, it is considered unproven by many and a hoax by some. That does not stop it. But surely we must ask why some thought systems prosper and others receive no audience or wither. Psychoanalysis is a set of ideas and practices claiming not only to be 'true' but to be a mental health remedy. If we are to believe some of its commentators, it is a system of disillusionism (Ladan, 2014) rather than a hoped-for cure like CBT.

DR can be said to contain a set of truth claims that are disillusioning, yet it makes no attempt to establish a form of psychotherapy or to make money. Many of its claims are brutalist and nihilist in nature, and this is not what people want, or want to believe. In the case of psychoanalysis, however, a minority are enchanted by its apparent depth and clinical promise, and spend considerable sums getting themselves trained in it and using it as the basis for treating individuals in distress. Sometimes its 'patients' know what they are buying into but sometimes they do not; of course, psychoanalysts do not believe in telling their customers explicitly in advance what it entails, how it allegedly works, that it has no convincing evidence base and that some serious thinkers consider it a hoax. It thrives because it appeals to an enchanted minority of believers, who then pass on their faith to unknowing consumers or to acolytes. I believe this to be unethical. Implicitly, many other therapists probably also believe it to be unethical – using an unsubstantiated theory and practice and selling it as a proven mental health benefit – but they cannot make accusations of unethical practice because they too are involved in theories and practices that are little better epistemologically or ethically. Indeed, nobody, it seems, wishes to make a fuss over the mis-selling of psychotherapy because at the consumer end there is enormous suffering (infinitely fuelled by the human condition) for which no cure exists. Nobody can face up to this, so consequently even government health departments continue to spend money on the ectoplasm of psychotherapy, adding spurious evidence-collecting rituals. Incidentally, many are comforted by the attention and warmth of therapists, and 'helped' by the placebo of seeing, for example, a psychodynamically oriented counselling psychologist with a doctoral title (who also has a significant investment, being on a salary scale that is well above the national average). Everyone appears to benefit from this watertight collusion.

Two things are in play here: (a) psychotherapists and counsellors are hopeful and romantic thinkers but poor epistemologists, that is, they do not know how to evaluate truth claims, nor are they even interested in doing so; (b) once immersed in the practice of and belief in therapy and dependent on this income stream, they cannot opt out of it without suffering from cognitive dissonance and shame and risking relative poverty. No matter how many clients they see who do not make much progress, they must convince themselves and hence their clients that all shall (eventually) be well. While true that all therapists receive supervision, their supervisors are also enmeshed in the same belief and economic system, and their focus is on relational nuances and micro-ethics, never on truth. DRs have to live in this money-oriented world and may sometimes have links with the mental health or academic fields, so they too are often in collusive situations. But, I argue, they recognise the problematic epistemology and shaky ethics involved here. That the DR pull away from illusions means that DRs can never quite join in with the game that others play so readily.

Human beings suffer due to deeply embedded factors. Most of us want to ignore the distressing aetiology and prognosis involved: our species is badly damaged and our prospects are poor. This seems too much for the average person to grasp and it is understandable that it is denied. But those who at least understand such a claim typically reject it not because it is untrue but because there is no relief or money in it. They recognise intuitively that even if true, DR is a hard road to endure. They will therefore dismiss it as untrue, while espousing another set of beliefs (like psychotherapy) that are largely untrue but optimistic and profitable. This, I argue, is unethical. An analogy may serve: if someone has terminal illness but consults another doctor in desperation, that doctor can confirm the terminal prospects or offer palliative help, or alternative remedies. A doctor who is religious might also hold out hopes of an afterlife. One who suffers psychologically and who consults a 'psychological doctor' will always be told that there is a variety of methods available, there is always hope and plenty of confirmatory evidence. Most psychological distress is nebulous and rarely terminal, and moods wax and wane. Eysenck (1952) was right to point out the slipperiness of psychoanalytic claims to success, and nothing has really changed, but he

94 Psychotherapy and depressive realism

was wrong to promote behaviour therapy (now transmuted into CBT) as the answer. We do not have the answer to the question of widespread mental distress because (a) we do not want to know the terrible gloomy truth, and (b) we are looking in the wrong places. But meanwhile, we can and we do hypocritically and unethically proceed to dupe and exploit suffering individuals: being duped and exploited is apparently preferable to looking at the disconsolate truth.

A mental health challenge

The radical DR believes that all is unwell and can never be well. The psychotherapist probably believes that all depression including the DR attitude stems from unhappy life experiences and can be cured (Stagg, forthcoming). The social materialist psychologist believes that capitalist society is responsible for most of our ills. And so on. One way of addressing these competing epistemologies is to list and consider them:

1   The purportedly illusion-free DR view of life as meaningless, painful and necessarily engendering suffering in all including (and perhaps especially) those who refuse to deny or downplay it.
2   Political-psychological views that regard social conditions (patriarchal, economic and other oppressions), as responsible for most psychological suffering, with the remedy lying in major socio-economic reforms or revolution.
3   The radically psychotherapeutic view of life which focuses on personal life events and lack of psychological skills as causing or reinforcing suffering, and therapy as restoring some degree of happiness.
4   The religious, spiritual or existential view that sees the predominant current lifestyle as wayward and in need of rebirth or re-enchantment.
5   The biological explanation that would seek causes in the genetic and neurological, and remedies in medical research, bioengineering and pharmacology.
6   A mixed but overall optimistic view suggesting that mental distress levels are not so bad, research will gradually identify causes, various remedies are available and improving all the time.
7   A modified, compassionate DR view might argue that mental distress will always be with us but can be pragmatically ameliorated by anything from assisted suicide to medication; probably not in any non-illusory way by religion or psychotherapy but neither can anyone be denied those comforts.

A mutual exclusivity is logically at work here. If (1) is true, most of the others are false; if (2) is true, most others are probably false, and so on. Clearly, (3) challenges (1) and implies that the 'DR problem' might evaporate if only all those DRs would submit to psychoanalysis or CBT. Conceivably, a radical version of (5) might one day identify biological roots of depression and/or DR, and instigate a programme to eliminate it. A dismal DR prediction, however, is that if we could convene a panel representing all these positions (and more), no agreement would ever be reached. Of course, I am saying nothing new here, and we could say the same if we changed the topic to war, crime, and so on.

Psychotherapy and the depressive realist

Introverted people seeking a career may quite naturally consider the helping professions, especially the quiet, dimly lit, often home-based, one-to-one situation in psychotherapy and counselling in which the inner world is the focus. Those who have had any therapy themselves (even with negative outcomes) often see a natural path from that into therapy training. The majority of therapists are presumably *somewhat* optimistic, which would seem to exclude the DR from their ranks, although a few crypto-DRs probably operate beneath the radar (Adams, 2014, being suggestive here). We face the difficulty that many clients are pessimistic and the therapeutic dyad is often out of synch. It is the prime task of the therapist to coax the depressed client towards the slightly sunnier uplands of perceived normality, or even of becoming a 'fully functioning person'. Some DRs will decide in advance of or during therapy that it is a false solution, but some may struggle to allow themselves to be converted to normal functionality or even cheerfulness. They will duly reveal their childhood hurts and everyday self-sabotaging strategies and the therapist will skilfully cajole and confront them. It may work, or appear to work, temporarily, but often enough the disparity between the two will result in stalemate and attrition. For Woody Allen and his ilk chronic psychoanalysis appears to be an expensive pastime made worthwhile for its narcissistic distraction value. It is possible that some humanistic therapists will empathically confirm the DR in his valid difference – 'you really do see the world quite differently from many others, and you have great integrity' – and perhaps regard the DR as a kind of social scapegoat, carrying the burden of the sadness of existence that others deny.

There are historical precedents for this latter scenario, in which therapy itself changes its theories and character. For example, homosexuality was once considered pathological, especially by psychoanalysts, but is now accepted as a validly different form of sexuality, with specialised theories and techniques sometimes being adopted in gay affirmative therapy, and ethical codes prohibiting gay conversion therapies. Clients with marked religious affiliations might once have been regarded suspiciously, given Freud's negative views on religion, but a multicultural and person-centred society now makes this scenario far less likely. Also, the concept of 'mad pride' argues that people with so-called mental health problems such as schizophrenia or Asperger's Syndrome are simply different or neuro-atypical and should be honoured as such. Laingian therapy treated the schizophrenic as a kind of heroic combatant against a mad, schizophrenogenic society. Now with DR, if it were recognised as a validly different worldview, therapists would recognise this and not try to change it. Their job would be to offer emotional support to DRs as a minority group struggling in an uncritically pro-optimism world.

96 Psychotherapy and depressive realism

This latter scenario is not so far-fetched if we are thinking of empathic and unconditionally acceptant person-centred practitioners, but CBT and psycho-dynamic therapists who are trained to look for depressogenic thinking and depressive defences might not adapt so readily to the envisaged DR-friendly social reality. Beck (2005) alerts her fellow CBT practitioners to challenging clients, for example, particularly those considered to have personality disorders. And Miller (2013) demonstrates unwittingly, I think, the analyst's inevitable power struggle with the DR, in this case the allegedly schizoid Samuel Beckett. However, consider that a majority of counsellors are mature women and are perhaps less likely to genuinely understand or accept a recalcitrant depressive worldview. The DR worldview in its refusal of illusions and placebos, and its resolute hopelessness, is also likely to challenge the very foundations of psycho-therapy and the professional identities of its practitioners. The radical DR sees no truth here at all, only exaggerated ideas and opinions masquerading pomp-ously as systematic procedures. The prospects for some sort of new DR-friendly version of psychotherapy being developed do not appear bright but McPherson and Baker (2013), as an exception, offer a form of acceptant spiritual life coach-ing and grief therapy in the context of expecting all human life to end within decades due to deadly climate change.

Were psychotherapy able to demonstrate its effectiveness in turning around the gloomy disposition of significant numbers of DRs, converting them into happy or at least lighter hearted people, we would still face the same scenario: we are all going to die, no God or other religious fantasies can save us, social and political absurdities and tragedies will continue, climate change or other disasters may destroy us. Perhaps, having confronted the origins of our DR in unhappy childhood experiences (Yalom, 2007; Miller, 2013; Stagg, forthcom-ing), we won't be too dismayed by all this and we will adopt a 'mature' attitude to social and existential problems. However, the chances of demonstrating that psychotherapy genuinely has such an effect in a majority of even sub-DR cases are extremely slim.

Note

1 The spelling of the author's name in Norwegian is Tønnessen but in Canada where he worked it is rendered Tennessen.

References

Adams, M. (2014) *The Myth of the Untroubled Therapist*. London: Routledge.
APA (2013) *Diagnostic and Statistical Manual of Mental Disorders (5th edn.)*. Arlington, VA: American Psychiatric Association.
Baker, C. & McPherson, G. (2013) *Extinction Dialogs: How to Live with Death in Mind*. San Francisco, CA: Taylen lane.
Beck, A.T. (1999) *Prisoners of Hate: The Cognitive Basis of Anger, Hostility, and Violence*. New York: Harper Collins.

Beck, J.S. (2005) *Cognitive Therapy with Challenging Clients*. New York: Guilford.

Dienstag, J.F. (2006) *Pessimism: Philosophy, Ethic, Spirit*. Princeton, NJ: Princeton University Press.

Ellis, A. (1996) *How to Stubbornly Refuse to Make Yourself Miserable about Anything – Yes Anything!* New York: Lyle Stuart.

Eysenck, H.J. (1952) The effects of psychotherapy: An evaluation. *Journal of Consulting Psychology*, 16, 319–324.

Feltham, C. (2010) *Critical Thinking in Counselling and Psychotherapy*. London: Sage.

Feltham, C. (2013) *Counselling and Counselling Psychology: A Critical Examination*. Ross-on-Wye: PCCS Books.

Feltham, C. (2015) *Keeping Ourselves in the Dark*. Charleston, WV: Nine-Banded Books.

Feltham, C. & House, R. (2016) The politics of counselling psychology. In D. Murphy (ed). *Counselling Psychology: A Textbook for Students and Trainees*. Chichester: Wiley.

Frankl, V.E. (2004) *Man's Search for Meaning*. London: Rider.

Frankl, V.E. (2010) *The Feeling of Meaninglessness: A Challenge to Psychotherapy and Philosophy*. Milwaukee, WI: Marquette University Press.

Fuller, P.R. (2013) *Surviving, Existing, or Living: Phase-Specific Therapy for Severe Psychosis*. London: Routledge.

Furer, P. & Walker, J.R. (2008) Death anxiety: A cognitive-behavioral approach. *Journal of Cognitive Psychotherapy*, 22 (2), 167–182.

Ghaemi, S.N. (2007) Feeling and time: The phenomenology of mood disorders, depressive realism and existential psychotherapy. *Schizophrenia Bulletin*, 33 (1), 122–130.

Gray, J. (2013) *The Silence of Animals: On Progress and Other Modern Myths*. London: Allen Lane.

Haaga, D.A.F. & Beck, A.T. (1995) Perspectives on depressive realism: Implications for cognitive theory of depression. *Behaviour Research and Theory*, 33 (1), 41–48.

Heinze, A.R. (2004) *Jews and the American Soul: Human Nature in the 20th Century*. Princeton, NJ: Princeton University Press.

Houellebecq, M. (2011) *Whatever*. London: Serpent's Tail.

Josselson, R. (2008) *Irin D. Yalom on Psychotherapy and the Human Condition*. New York: Jorge Pinto.

Kabat-Zinn, J. (2013) *Full Catastrophe Living (Rev. edn.)*. London: Piatkus.

Ladan, A. (2014) *On Psychoanalysis, Disillusion, and Death: Dead Certainties*. London: Routledge.

Lambert, M.J. (1992) Psychotherapy outcome research: Implications for integrative and eclectic therapists. In J.C. Norcross & M.R. Goldfried (eds). *Handbook of Psychotherapy Integration*. New York: Basic Books.

Langs, R. (2007) *Beyond Yahweh and Jesus: Bringing Death's Wisdom to Faith, Spirituality and Psychoanalysis*. New York: Jason Aaronson.

Layard, R. (2011) *Happiness: Lessons from a New Science (Rev. edn.)*. London: Penguin.

Layard, R. & Clark, D.M. (2014) *Thrive: The Power of Evidence-Based Psychological Therapies*. London: Allen Lane.

Lilienfeld, S.O., Ritschel, L.A., Lynn, S.J., Cautin, R.L. & Latzman, R.D. (2014) Why ineffective therapies appear to work: A taxonomy of causes of spurious therapeutic effectiveness. *Perspectives on Psychological Science*, 9 (4), 355–387.

Maslow, A.H. (1968) *Toward a Psychology of Being*. New York: Van Nostrand.

Miller, I. (2013) *Beckett and Bion: The (Im)Patient Voice in Psychotherapy and Literature*. London: Karnac.

Nussbaum, M.C. (1994) *The Therapy of Desire: Theory and Practice in Hellenistic Ethics*. Princeton, NJ: Princeton University Press.

Pretzer, J.L. & Walsh, C.A. (2002) Optimism, pessimism, and psychotherapy: Implications for clinical practice. In E.C. Chang (ed). *Optimism and Pessimism: Implications for Theory, Research, and Practice.* Washington, DC: American Psychological Association.

Purton, C. (2014) *The Trouble with Psychotherapy: Counselling and Common Sense.* London: Palgrave.

Robertson, D. (2010) *The Philosophy of Cognitive-Behavioural Therapy (CBT): Stoic Philosophy as Rational and Cognitive Psychotherapy.* London: Karnac.

Schutz, W. (1979) *Profound Simplicity.* London: Turnstone.

Smail, D. (1993) *The Origins of Unhappiness: A New Understanding of Personal Distress.* London: Harper Collins.

Stagg, R. (forthcoming) When the desert starts to bloom: Humanistic psychology and depressive reality. *Self and Society: An International Journal for Humanistic Psychology.*

Tennessen, H. (1966/67) Happiness is for the pigs: Philosophy versus psychotherapy. *Journal of Existentialism,* 3 (26), 181–214.

Wampold, B.E. & Imel, Z.E. (2015) *The Great Psychotherapy Debate: The Evidence for What Makes Psychotherapy Work (2nd edn.).* New York: Routledge.

Weatherill, R. (2004) *Our Last Great Illusion: A Radical Psychoanalytical Critique of Therapy Culture.* Exeter: Imprint Academic.

Webb, D. (2010) *Thinking about Suicide: Contemplating and Comprehending the Urge to Die.* Ross-on-Wye: PCCS Books.

Wertheimer, A. (2014) *A Special Scar: The Experiences of People Bereaved by Suicide.* Abingdon: Routledge.

Whitaker, R. (2011) *Anatomy of an Epidemic: Magic Bullets, Psychiatric Drugs, and the Astonishing Rise of Mental Illness in America.* New York: Broadway.

Yalom, I. (2007) *The Schopenhauer Cure.* New York: Harper Perennial.

Yalom, I. (2011) *Staring at the Sun: Overcoming the Dread of Death.* London: Piatkus.

Yalom, I. (2012) *The Spinoza Problem.* New York: Basic Books.

Chapter 7

The socio-political domain
and depressive realism

'There are criticisms of American society that the neurotic can make as well as anyone, perhaps better' (Alexander, p. 322). This linkage of the depressive poet Sylvia Plath with politics makes the point well. We are, as the cliché goes, social animals, born into and dependent on early attachments, close relationships and complex social networks with deep historical roots, neurological ties and inescapable economic and symbolic webs. We romanticise our interdependence and also recognise that hell can be other people, on all levels. As Seneca said 2,000 years ago, 'We are mad, not only individuals, but nations also' (Humphrey & Lifton, 1984, p. 57). Mathy (2011), for example, writes of France as suffering from a 'national depression'. Terminology is often a challenge and the chapter heading requires a brief explanation. I intend here to refer to matters that might elsewhere be divided into politics, political philosophy, economics, social and cultural theory, feminist and queer theory, sociology and environmentalism. Of course, that is impossibly wide territory, and this is without complicating it with social psychology, criminology, anthropology, demography. We might convert these terms into the world around us, the lifeworld, the social world and the structures of civilisation. Bennett (2001) offers an analysis of these matters in which the term 'cultural pessimism' covers everything I refer to here; and see also Liddle (2008). While some appear highly active in and impassioned about shaping the world politically and economically, the majority arguably endures it or is baffled by its complexity.

Everyday news

Not everyone reads daily newspapers, watches television or other online sources of news, but it is an extremely common practice and acts as a major barometer of social trends (not to mention a defence against anomie and a way of structuring non-work time). At the time of writing, a selection of random examples: an American journalist was beheaded by the ISIS group in Syria; further air strikes take place in Gaza; there are further reactions to the shooting by police of a black teenager in the United States; trouble or tensions continue in Ukraine, the Central African Republic, South Sudan, Egypt and North

Korea. It is mostly bad news, mostly involving violent males, much more of the bad than the good, neutral or trivial. The death of Indian yoga teacher B.K.S. Iyengar, although a death, is perhaps the main exception, reminding us of what seems a decent man in a mad world. Somehow alongside and between atrocities most of us conduct ordinary non-dramatic lives (especially those of us who live outside so-called trouble-spots) of business as usual. But even those of us relatively unaffected in a direct way by brutal events derive some of our sense of the world from them. We live in, and we know we live in, a patriarchal civilisation afflicted by tribal conflicts. We know that most of this unrest is in certain volatile parts of the world. But we are aware, too, that terrorist incidents, major accidents or natural disasters can happen anywhere at any time. We are confirmed in the finding of Baumeister et al. (2001) that bad is stronger than good. We could, and some do, refuse to read the daily news; we know, after all, that things don't appear to get better. The media have sometimes been asked to include more positive stories (not to mention royal and celebrity marriages and births) by way of balance, but either they ignore such requests, or they cannot find sufficient positive balance or news coverage reflects what people actually want to hear.

Soroka (2014) refers to an established chicken and egg problem of journalists stoking fear and negativity in news content and readers expecting it. His research entails the compilation of a Lexicoder Sentiment Dictionary which was used to count and analyse negatively toned words found in media reports. These showed about twice as many negative as positive stories as measured by negativity in the 'real world'. Soroka asks whether the negative bias has long-term detrimental effects and decides it probably has but believes that this will be corrected in time. What analyses like these cannot do is evaluate the effects of information overload as a negative. The events I have mentioned above, from 2014, are transiently impactful and distressing but also merely the latest bad events, probably soon forgotten. Fed constant global threats and digested scary health research and advice by the media, it isn't surprising if we become desensitised and anxious and exhausted by turns. Etchells (2015) is one of many to look at relevant variables and ask how we can judge whether or not things are actually getting worse, citing a survey in which 71% of respondents considered the quality of life to be declining.

Injustice

As Schopenhauer puts it: 'People have always been discontented with governments, laws and public institutions; for the most part, however, this has only been because they have been ready to blame them for the wretchedness which pertains to human existence as such' (1851/1970, p. 154). In an often post-brutal world of liberal education, human rights and the belief that we are entitled to progress, we are sensitive to what we perceive as injustices and infelicities. The rhetoric and force of moral argument has seemingly triumphed over brute force

The socio-political domain and depressive realism 101

and allows us to complain vocally about and seek to change anything we do not consider just. Yet so many competing claims to worse suffering exist that it is hard to know where one would begin to seek comprehensive justice, some arguing, for example, that the depression experienced by black people outweighs that of depressed white people (Cvetkovich, 2012). Those committed to fighting for 'social justice' may conveniently link arms with critical theory scholars in their conviction that the cause of oppressed groups is axiomatically morally compelling, while refusing to consider critical counter claims, problems of complexity, human nature and entropy.

Most of us would rather live in a world where we are protected by the state from gross injustice and barbarism. The law protects the weak against the callous strong, up to a point. Law and moral outrage defend us against murder, rape, robbery and other crimes but they cannot entirely prevent such crimes; they can only stigmatise, outlaw and punish. Your right not to be raped, unfortunately, cannot prevent someone from raping you if he is able and determined to do so. Any young man with a pathological, inchoate grievance, who is able to obtain guns, can walk into a school and kill several children. A drunk driver can hit you and leave you in a state requiring lifelong medical attention. Most such brutalities are perpetrated by men and reflected in prison populations worldwide. Yet we easily conflate our emotional attachment to legal and human rights with the magical thinking that protests we must never be hurt. We fail to notice that we live in a world in which natural disasters and fatal accidents can happen (just as they do in 'nature'), and against those who are disturbed, aggressive or psychopathic enough to rape and kill us there is no ultimate protection. We limit our risks but take our chances.

Perhaps we also fail to notice or we are not honest about the fact that there are always, and always will be, harmful events and circumstances and unfair social arrangements. The single most startling fact of injustice is that a miniscule percentage of the rich own over half of the world's wealth (Farmer, 2004). The extreme left seek to control the savagery of extremes of unfairness, and the extreme right want us to take our chances against each other and rely on our own resources (Asma, 2013). In the perennial argument that attaches to these political positions, both offer remedies. Hobbes was right to recognise the forces of brutality that underpin natural human existence and require law and order to keep in check. In a sense, politicians of all stripes are correct in identifying selective causes and offering selective remedies. The public, whether politically engaged or passive bystanders, imagines that politics takes care of all such matters. Insofar as individuals have insecurities, grievances and experience injustices, they all lean towards certain promised political solutions, never mind that complete solutions in reality are seldom if ever forthcoming. Almost everyone seems to emotionally and amateurishly associate perceived injustices with a range of tenuous causes and touted remedies. The so-called intelligentsia produce articulate theories of injustice and remedial proposals, both grandiose and pragmatic, both tightly reasoned and impassioned. Politics represents hope. But as Gray puts

102 The socio-political domain and depressive realism

it: 'politics is only a small part of human existence, and the human animal only a very small part of the world' (2010, p. 16).

Very few, however, take the nihilistic or tragic reasoning route. As Schopenhauer puts it, the wretchedness of existence itself is to blame, or in Beckett's terms our earthly location permits of no cure for our many ills. DRs readily accept this. But critics of modern society who want to deconstruct standard psychotherapy, politics, religion and so on, quite commonly accept part of the DR analysis but stop well short of nihilism. Marxists want to blame capitalism for all our immiseration; feminists blame patriarchy; critical psychologists want to blame capitalism for our psychological ills; eco-warriors want to blame consumerism; anarcho-primitivists want to blame industry and agriculture; and all have their proposed remedies, most involving some partial regression to idyllic visions of an imagined past and/or of reparations for suffering. Some thinkers inspired by evolutionary biology and psychology claim the mismatch between our hunter-gatherer existence over 10,000 years ago is responsible for our present malaise. None of these can accept the idea that human existence, or even sentient existence itself, *inexorably* leads to suffering and misery. It looks doubtful, for example, if we can ever be free of the ravages of mental illness that torment an unlucky section of humanity: this itself is a form of natural injustice. The majority barely clings to the hope that conventional politics, however flawed, will sort out all our ills.

The capitalism-socialism impasse

It seems that the unfettered economic efforts of the most motivated can make them personally rich and stimulate national economies, including along the way the creation of employment. The underlying philosophy of human nature is clear, too, that entrepreneurial talent, risk and hard work create wealth, and those who are unwilling to take risks and work hard cannot expect significant rewards. Desire and greed are motivators. Trade, the origins of capitalism, lies many thousands of years in humanity's past. Capitalism now requires vast numbers of subservient workers and 'hungry' consumers; it creates huge social divisions, sometimes destroys communities, and can flout health and safety measures; it relies on creating illusions of need by deceptive advertising and fashion trends. The 'finance industry' thrives on deceptively juggling money while producing little or nothing substantial. The most ruthless capitalists have no social conscience. Capitalism has come to seem like the very air we breathe, with no credible alternative (Fisher, 2009). These are just some of the charges against it.

Socialists of various stripes like to believe that human nature is good, or that there is no human nature and we simply construct ourselves politically. In this view capitalism (as well as all other forms of economic and political organisation) is a kind of cancer spread by the wicked greedy few, and has to be stopped or severely restrained. Soviet communism did not turn out well and few socialists wish to repeat the experiment. South American socialism appears slow,

The socio-political domain and depressive realism   103

unreliable and unpromising. Scandinavian-style socialism is invariably held up as a beacon of hope but it still rests on tight state control, high taxes, propaganda and not least on very small populations. Arguably socialism can only work with relatively small, trusting groups; perhaps ancient hunter-gatherer tribes succeeded in internal reciprocal altruism but even they did not co-operate easily with other tribes.

We think there has to be an answer but we certainly haven't found it, tweaking, dissembling and over-correcting being the best we can apparently do. We may romanticise human nature and long for a utopian future but we must realise it isn't coming any more than Jesus is returning. If planned socialism worked well, one would expect democracy to install it by popular vote but the majority does not like high taxes, heavy bureaucracy, constrained freedoms, low rewards and the bland culture that often results from it. Nor is the majority clearly pro-capitalist, showing an instinctive revulsion against the inequalities and unfairness spawned by runaway capitalism. Some political philosophers, anthropologists and anarchists continue to weigh up the merits of stateless, hunter-gatherer style self-rule contrasted with the Hobbesian defence of the contractarian state authority (Widerquist & McCall, 2015). Whatever system is installed, those administering it soon appear at least partially corrupt and incompetent. While huge multinational corporations thrive by exploitation of labour, tax evasions and other strategies, they always bring yet further injustices. Human nature is an unreliable mixture of goodness, wishful thinking, denial and selfishness, is always at the mercy of the natural environment and its downsides are multiplied by mass societies.

Democracy

Where optimists see hope for real change in every election, DRs see merely another farce playing out. Whether it is Mandela in 1994 ('free at last'), Blair in 1997 ('things can only get better'), or Obama in 2009 ('yes we can'), the great hopes soon turn to ashes of disappointment as hypocrisy, hubris, impotence or incompetence become apparent. Some leaders are better than others, but most turn out to be either routinely or extraordinarily bad. But in essence democracy, the right to vote and change governments, is idealistically about the people's (or the majority's) right to govern themselves by voting for political parties whose principles and manifestos they approve of. This system entails a trust in the electorate to be as informed, engaged and fair as possible; or rather, fairness is not a requirement, since everyone is at liberty to vote to protect their own self-interests. Engagement is problematic, with many not using their vote, out of apathy or protest. Democracy tends to look better than dictatorship or totalitarian regimes and often is, at first at least. Corrupt, incompetent or wrongheaded administrations can be replaced by another party for a few years. However, it is now commonplace to observe in many democratic nations that democracy is ailing for many reasons, including politicians being regarded as out of touch with the electorate, impotent and failing to match manifesto promises with results. Rich individuals and multinational corporations assert their power (Plummer, 2014). National governments are at the mercy of volatile international political trends. Multicultural societies splinter away from traditional bipolar class structures into multi-interest groups. And often, little real differences manifest between parties. As Mair (2013) observes, moves towards European homogeneity appear to reduce citizen participation in democracy. What was once the vibrant institution of democracy has arguably become simply the latest failed means of running mass societies, a view that fits well with an entropic theory of all institutions as well as a misanthropic view of human nature.

Geopolitics

The vast majority of us know of international events and tensions only via the media; and even those living in a war zone only really know their own local tragedy. Yet we realise that events and trends in other parts of the world threaten us as potential wars, as terrorism on home soil, or as increasing refugee immigration and its unsettling socio-economic effects. In general, at our moment in history, the greatest instability is in the Middle East and Africa, and refugees typically head northwards and westwards to escape persecution, death, poverty, hunger and disease. (In the last major ice age this migratory pattern was the reverse, that is, from north to south.) This migratory trend will only continue with climate change. Some fundamentalist Muslim groups are energised to attempt caliphate-building by aggressive expansion and terrorism. International economic downturns threaten Western, indeed global stability, and publications warn us constantly of the decline of one bloc or another.

Even in advanced economies like Japan, DR observers see signs of cultural collapse. Japan has a large (127.6 million) and ageing population (23% over 65), but its population is in slow decline as young people increasingly spurn relationships and pronatalism. Websites show us that Japan appears in top ten lists for most introverted and pessimistic nations, and the Japanese suicide rate puts it at seventh in the world. But Japan is overshadowed by China, its vast population and economic outreach. China has many internal problems, including a high suicide rate, but no-one can deny its international ambitions. Russia, for all its assertiveness on the international stage, suffers from vast inequalities in wealth, and extensive internal problems of human rights, a declining population and high levels of depression and suicide.

As Mearsheimer (2014) argues in what is known as a realist (indeed 'offensive neorealism') paradigm in politics, the great powers are always anxious to compete for security in an anarchic world situation, and to retain their power if not extend it blatantly or surreptitiously. While we generally impute evil or aggressive motives to nations engaging in bids for power, a simple geodeterminist view suggests that it was ever thus, based on factors of physical geography, land and sea barriers and limited resources. Marshall (2015) indeed expands on this view

The socio-political domain and depressive realism 105

to show how sheer geographical constraints, historical tribalism, competition for resources and strategic alliances and treaties conspire to produce ongoing tensions and wars. This mixture of geodeterminism, inertia, international accidents and occasional, apparently wise choices made by politicians, constitutes the lumbering nature of human history unfolding in ways we may hopefully regard as progressive but which often look frighteningly random.

Climate change

I look briefly at climate change as one of the threats to our future in Chapter 8, but here I touch on some of the social and economic issues involved. Global warming does appear by most scientific accounts to be real and to be linked with humanly generated, unsustainably high carbon emissions. Its combination of potential climatic and demographic devastation, urgency and denial, arguably makes it one of the most challenging of events ever. According to Ponting (2007), human activity has been acting on the natural environment for thousands of years. The greenhouse effect was noted in the early 19th century, and the topic has been on the international agenda for several decades. It highlights our unsustainably consumerist way of life and our inability to think and act co-operatively and in a timely fashion. Like the legendary foolish frogs that boil to death in a pan of water, not jumping free because they do not notice the gradualness of the lethal heating process, human beings are similarly foolish and unable to take necessary steps.

Bjørn Lomborg's (2001) *The Skeptical Environmentalist* positioned him according to some as a climate change denier. Lomborg, however, has argued that he takes seriously the increase in anthropogenic climate change but wants to get it in proportion and to prioritise nations' expenditure on the most significant and pressing needs such as clean water for the developing world. Lomborg is not obviously driven by a capitalist agenda but has been accused of minimising threats from climate change. But he is far from alone, blatant denialists ridiculing claims that we are approaching disaster, and many others being simply unwilling or unable to respond with due urgency. In this last sense, our own anthropogenic disaster scenario is sometimes compared with the collapse scenarios of past civilisations that have created their own demise in a fatal mixture of denial and hubris. Writers from Edward Gibbon through Oswald Spengler, Arnold Toynbee and Jared Diamond have documented or interpreted causes of civilisational downfall but we seem none the wiser today. NASA maintains a Near Earth Object Program to scan for asteroid threats, yet we remain hypoanxious about threats much closer to home.

Tragic pluralism

Or should that be 'pluralistic tragedy'? Here is my meaning. The human species has evolved from separated small nomadic numbers into a vast population of over 7 billion covering most of the earth, increasingly living in dense cities in over 200 nations, speaking 6,000 languages, highly technologized, still tribalistic and violent, interconnected but divided by many religious, political, economic and other tensions. We have to choose a path and whichever path we take we create and encounter further problems. Given the availability of weapons of mass destruction, constant monitoring must take place, threats must be responded to and uneasy diplomacy attempted. Nothing can stand still, and geopolitical realignments abound. We negotiate uneasily between tendencies towards large totalitarian states and fragmentation into smaller units at the popular will. The antagonistic structure of left- and right-wing (or cultural Marxism and capitalist hegemony, to use some of their own insults for each other) runs deep and little rapprochement seems possible. It is not only that history is the nightmare we are trying to extricate ourselves from, but that collective human existence is as unstable as geological and ecological arrangements. It seems we needed the horrors of the Holocaust to teach us about the dangers of dictatorship and race hatred, and its scar lives within us collectively and prophylactically but is no guarantee against similar or worse horrors to come. We cannot know to what extent Pinker's (2011) analysis of the decline of violence is reliable (John Gray is dismissive), but we are sensitised to outbreaks of violence and war remaining forever possible.

The Joseph Rowntree Foundation (JRF) conducted a major online opinion poll of 3,500 respondents on perceived 'social evils' in the 21st century which identified diseases of prosperity, poverty and inequality, decline in moral values, decline of the family, individualism, fear and distrust among other evils. Taylor (2009) attempts to distil these into attitudinal groups: *hierarchical* ('I do what I'm told'); *egalitarian* ('I will do what the group does'); *individualistic* ('I do what I want'); and *fatalistic* ('It doesn't matter what I do'). DR clearly lines up as fatalistic here but probably also as individualistic. The hierarchical is contemptible and the egalitarian group is absurdly optimistic. So-called social evils change from time to time but all emanate from underlying anthropopathology. Exercises such as these always assume that socio-political trends cause social problems, that they can be identified and remedied. Bodies like the JRF cannot allow that dismal human nature and inescapable conditions of existence might always sabotage whatever positive arrangements we put in place. It may sometimes matter in small ways what I do but in the long run it doesn't.

We speak of the human species and often romantically as one species. But we also speak in terms of continental and nationalist entities, the developed and developing world, of historico-cultural tribes, races and ethnicities. We are accustomed to religious divisions, separation of religious and secular worlds and to political left and right wings, with labels for political extremism. Often countries are tacitly divided by regional, tribal and class interests and historical fractures. Current multicultural ideology favours the notion of a rich diversity of cultures, ethnicities, as well as sexualities (LBGTQ as well as heterosexual and asexual), degrees of disability and difference, all characterised by an ill-defined equality (see West, 2015). We have a longstanding 'battle of the sexes' (now genders).

Academic sociology, criminology, economics and psychology prove poor value for money, producing little of real use. Science, religion, the arts and humanities continue to fail to agree on many matters. At the level of individual differences, we have psychology's 'Big 5', or more simply the divisions between optimists and pessimists, extraverts and introverts and so on. But beyond this we have hard-to-categorise differences in personality, perceptions and worldview: no two of us, not even twins, see the world in exactly the same way. We are all idiosyncratically hardwired individuals in a mass species of over seven billion, torn between allegiances and a utopian fantasy of oneness. Cioran refers to our 'odyssey of rancor,' spending our 'sleepless nights in mentally mangling our enemies' (1996, p. 57) and argues that 'everything wounds and insults us' (p. 78). It is our conceit that utopia awaits the civilised but the reality is otherwise.

DR as 'patriarchal'

I am searching for a better term here and I am mindful of lack of 'evidence', and critiques of perceived essentialism. In parallel with millennia of male-dominated societies we have had an underbelly of values held to be more feminine. Let me argue that where men have been prominent in tribalism, violence, ambition, rationality, detachment, risk-taking, crime, alcoholism, suicide and technology, and have died a little younger than women, women (and sometimes artists and gay men) have tended to represent nurturance, intuition, communicativeness, emotionality, romanticism, aesthetics and spirituality. Mundane cynicism is associated with men rather than women, as in 'grumpy old man'; and the phrase 'beta male misanthropy' suggests that some strains of DR emanate from men who are losers. We could propose emptily sexist arguments about the 'better sex', or suggest some ultimate 'equality', but my observation is that most women and men roughly fit the above schema.

Women are evidently more prone to low self-esteem, depression, panic attacks and hormonal mood swings, and they have been socio-economically oppressed. The feminist fight for full equality, which fuels hope, may be partly responsible for women not tending to be depressive realists, while men who apparently 'have everything' realise that such possession does not satisfy. Women, biologically primed for pregnancy, giving birth and nurture, are domestically stable and future-oriented, while men on average have more mixed feelings about domestic commitments and monogamy. Work by Taylor (2003) is suggestive of biological and social explanations for women's better coping via oxytocin release and social connectedness than men's greater solipsism; in our evolution, fight or flight mechanisms may have worked for men but not for women with children to tend to. The philosopher Christine Overall (2003, 2012) also lends weight to the gender case put here by supporting both prolongevity and procreation, if making a small, environmentally-informed plea for smaller families.

108 The socio-political domain and depressive realism

A majority of philosophers have been male, and often celibate or uncommitted to others. Ancient Greek and Roman philosophy was not especially kind to women, sometimes attributing evil to them (Songe-Møller, 2002; Gilligan & Richards, 2009). Some exceptions can always be found to patriarchal dominance, its evil and suffering, but women are much more often perceived as victims. Sylvia Plath is celebrated as a literary suicide and some feminists have sought to apportion male blame in her case, although this remains disputed. Sarah Perry (2014), however, also appearing online in her website as theviewfromhell or Sister Y, is a rare, sharp philosophical thinker with distinctly DR views on birth and suicide. Women have usually promoted the soft values of non-violence and compassion. But the downside is that they have also promoted euphemism and embellishment, preferring kindly words and censorship and distracting decoration, to harsh realities and bare furnishings. Many men have given free rein to execration, violence, slobbish habits and scruffy habitats. Violent films attract male not female audiences, and arguably it is mothers who foster the vision of life as a fluffy pink nursery with soft furnishings, sweet music, romance and happy endings. Life has largely unhappy endings – the illnesses, ugliness and bereavements of old age and grisly death and funerals – but, so I argue, a gender difference attends such observations.

In terms of intergender issues, let us remember certain critical paradoxes. Sex is one of the relatively few activities brightening up life for many of us, yet sex frequently leads to unintended procreation. But celibate mystics including the Buddha and St Paul demonstrate the nature of sex as an obstacle to enlightenment, one of the very few hopes of escape from DR. Overall (2012) argues that since women are more pronatalist than men, bear more responsibility for birth (which is painful) and for child care (which can be an economic disadvantage and sometimes boring), they deserve a greater say in debates on procreation. Yet some radical feminists have defined penetrative (or PIV/penis in vagina) sex as intrinsically violent and unwelcome.

DR as right-leaning?

Inevitably, some suspect DR of being aligned with a right-wing take on life. The emphasis on determinism and fatalism, and corresponding diminishment of hope may conjure up a picture of sociobiology, positivism and misanthropy that looks very suspicious. One only has to make some easy associations. Schopenhauer was certainly misogynistic, if we can use such terminology retrospectively; he was known as selfish and quarrelsome, yet has informed subsequent political thinking (Neill & Janaway, 2009). Kierkegaard was a tortured, single, childless man living on an inheritance and defending individualism. Williams (1987) notes that the Italian Far Left in the 1960s were advised not to follow only Gramsci but to take seriously Leopardi's insight into the passivity of suffering. Nietzsche has famously been blamed for the rise of Nazism and Heidegger heavily implicated in it. Freud, if we consider him a pessimist, spoke of humanity as 'trash' and freely used the 'man is a wolf to man' epithet. In his youth, Cioran was associated with the Romanian Iron Guard, a fascist party. Zapffe was an avowed antinatalist who espoused environmental conservation in an elitist manner, and also hoarded supplies in case of some endtimes scenario. Larkin was considered blatantly racist, sexist, misanthropic, was friendly with Margaret Thatcher and his father even attended Nuremberg rallies and took him along. Houellebecq has been accused of Islamophobia, sexism and misanthropy generally. The caricature of grumpy old misanthropist appears to fit well with a depiction of right-wing depressive realism, if not a miserly Scrooge figure harbouring an intellectual hatred of humanity and wishing a hastening of its annihilation.

On the other hand, Beckett fought for the French resistance (which he described as 'Boy Scout work') and he wrote the play *Catastrophe* (1982) in support of Václav Havel, imprisoned in Czechoslovakia. Both Adorno and Brecht were somewhat at odds with Beckett's perceived apolitical stance. In Boxall's (2002) terms, however, it is at least questionable whether Beckett was quite as apolitical as legend has it (and see Sussman & Devenney, 2001). He was also known to be kindly and generous in person. Sartre briefly adopted Maoism. Jean Améry was active in the Belgian resistance movement and tortured by Nazis. Even Ligotti has identified as a socialist. Insofar as we think of Diogenes as spurning possessions and status, he is not a representative of right-wing greed and pomposity. Gautama Buddha may have regarded all life as suffering and illusion but compassion was a very large part of his nature.

As the painter Francis Bacon put it, however: 'I have always tended to vote for the Right because they are less idealist than the Left and therefore one is left freer than one would be if encumbered by the idealism of the Left. I always feel that for me the Right is the best part of a bad job' (cited in Lewis, 2014, p. 190/570). Houellebecq has one of his characters in his listlessly political novel say, 'I was about as political as a bathtowel' (2015, p. 39).

Depressive realism, I would argue, is not apolitical but metapolitical, or so instinctively critical of politics like all other human endeavours as to entirely shrink from it. Plato and many since have argued for politics as necessarily involving a noble lie, as entailing 'dirty hands' and being merely the 'art of the possible'. Increasingly, however, we see that politics of whatever kind is rooted in flawed systems whose flaws, in spite of small temporary improvements at best, lead to further suffering. One system may be replaced by another that initially seems more hopeful, fairer or more efficient but its flaws soon become apparent. Economics, the 'dismal science', is also a failed, hopeless 'science'. We cling tenaciously to political hopes, however, all the more as religion wanes in credibility, since a farcical politics feels better as a Zapffean anchor than an anarchistic vacuum.

The equality and happiness wars

The United States Declaration of Independence enshrined among other things the right to pursue happiness. It is a document of its times (1776) but still reflects preoccupations with wealth and happiness (even if happiness at that time had connotations of self-worth, dignity and well-being rather than hedonism). The Declaration does not mention any right to express unhappiness (unless freedom includes the right to do so), to remain unhappy or to criticise one's society as depressing. No mention is made of the right to pursue unpalatable ideas, including those of atheism and inequality. It has been fashionable of late for politicians to debate happiness rather than wealth as the key indicator of a nation's success. As part of this trend, consider the *World Happiness Report* (one of whose authors is Lord Richard Layard). Rather often, Denmark ranks as the world's happiest country, according to measures of satisfaction with life. Danish culture is built on once strong farming values and strong unions, which have promoted a welfare state paid for by very high taxation. Modern Danes are accustomed to this from childhood and support it. But it means that in a nation of only 5.6 million people, a third are state employees and another large section of the community (children, students, parents on leave, the unemployed, sick and disabled and pensioners) have to be supported. High taxation of even quite low levels of income, plus high sales tax, inheritance and other taxes, means that Danes tend not to have high disposable income, which is associated in turn with a so-called *hygge* lifestyle, essentially an indoor one. Shops close half way through Saturday, people do not often eat out and some foreigners perceive Denmark as bland, smug and boring, even in wonderful Copenhagen. One middle-aged Syrian refugee told me that he had never considered suicide before but found himself brooding on it in Denmark, which he found cold and unfriendly by Mediterranean standards. But not even the finding that Danes are large consumers of antidepressants dissuades socialist dreamers from the happiness hype.

Unfortunately, it is all too evident from the inside that Denmark is *not* a particularly happy country, and if indeed it was we might expect to see foreigners queueing to move there. But among those, for example, who espouse happiness based on an egalitarianism that is facilitated by very high taxation, we do not see prominently wealthy happiness-espousers willing to pay at 55% and more taxes on their incomes as well as on their multiple properties, and high sales tax. They do not put their money where their mouth is; they are either fainthearted socialists or hypocrites. The DR is inclined to see through false claims made by public relations. The DR in Denmark sees plainly that the happiness brand is a lie, that Danish socialism isn't working nearly as well as its propaganda or works only at the cost of vibrant individuality. Where Kierkegaard advocated existential individuality and opposed 'levelling' in the 18th century, Danes today live in a socially flattened, homogenous society as well as in a flat, grey landscape. The so-called *Janteloven* principle suggests that individual Danes do not like to stand out. This does not mean that Denmark is a dreadful country but it is very far from any silly, public-relations promoted utopian fantasy, like most other countries. The American dream is real, if at all, only for a few sections of the population. But fantasy-dependent foreign socialists will not give up the delusion of happy and orderly Denmark. Fukuyama (2012) in his wide-ranging analysis of the history of politics retains the same fantasy of 'getting to Denmark' as a watermark of political and economic aspiration. I have examined many of these claims in Feltham (2015).

Snowdon (2010), although not DR-inspired, dedicates an entire book to examining and refuting the claims of Wilkinson and Pickett (2011), offering a very different interpretation of social trends that pricks the standard optimistic left-wing bubble. Snowdon rightly, I think, charges these authors as well as Oliver James (2007), Richard Layard (2011) and others of distorting views and statistics to fit their ostensibly equality-espousing and allegedly evidence-based agenda. Layard's mission is to spread the 'science of happiness' and James's to challenge 'affluenza' and 'selfish capitalism'. Interestingly, American happiness gurus like Barbara Fredrickson and Martin Seligman, also quite capable of bending statistics to suit their own dubious arguments, are far less concerned with the happiness-*equality* connection, which would not go down well in the United States.

The most depressing aspects of all such debates however are (a) that authors on both sides of the political divide stubbornly maintain their positions no matter what; (b) statistics and 'evidence' are thrown around by both sides regardless of everyday experience, with a 'blind them with science' abandon; (c) authors of such left-wing views are overwhelmingly privileged and affluent themselves and, disappointingly but predictably, left-wing prophets of greater equality rarely if ever demonstrate in their own lives solidarity with the worse-off by shedding their own luxuries; (d) nothing ever changes significantly as a result of these debates.

Another form of happiness critique is to be found in the writings of certain philosophers and critical theorists. Cvetkovich (2012), for example, promotes the 'affective turn' which is driven by queer theory and seeks recognition of depression as a public feeling, indeed as a form of politics. Similarly, Ahmed (2010) presents a critique of happiness based on its demanding character and unattainability, and Berlant's (2011) view of cruel optimism powerfully confronts the myths of upward mobility towards the good life of materialism. Some research suggests that the happiest countries may also have high suicide rates (Daly et al., 2011). Affect studies includes recognition of 'precarity', or the job and economic insecurity of many low-paid workers today. We have become accustomed by the self-help, personal growth movement and positive psychologists, and now some governments, not to hold only the right to pursue happiness but the *duty* to do so, however delusory this agenda is (Bruckner, 2000).

Perhaps the contemporary progressive, egalitarian and happy agenda is not quite the majority view we are led to believe. Pessimism is reviled and yet we have an extensive international vocabulary for the myriad nuances of DR. Walter Benjamin labelled as *linke melancholie* the tendency of left-wing intellectuals to look back nostalgically and impotently to past socialist ideals (Pensky, 1993). Bowring's (2008) excellent account of melancholy alone provides us with terms pointing to loss, longing, dissatisfaction, malaise, ennui and mortality salience. These include *chou* (Chinese), *kaiho* (Finnish), *Weltshmerz* (German),

112 The socio-political domain and depressive realism

kanashii, aoneko, wabi sabi (Japanese), *saudade* (Portugese), *toska, tošno* (Russian), *duende* (Spanish) and *hüzün* (Turkish). It may be that poetic folk terminology echoes the perverse abundance of dismal themes and refrains in art, literature and music, as also catalogued very well by Bowring. But the translinguistic sense of unhappy longing may signify the deep unconscious pull of insecure but vital animal life – 'paradise lost' – we sacrificed in our artificial and cerebral ascent to alienated magnificence. Social animals we may be, but we are far from being or ever becoming happy bunnies.

A flip side to the above appears in the work of some happiness researchers. Bergsma et al. (2011) argue on the basis of an analysis of over 7,000 Dutch citizens that 'high levels of distress do not necessarily exclude happy moods' even though overall those with a diagnosis of mental disorder are less happy than those without. They found that those with alcohol abuse disorder are as happy as those without a mental disorder and people with a single phobia do not necessarily feel unhappy most of the time. Even some of those with major depressive disorder, it seems, report some times of happiness. Overall, 68.4% of those with a mental disorder often or always felt happy compared with 89% of those without. This research was conducted in Holland, and the authors speculate that Dutch society is very supportive generally and offers good mental health care. The gravest flaw in such research is reliance on self-reports of happiness during the previous four weeks, and rather blunt choices ranging from 'never felt happy' through to 'always happy'. We may say that positive psychologists want to find that happiness is more common than pessimists think and also that positive psychology has a greater understanding of happiness and of the mechanisms to extend it further. But DRs are always likely to point to the rarity of happiness and to disbelieve those who claim to be happy, as well as doubting research linking happiness with longer life (Liu et al., 2015). Both groups have a very strong bias.

One of the accounts of happiness versus unhappiness that comes closest to thoughtfully well-balanced is that by Bok (2011). She examines the views of the classic philosophers and questions of luck, meaning, measurement of happiness, temperament, durable happiness and the place of illusion in happiness. She cites the research of Veenhoven (2004) that finds that globally the majority report being happy, including those living in the slums of Calcutta. She chides critics of modern civilisation (mentioning explicitly Rabindranath Tagore and Theodor Adorno) who argue that it has increased misery, citing the well-worn reports that Scandinavians, the Dutch and Swiss are usually at the top of national happiness surveys. She is also critical of Sigmund Freud and Bertrand Russell for propounding the view that unhappiness is our true state and that those claiming to be happy are deluded. One compelling reason for this bias is suggested by a historian, J.M. Roberts (1999): the 1920s, when Freud and Russell formulated many of their negative views, experienced much greater poverty and disadvantage. Since then material and health conditions have improved considerably, particularly for women. Bok contrasts the 'discordant claims' of the 'dark

The socio-political domain and depressive realism   113

backdrop of suffering, injustice, and death', with both 'feel-good messages' and the genuine 'potential for happiness' (p. 178). The human condition has assuredly bipolar aspects and all of us seem susceptible to innate bias and illusions both positive and negative.

Dark truths of the human condition

Oddly, those who reject the principle of human nature usually assume that our societies are mysteriously driven by co-operation, love and the common pursuit of happiness. Decency is the principle that tacitly substitutes for human nature in the common Leftist worldview, happily spanning every aspect of society: deep down we all love each other and share a desire for the consensual good life. Unfortunately, this view overlooks not a few unconscious kinks in our make-up. People fall in love and spend decades together but sometimes cheat on each other, or have open conflict. Relatively rarely perhaps is 'I wish you were dead' spoken but it is probably thought from time to time, just as many of us sometimes think of ourselves 'I wish I were dead'; and suicide and partner violence and murder are well documented. Parents and children love each other but sometimes come to be estranged and hate each other. The scathing views of the mothers of Cioran and Houellebecq towards their famous male offspring are well known but must be replicated in many other anonymous cases. Strategic infanticide is not uncommon in some parts of the world today. Matricide and patricide are relatively rare but unconsciously many adult children must sometimes wish their meddlesome, unproductive and obstructive parents dead so that inheritances can flow and financial problems be eased. Governments, too, while welcoming new births with family-friendly policies in order to boost population and support the tax-paying workforce, are unconcerned about the casualties of mass education, work and war, and count on citizens' deaths to make population space and release death taxes.

Hate crime and violent crime is something reprehensible perpetrated by other people, a small deviant class, mainly men – this, at least, is the commonly held view. But Miles (2003) argues that we must reckon fully and realistically with our barbaric evolutionary heritage; and Buss (2006) uses case study research to suggest that fantasising harm and death to others is extremely common. Freud would have agreed with such assessments of human nature, acknowledging that unconsciously, 'safely' repressed, we sometimes harbour destructive and taboo-breaking wishes not only towards enemies but also towards loved-ones and ourselves. Today's ascendant coalition of groups opposing racism, sexism, homophobia and anti-religious views, and championing equality and human rights, want to abolish not only outward physical violence and its verbal scaffolding but also vocal and mental hatred. This amounts to an unrealistic and dangerous totalitarian agenda for the fantasised good, the mechanism for which is suppression not understanding. That we all have a barbarous dark side that can be triggered in certain circumstances is a thesis denied or ignored by many

114 The socio-political domain and depressive realism

but recognised by so-called misanthropes, anthropathologists and DRs. Ironically, opponents of the concept of (often dark) human nature unwittingly force a mental illness status upon those who notice weird and hateful thoughts in their own heads and conclude that they are uniquely perverse and unacceptable individuals. In other words, denial breeds another layer of depression in the same way that sin-focused puritanical religions have caused inauthentic behaviour and created neurotic minds.

The wisest course might be to avoid proclaiming any worldview at all, particularly if it diverges from pro-life and business-as-usual sympathies, and especially if one is thin-skinned. But even those avoiding labels themselves, such as Gray (2010), tend to be labelled dismissively by others. Perhaps there is a hierarchy of dreaded labels that include, at the ignominious end of the scale, crackpot, conspiracy theorist, fascist scum, loony leftist, sinner, infidel or nihilist. In the USSR anyone could be hospitalised for holding anti-communist views in the era of political abuse of psychiatry from the late 1940s, a practice Solzhenitsin likened to the use of Nazi gas chambers. 'Sluggish schizophrenia' was invented as a primary diagnostic category to cover such punitive actions. Ironically, in the United States it has also been inadvisable to be too openly unhappy, shy ('socially phobic') or atheistic, implying a rejection of the norms of extraverted American happiness, for which rampant medication is often the remedy (Ehrenreich, 2010; Frances, 2014). As Perry (2014) asserts, it is often unsafe to voice the (DR) view that life may be so bad that suicide is quite a rational option, and it is illegal to assist anyone in suicide. The explicitly dissenting DR may find himself between the openly angry 'Why don't you kill yourself?' and the more common censorship by silence. It may be a dreadful confession that although the DR bites the pro-life hand that feeds him, he shamefully craves some modicum of social approval: 'please tell me I'm not crazy'.

Conclusion

Depressive realism sees a large dose of biological determinism in our constitution, marvels negatively at human folly and denial and predicts mixed business-as-usual and disasters to come. Few DRs are likely to be political activists of the right or left, indeed they are likely to be politically passive. We cannot know what the explicit political affiliations of the average anonymous DR are: probably none. The likeliest explanation is perhaps that DRs are passively 'happier' with a status quo since any socialist commitment would require naïve optimism, belief and action that would challenge nihilistic apathy and a pessimistic view of the future. Similarly, any capitalist commitment would require belief in competition, lies and acquisition. The DR may also intuit that behind the idea of even a DR worldview, no consensual world as such exists, only 'infinitely many worlds' (Gabriel, 2015) as perceived by billions of humans, each with a tenuous grasp of history and politics, if any, and all informed, misinformed and swayed by tendentious media.

The socio-political domain and depressive realism   115

Living in 21st century civilisation entails a neo-Faustian bargain. In return for your 'soul' (or at least your fundamental authenticity, let's say), you will receive extensive benefits. Immortality isn't yet available but relative affluence, a well-distracted sense of amortality and longevity are clear benefits. Freud (1908/2001) understood the bargain involved in surrendering thus, repressing the depths of our instincts and giving huge status to the superego. Society will soothe your anxieties if you smile rather than frown, and always reply 'Fine' to the meaningless 'How are you?' An occasional, darkly leaky 'Mustn't grumble' may be tolerated. Endorse the status quo, have children and don't talk about suffering and death. Absolutely avoid 'that odd shit' spoken by weirdos like Rust Cohle (see Chapter 4). For the superior neo-Faustian package of enhanced benefits, help to boost capitalism with entrepreneurial projects; support (indeed be part of) religion, psychotherapy, the self-help industry and the rhetoric of well-being and flourishing; distance yourself from civilisation's discontents, especially DRs; do not get visibly ill, old or die, or be very discreet or upbeat about it when it happens. If you ever consider defecting to the DR club, you may rapidly lose all benefits.

References

Ahmed, S. (2010) *The Promise of Happiness*. Durham, NC: Duke University Press.

Asma, S.T. (2013) *Against Fairness*. Chicago, IL: University of Chicago Press.

Baumeister, R., Bratslavsky, E. & Vohs, K.D. (2001) Bad is stronger than good. *Review of General Psychology*, 5 (4), 323–370.

Bennett, O. (2001) *Cultural Pessimism: Narratives of Decline in the Postmodern World*. Edinburgh: Edinburgh University Press.

Bergsma, A., ten Have, M., Veenhoven, R. & de Graff, R. (2011) Most people with mental disorders are happy: A 3-year follow-up in the Dutch general population. *Journal of Positive Psychology*, 6, 253–259.

Berlant, L. (2011) *Cruel Optimism*. Durham, NC: Duke University Press.

Bok, S. (2011) *Exploring Happiness: From Aristotle to Brain Science*. New Haven, CT: Yale University Press.

Bowring, J. (2008) *A Field Guide to Melancholy*. Harpenden: Oldcastle Books.

Boxall, P. (2002) Samuel Beckett: Towards a political reading. *Irish Studies Review*, 10 (2), 159–170.

Bruckner, P. (2000) *Perpetual Euphoria: On the Duty to be Happy*. Princeton, NJ: Princeton University Press.

Buss, D.M. (2006) *The Murderer Next Door: Why the Mind is Designed to Kill*. New York: Penguin.

Cioran, E.M. (1996) *History and Utopia*. London: Quartet.

Cvetkovich, A. (2012) *Depression: A Public Feeling*. Durham, NC: Duke University Press.

Daly, M.C., Oswald, A.J., Wilson, D. & Wu, S. (2011) Dark contrasts: The paradox of high rates of suicide in happy places. *Journal of Economic Behavior & Organization*, 80 (3), 435–442.

Ehrenreich, B. (2010) *Smile or Die: How Positive Psychology Fooled America and the World*. London: Granta.

Etchells, P. (2015) Declinism: Is the world actually getting worse? *The Guardian*, 15 January.

Farmer, P. (2004) *Pathologies of Power*. Berkeley, CA: University of California Press.

Feltham, C. (2015) *Keeping Ourselves in the Dark*. Charleston, WV: Nine-Banded Books.

Fisher, M. (2009) *Capitalist Realism: Is There No Alternative?* Winchester: O Books.

Frances, A. (2014) *Saving Normal: An Insider's Revolt against Out-of-Control Psychiatric Diagnosis, DSM-5, Big Pharma, and the Medicalization of Everyday Life*. New York: Harper Collins.

Freud, S. (1908/2001) *Civilisation and Its Discontents*. London: Penguin.

Fukuyama, F. (2012) *The Origins of Political Order*. London: Profile.

Gabriel, M. (2015) *Why the World Does Not Exist*. Cambridge: Polity.

Gilligan, C. & Richards, D.A.J. (2009) *The Deepening Darkness: Patriarchy, Resistance, and Democracy's Future*. New York: Cambridge University Press.

Gray, J. (2010) *Gray's Anatomy: Selected Writings*. London: Penguin.

Houellebecq, M. (2015) *Submission*. London: Heinemann.

Humphrey, N. & Lifton, R.J. (eds) (1984) *In a Dark Time*. London: Faber & Faber.

James, O. (2007) *Affluenza*. London: Vermilion.

Layard, R. (2011) *Happiness: Lessons from a New Science (Rev. edn.)*. London: Penguin.

Lewis, D. (2014) *No More Nature: Nihilism in the Works of Francis Bacon and Samuel Beckett*. Amazon Media EU S.a.r.l.

Liddle, R. (2008) *Social Pessimism: The New Social Reality of Europe*. London: Policy Network.

Liu, B., Floud, S., Pirie, K., Green, J., Peto, R. & Beral, V. (2015) Does happiness itself directly affect mortality? The prospective UK million women study. *The Lancet*. Doi: org/10.1016/S0140–6736(15)01087–9.

Lomborg, B. (2001) *The Skeptical Environmentalist: Measuring the Real State of the World*. Cambridge: Cambridge University Press.

Mair, P. (2013) *Ruling the Void: The Hollowing of Western Democracy*. London: Verso.

Marshall, T. (2015) *Prisoners of Geography: Ten Maps That Tell You Everything You Need to Know about Global Politics*. New York: Elliott & Thompson.

Mathy, J.-P. (2011) *Melancholy Politics: Loss, Mourning, and Memory in Late Modern France*. University Park, PA: Penn State University Press.

Mearsheimer, J.J. (2014) *The Tragedy of Great Power Politics (Updated edn.)*. New York: Norton.

Miles, J. (2003) *Born Cannibal: Evolution and the Paradox of Man*. London: IconoKlastic.

Overall, C. (2003) *Aging, Death, and Human Longevity: A Philosophical Inquiry*. Berkeley, CA: University of California Press.

Overall, C. (2012) *Why Have Children? The Ethical Debate*. Cambridge, MA: MIT Press.

Pensky, M. (1993) *Melancholy Dialectics: Walter Benjamin and the Play of Mourning*. Amherst, MA: University of Massachusetts Press.

Perry, S. (2014) *Every Cradle is a Grave: Rethinking the Ethics of Birth and Suicide*. Charleston, WV: Nine-Banded Books.

Pinker, S. (2011) *The Better Angels of Our Nature: The Decline of Violence in History and Its Causes*. London: Allen Lane.

Plummer, J. (2014) *Tragedy and Hope 101: The Illusion of Justice, Freedom and Democracy*. London: Brushfire.

Ponting, C. (2007) *A New Green History of the World: The Environment and the Collapse of Great Civilisations*. London: Vintage.

Roberts, J.M. (1999) *The Twentieth Century: The History of the World, 1901–2000*. London: Viking.

Schopenhauer, A. (1851/1970) *Essays and Aphorisms*. London: Penguin.

Snowdon, C. (2010) *The Spirit Level Delusion: Fact-Checking the Left's New Theory of Everything*. Ripon: Little Dice.

Songe-Møller, V. (2002) *Philosophy without Women: The Birth of Sexism in Western Thought.* London: Continuum.

Soroka, S.N. (2014) *Negativity in Democratic Politics: Causes and Consequences.* New York: Cambridge University Press.

Sussman, H. & Devenney, C. (eds) (2001) *Engagement and Indifference: Beckett and the Political.* Albany, NY: State University of New York Press.

Taylor, M. (2009) Reflections on social evils and human nature. In D. Utting (ed). *Contemporary Social Evils.* Bristol: Policy Press.

Taylor, S.E. (2003) *The Tending Instinct: Women, Men, and the Biology of Relationships.* New York: Owl Books.

Veenhoven, R. (2004) Happiness as an aim in public policy. In A. Linley & S. Joseph (eds). *Positive Psychology in Practice.* Chichester: Wiley.

West, E. (2015) *The Diversity Illusion: What We Got Wrong about Immigration.* London: Gibson Square Books.

Widerquist, K. & McCall, G. (2015) Myths about the state of nature and the reality of stateless societies. *Analyse & Kritik*, 1 (2), 233–257.

Wilkinson, R. & Pickett, K. (2011) *The Spirit Level: Why Greater Equality Makes Societies Stronger.* London: Bloomsbury.

Williams, B. (1987) *An Introduction to Leopardi's Canti.* Leicester: Troubado.

Chapter 8

Science, technology, the future and depressive realism

The science I refer to here is natural science, which includes physics, chemistry, biology, astronomy and earth sciences. The bid for the social sciences to be regarded as having equal status has almost certainly failed. We can pursue better knowledge of anthropology, economics, politics, society and psychology, but we cannot conceal the distinction between hard and soft sciences. Nor can we conceal the suspicion that the former are much more reliable than the latter, yet we face ongoing contests between them. Rose (2014) may persist in naming Adorno's critical theory 'melancholy science' but this view has little place here. Science is recognised as difficult and is generally not part of everyday discourse and distraction for the majority, unless in the form of science fiction, popular science, medical treatment and technological appliances. However, in this chapter I intend to discuss science in its wider, applied context of science, technology, engineering and mathematics (STEM) as the most powerful 'movement' taking humanity into the future.

The importance of science and technology for DR lies in the combined forces of historical toolmaking, speculation, rationality, knowledge acquisition, scientific progress and technological dominance. The argument repeated here is that this movement has superseded mythology, religion and emotionality in human affairs. We cannot simplistically suppose that science has any finality about it, but rather that it does utilise a superior epistemology and produce verifiable outcomes. We can honour the 'pessimistic meta-induction from the history of science' that all science is provisional and chronological exceptionalism is to be avoided, without pretending that earlier forms of knowledge must have equal value. The paradox that should engage DRs is that while science and technology have in many ways reduced our ignorance and suffering, they also add new burdens to the human condition incrementally.

The Bible has it that evil came into the world following Adam's disobedient eating from the tree of knowledge. In the Greek myth of Prometheus, Zeus is tricked by an inferior meat offering and has fire stolen from him, which triggers divine wrath in the form of Pandora and eternal torment being sent to mankind. We do not know how and when the precise mechanisms arose whereby human beings became significantly more intelligent than other species

Science, technology, the future and depressive realism   119

(see Chapter 1) but Taylor's (2010) thesis of the artificial ape is most promising. Manipulation of the environment, fire-capture, cooking and tool-making (going back to about three million years) in association with changes in the brain and consciousness led slowly but inexorably to language, mathematics, thought, knowledge acquisition and transmission and to advanced science and technology. McClellan and Dorn (2006) show extensively how technology, science and history have intertwined.

Cosmology currently teaches us that life began with the Big Bang, not with God; geology displays the longest-term foundations and changes in the earth's structures; biology reveals that we evolved over millions of years and were not created a few thousand years ago; archaeology shows some of how we developed human societies and technology and how large scale extinction events occurred; genetics demonstrates how inherited traits are coded, modified and passed on across generations; neurology how our brains process information; medical science detects the causes of diseases and looks for cures; climate science shows patterns of climate change including man-made worsening conditions; engineering and technology constitute solutions and inventions for practical problems, including possible long-term radical post-human modifications and space travel; and physics and cosmology reveal the underlying laws of all matter from the smallest to the largest of phenomena.

As we know, science has many unintended negative consequences and problems, and it is never final. As far as we can tell, however, it is so far the best instrument we have for discovery, survival and prediction. While science and technology reveal the wonders of the universe and we invent our own wonders, the dark side is also confirmed: that a great deal about us is determined in kluge-like ways that are resistant to change efforts, that we must age and die, the earth will eventually perish, as will the sun. The scientifically based certainty as to total and unavoidable extinction, and the probability of at least partial extinctions in the meantime, has been intuited by prophets for millennia. Now we have better, more accurate predictions and some possibility of forestalling some disastrous events, but we must live with the anxiety of possible disasters, and some philosophers like Lyotard and Brassier have suggested that even the longest-term certainty of extinction radically alters human self-understanding now. In other words, we are faced with the certainty of our own long-term annihilation as a species regardless of what we try to do about it. Not only will we perish but we will have no means of leaving any sign that we ever existed, a prospect that engenders a dreadful sense of futility in some human beings: *all this is ultimately for nothing* (Krauss, 2012).

Just one example of how technology transformed our lives for the better but simultaneously, probably, for the worse, can be seen in extensive night lighting (Koslofsky, 2011). European installation of street lighting from 1660 both changed terror and vulnerability associated with the night and its crime patterns, and made for increased opportunities for civic life in theatres, bars and cafés, as well as extending working hours and productivity, until today's so-called

24/7 culture. But it has also led to distorted leisure, sleep problems, mesmerisation by constant television and light pollution. All such advances contain an unforeseen downside, a new set of problems. Again, this seems to be in our nature, constantly to address and solve problems technologically, thus always having practical goals and satisfactions that rescue us from contemplation of our ultimate meaninglessness.

First we have to concede that God was a myth all along, but then we would have to live for however many thousands or millions of years with the realisation that humanity will one day be as if it had never existed and is pre-programmed to perish entirely; and if the antinatalists have their way, our collective demise will arrive in a much shorter time span. But perhaps a majority of us lean towards short-term 'human adaptive optimism', a humanistic faith in our ability to problem-solve. The religious can deny scientific findings, replacing them with delusions of posthumous existence and meaning. Scientists can apparently take in these prospects phlegmatically; most of us realise that the timescales involved have no bearing at all on how we live our individual lives; and the most optimistic of scientists and posthumanists can come up with ultimate fantasy-survival scenarios.

The rationalistic neurosis of science

The philosopher of science Maxwell (2004) has argued that natural science suffers from 'rationalistic neurosis'. Scientific laws are totalitarian by nature and ignore rival theories. Scientific investigation has become detached from social aims and goals, or what Maxwell calls aim-oriented empiricism, or wisdom. A large part of science's institutional neurosis, says Maxwell, is seen in its clinging to self-preservation. The main problem with Maxwell's view is that a consensually agreed scientific aim which is subservient to social ends only must come to resemble Soviet era science, dictated to by central government and detached from free enquiry, parallel to socialism suppressing free markets. The Stalin-approved distortion of genetics research by Lysenko in the 1920s to 1950s is but one example of this (de Jong-Lambert, 2012). Protecting or diverting science from misuse is a necessity but finding the line between wise control and Luddite, anarchistic and socialist suppression of science is far from easy.

Generally speaking, scientists are not notably depressed as individuals, notwithstanding exceptions like Isaac Newton, Charles Darwin and David Bohm and an average share of suicides. Competition for scientific jobs and the suggested tendency for scientists not to be in touch with their (or others') feelings – indeed often belonging on the Autism Spectrum Disorder scale (Baron-Cohen et al., 2001) – could suggest some degree of alienation and susceptibility to depression, but the rational and problem-solving nature of scientific temperament may mitigate this. Newton certainly experienced a depressive crisis in 1693, about which the novelist John Banville (1999) speculates. Following a fire in Newton's study, the loss of all his scientific papers would mean nothing at all: 'It's not the loss of the precious papers that will drive him temporarily crazy but the simple fact that *it doesn't matter'* (Banville, 1999, p. 2, italics in original). Counterfactual histories of science would simply have taken us in different, haphazard directions toward the same, ultimately pointless end. Newton is hailed as one of the greatest scientific geniuses ever but he was also obsessed with alchemy and religion. Science along with philosophy has generally been in the forefront of challenges to outmoded religious conceptions of the universe, and Darwin and others suffered from their own discoveries. Scientists are much more often atheists than religious believers. They are largely dedicated to the pursuit of truth or truths and their promotion, above any attachment to prized but erroneous worldviews. Exceptions are, of course, found among occasional fraudsters and some of those with commercial interests.

Humankind's evolution, driven as it always has been by prosthetics, technology, reason, knowledge and science, is inseparable from science and technology (Taylor, 2010). Tools for hunting and farming, fire use, clothes, pottery, weapons, building, mean of transport, mining and writing, all led to ever more refined, complex and mass-produced artefacts. Diamond (1998) has demonstrated convincingly the powerful linkage between history, geography and technology (which he dubs 'necessity's mother'), with Europe luckily situated to develop farming before gaining a massive advantage in technological progress which included gunpowder. From about 1760 Britain was the main home to the industrial revolution, but American industrial development grew rapidly thereafter. Rather than attributing intentional merit or evil to all such phenomena, it may be truer to regard them as 'one damn thing after another'.

The myths of Adam, Prometheus and Frankenstein attest to the centrally perilous role of human ingenuity. Despite heartfelt pleas by McGilchrist, Zerzan and others, there is little realistic prospect that we will voluntarily and *en masse* relinquish or reduce our investment in a technical-rational way of life. Disenchantment is the way forward, hopefully linked with pragmatic new mindsets. Bennett (2001) argues that the threats from science, coupled with its own decline, as challenged by 1970s countercultural luminaries such as Roszak and Capra, show that it is merely one part of a general cultural decline. Meanwhile, the long-term trend of scientific dominance may result in tragedy or in sustained progress. One small current example of a major bifurcation in human development is medical inventions like cochlear implants that can improve lives but the expense of which can probably only yet be met by the rich. On ideological and economic grounds some sections of any population may pursue and secure far better technologically-assisted bodies, lifestyles and lifespans, which radical socialist commentators fear will even lead to the emergence of different species. Whether this becomes another protracted left-right tussle or a survival-of-the-fittest *fait accompli* remains to be seen.

Darwin

Charles Darwin ranks as a giant of science and remains something of a devil in the eyes of diehard creationists. Important not only for his specific contributions to biology, he is key to our discussion of DR because the theory of evolution marks the decisive break with religious mythologies founded on the God-given distinctiveness of humanity. While others were working along similar lines in the 19th century, Darwin almost single-handedly put together the first jigsaw that demonstrated we have evolved from other life forms, that this took an unimaginably long time, but ultimately we are, however clever and dominant as a species, animals who must eat and drink, copulate, suffer, die and disappear. Darwin delayed completion and publication of *On the Origin of Species* in 1859 because he realised its implications but did not want to believe what his discoveries showed him, that the Bible was incorrect and God was improbable. He did not wish to upset his pious wife, nor did he want to have to face the fact that his beloved daughter Annie who died at the age of 10 altogether ceased to be rather than ascending to heaven. Let us remember, too, that Darwin like all of us was of his own time, and critics who impute Social Darwinism and wilful sexism to him are off the mark.

It is as I write 157 years since Darwin published his world-changing book and in spite of its initial shockwaves it has taken many decades for its full implications to percolate through to widespread – but far from universal – acceptance. It was not, of course, Darwin's intention but Dawkins' (1978) *The Selfish Gene* went on to popularise the notion of self-replicating genes that have no concerns about any larger purpose, and Dawkins has been in the vanguard of the so-called new atheists. Nature's pitiless indifference is now a clear rival with disobedience to God for an explanation of why our world is as it is. Meaninglessness was the focus of Nietzsche and subsequent existentialists, but the struggle for survival in Darwinian evolutionary theory supports and informs this. As well as this, we inherit from Darwin the many advances in evolutionary biology and genetics, just one of which – evolutionary psychology – promotes the view that ancient behavioural patterns still influence us: we are hence in Ligotti's (2010) term *puppets.*

Darwin can certainly be regarded as a genius, but he is also only part of a relentless logical exposure of the workings of life in which we are merely conscious cogs or fortuitous materialist outcomes. The Darwinian accent on contingency has led some commentators to liken his theories to Buddhist philosophy, to which he would have had access and which also harbour a scheme of meaninglessness, if softened by compassion. Dawkins and his scientific colleagues stress the natural wonders that are revealed by scientific investigation but accompanying these is the inevitable recognition that we are no more than self-conscious replicators in a non-teleological, expanding and entropic situation. Even atheistic scientists like Tallis (2011), while having to accept evolutionary theory, seem not fully capable of understanding that evolutionary time alone has led to human beings and explains much of our stubborn and damaging behaviour.

Aside from creationists, there are those who support Darwinian science but dislike the reputation for bleakness that it generates. Levine (2006) is one of these, who emphasises Darwin's love of nature and life, in spite of losing three of his ten children, suffering much illness and knowing acute depression. Levine, a professor of English, not science, has as his agenda the re-enchantment allegedly needed by our secular world. American society sees disenchantment where 'a mindless algorithm replaces an intelligent creator, and the world empties out of meaning' (p. 24). One kind of 'Darwinian passion for reason misses an important element in Darwin, the quality of affect and of awe' (p. 202). Levine can forgive Darwin for his uncomfortable but of-their-time views on eugenics, underlines his kindness and middle class gentility and seeks to restore him as a 'romantic materialist' rather than a mere collector, cataloguer and reductionist. Using copiously many enchantment-like terms – awe, mystery, joy, diversity, the sublime and love – Levine unintentionally demonstrates that it is only through his own romantic, compulsive poetic selection, his personality dependent realism, that he himself can see and describe the world. Sadly, this plays into the tired dichotomy of science versus art, of left brain versus right (McGilchrist, 2009), with all of us being puppets of our predetermined personality types. Each of us thinks we hold the right view or see the bigger picture. None of us can grasp the complexity of this existence we inhabit. It is not wholly enchanted, disenchanted, mechanical, marvellous or depressive. We know more and more of it in scientific terms but simultaneously we realise how infinitely complex it is. Words are merely feeble, limited tools for symbolising what we think we know so far. Thomas Hardy's novels were influenced by Darwinian themes in their story line but the emotional artistry, the power to enchant, is another matter. Contrary to the Darwinian celebration of teeming biodiversity, a writer like Beckett prophetically observes an increasing loss of biodiversity: in the lessness of this existence the planet becomes parched, as all planets must.

Dangerous science

That knowledge is the road to sin and suffering is the doctrine we have inherited from various sources over thousands of years. Ideas about mad, hubristic scientists abound. We are familiar enough with the concept of bad science but mad scientists hold far greater fears for us, echoing perhaps the exploits of much earlier evil wizards and witches, and Faustian characters. Clegg (2010) reminds us of the panoply of mad scientists in literature. First, he considers the motivations for and work at CERN, near Geneva, and its theoretical dangers, especially in the Large Hadron Collider and its potential to create a microscopic black hole. He goes on to examine the Manhattan Project, the creation and use of the atomic bomb in the 1940s and the ever-present risk of mutually assured destruction. Clegg adds to the list of science's arsenal of mass destruction projects and products climate change, extreme biohazards, the 'gray goo' produced by runaway nanobots, large scale computer failure or 'information meltdown' and natural pitfalls. On runaway climate change, Clegg writes flatly that 'it's depressing. I wish it were different. But it isn't (Clegg, 2010, p. 137). A chapter is also devoted to posthuman developments, the current scenario in which the artificial ape that learned to cook can now extensively improve his own body and fashion our environment to our perceived needs. Consider thalidomide as an improvement attempt gone badly wrong, or our extensive dependence on life-extending drugs and surgery; add to this the internet, the drive towards artificial intelligence, robotics and towards the conquest of ageing and death (Garreau, 2005; Zhavoronkov, 2013). All scientific developments carry some short-term dangers and risks of accidents and misuse, but it may be the long-term unintended consequences we should worry about most.

The Nobel Laureate and discoverer of Vitamin C, Albert Szent-Györgyi (1970) laments that science, including some of his own work, is often exploited for destructive ends. He suggested that stupidity in human affairs is additive and can sway intelligence. It is not science that destroys but human beings in their trance-like stupidity and violence (or anthropathology as I have called it). But Szent-Györgyi is clear that 'if the fruits of this research were taken away, civilization would be back in the stone age' (p. 72), and not in the good way imagined by some. The anarcho-primitivist John Zerzan believes that only the forceful rejection of science and technology can save humankind; only a return to a pre-agricultural age can reverse the horrors inflicted by dehumanising science and technology (Zerzan, 2002). There is probably very little popular taste for such a retrogressive step, despite Zerzan's often perceptive analysis of our civilisational pathology.

The future and depressive realism

The future is a curious entity. Given the nebulous, problematic nature of time, we should pause to consider how much we take the future for granted. It is an indelible part of human consciousness, yet if you or I died tonight it would altogether cease to exist from our point of view; and if we could know that our collective future entailed decimation and obliteration by one catastrophe or another we would likely find this collectively a depressing prospect (Scheffler, 2013). Perhaps those who are religious assume their future will necessarily be one of non-specific posthumous survival. Perhaps most of us either cannot or do not want to think too far ahead; after all, we recognise how much things can change and we are, like other animals, mainly focused on the biological and practical present and its temporal hinterland.

If we care to, we can discover some very worrying future scenarios, coming not from traditional and erroneous religious prophets of the endtimes (Stone, 2000) but from eminent scientists and science writers (Gardner, 2012). Climate change and science history literature tells us often that without urgent action temperatures are rising and within decades catastrophic changes will trigger a decimation of world population (Oreskes & Conway, 2014). The direst of such predictions comes from those whose reading of climate change trends causes them to speak in terms of near-term human extinction. McPherson and

Baker (2014), for example, are sure that the earth will become uninhabitable by humans between the years 2030 and 2050. In this view, climate scientists suppress the true depth of negativity concerning climate figures, and trends are now irreversible and lethal. In this scenario, we should regard our situation as hospice-like: no, there is nothing we can do to rectify the situation, and yes, we are all going to die, probably horribly and very soon. Rather than panic, depression or suicide, they advocate a profound spiritual acceptance.

The British Astronomer Royal, Martin Rees (2004), asked whether we can survive the present century, given the number and variety of threats facing us. Mark Lynas (2008) has predicted that if left unaddressed climate change will propel the earth to catastrophic average temperatures with globally devastating results for humanity; and as we can see, governments have taken woefully insufficient action to forestall even the least increases. Conflicting optimistic accounts suggest utterly different versions of this earthly existence – it will be eternal, and ever better. Meanwhile closer to DR, parents and lovers facing their own extinction will think of those loved ones to be left behind, and grandchildren, but it is difficult to imagine many generations ahead. The pessimists among us will fret about climate change and its likely negative impact on our collective future. The bitter nihilists may think 'good riddance' when doomsday scenarios are published. Survivalists, or preppers, will continue to store ammunition, food and supplies in their concealed hideaways. Posthumanists are busy taking the mega-vitamins, reading the research about medical, technological and space travel advances and making arrangements for their own cryonic storage. My guess is that the majority of humanity thinks little of the general future, and certainly not of the distant future, any more than the general disaster we may be heading for in a 'mini ice age' within decades, or that we are already entering the next actual ice age. Few species have ever survived longer than some millions of years and we are broadly at that point now, with some giving us 10,000 years left. These are all pictures of much more imminent demise than the fairly well-known figure of 6 billion years in the future when the universe will die.

Closer to home again, we know that the Yellowstone caldera in Wyoming is roughly due for a massive eruption that would have worldwide catastrophic consequences. Anyone predisposed to anxiety about endtimes can consult numerous related websites. Barry Schwartz on AlterNet, for example, lists the top biggest threats to human existence, in order of significance, as climate change, biodiversity loss, bee decline, bat decline, pandemic, biological/nuclear terrorism, supervolcanoes, asteroid impact, the rise of the machine and the parasite *Toxoplasmosa gondii*. Anti-microbial resistance is high on many lists. All this bad news that hasn't yet happened is exhausting and since much of it is vague, contradictory and the information on which it is based in highly technical, we tend to turn off. We can only live in the present and near-present.

As we have seen, those labelled depressive are deemed guilty of depressogenic thinking about the future: pessimism is a hallmark of the depressive's self-fulfilling prophecy with regard to his own life. But the DR accurately and unflinchingly grasps the mortality of himself and all living beings, he knows that he will die and cease altogether to exist. He is under no romantic illusions about the limitations of life. He may or may not downwardly distort his own prospects of happiness. When it comes to the DR worldview and how it relates to the future of society, humanity, earth and the cosmos, we are entitled to pause to consider the accuracy or inaccuracy involved.

Human progress

The idea of collective social, moral and technological progress is, if not universal, extremely prevalent and progress deniers are often regarded as outright cynical or ridiculous. Who can deny advances in medicine and dentistry, for example, in the reduction in infant mortality and toothache? Or a decline in many forms of violence and the growth of human rights? I grew up in a household where both parents chain-smoked and died of cancer, where they stayed together in a pre-divorce era, in spite of a probable emotional chasm after over thirty years of marriage and in a home where I was casually smacked from time to time. Today much of that has changed among populations of non-smoking, freely separating and non-violent adults. Racism, sexism, homophobia and other negative attitudes have also changed considerably.

Just as we look back at so-called early history and primitive societies, we tend to look back just decades or centuries and shake our heads at our near-ancestors' lack of enlightenment compared with ourselves. What we cannot see is the future, from which perspective our descendants will shake their heads at our insane eating habits, stultifying jobs, economic inequality, carbon emissions, wars and superstitious religious beliefs. Indefinite moral and intellectual progress is always assumed, with time's arrow flying ever-upward. Our descendants will perhaps travel by superior, non-polluting means; take trips through space; live much longer and disease-free lives and enjoy greater self-fulfilment. We can't achieve this yet but they probably will (climate change or other disasters permitting), but presumably *their* descendants will also look back on them one day with amusement and disbelief, too. This is to imagine a future of steady material and technological progress, of course, but if we allow ourselves this vision, where does it lead? Infinite linear progress is a possibility, give or take various obstacles and setbacks. Suspend the negative idea of disastrous reversals in human fortunes and picture this infinite progress: perhaps it will just keep on gloriously unfolding, with humans forever solving temporary problems.

If we agree that DR is centrally concerned with the reality-or-illusion (or truth versus untruth) question, we confront ultimately the Buddhist, wholesale *maya* view. That is, that *everything* humanly perceived is illusion (see Nöe, 2002, for an interesting view of the visual world as illusion). Discredited myths, hopes that came to nothing, are easy to see through. Contested realities, or phenomena with no or few illusory qualities, might be said to include God, monarchy, Marxism, democracy, celebrity, psychotherapy, marriage, equality (see Feltham, 2015).

However ruthless each of us regards himself or herself as being in relation to sceptical examination of truth claims, all of us have our sacrosanct areas of belief. No unenlightened person (if enlightenment exists) can bear the reality of an illusion-free life, although Rosenberg (2011) claims otherwise. In his view, there is no God, no purpose or meaning, no free will and so on, with only science and 'nice nihilism' as our guides. Contra Eliot's famous wisdom, humankind *can* bear more (nihilistic) reality than we think.

We cannot know very much about the future. One would envisage setbacks, even world wars and worldwide natural disasters. But the human spirit inevitably aspires to a tension-free life. However, it may be that the future is likely to expose more and more of our cherished beliefs, myths and illusions for what they are, taking us into progressive disenchantment and ever closer to nihilistic territory. We will then be challenged to deceive ourselves anew, to find enlightenment sooner or later, and after all, love conquers all – this is how it is commonly seen. Is it defeatist to ask what it's all for? Survival and discovery are the prosaic explanations. The alternatives to infinite progress are inadvertent or intentional species self-destruction on the one hand and likely everlasting adversity-overcoming on the other. Long-term futures can be interpreted as futile, as being in our very nature, or as irresistible challenges. A hardline DR view will take the position of futility: further human adventures are folly, merely extending suffering. A moderate DR view might accept a vision of a future filled with new illusions and tragedies but a future nonetheless. I think depressive realism would be at odds with the romantic re-enchantment agenda of wistful retro-ecophilia.

Our children's future

What is a DR parent to make of the future? Crawford (2010) regrets having had two daughters but at the same time loves them. However, he cannot offer them any solace or hope. While I do not regret having had two sons who I love, I cannot but see the ways in which they suffer. Familial love, however strong, cannot banish awareness of negatives. The sharpest and most painful of realisations about one's own children is that they must one day die; one day they, like you, will lie on their deathbed, lonely, fearful, old and infirm, and pass into nothingness. But in the meantime they must face some of the same challenging things we have faced and probably many different challenging scenarios, too.

Like many other so-called (British) baby boomers I grew up in a post-war era of hope and relative prosperity, free education and social mobility, free health care, increasing social freedoms and aspirations to peace and plenty. In contrast, my children like their peers carry heavy student debts for decades, struggle in the employment market, cannot afford to buy their own homes, face longer working lives and poor pension prospects. Geopolitical instability continues apace. If climate change predictions are accurate, they may face grim environmental and social conditions, dystopia rather than sunny uplands. To what extent they have benefited from advanced technology (television, endless videos and video games, social networking) is hard to say, and although they may receive better treatment for cancer and other diseases, they will also face new epidemics and uncertainties. The assumptions of linear and limitless progress are probably unfounded, and our children may well experience new dark ages rather than the continuing bounties of the Enlightenment and capitalism. If many of us have been lucky enough to live relatively untouched by major wars and natural disasters, they may not be so lucky. No doubt this may be regarded as the crackpot pessimistic logic of the DR, but the longer we live free of major volcanic activity, drastic climate changes, asteroid impacts, incurable disease epidemics and so on, the greater become the chances that they will occur for future generations.

The future holds at least three sets of intriguing possibilities. The first is that humanity extends its reach of the universe, gradually exploring the nearer planets, colonising some and moving on as far as possible. I envisage a morally chastened humanity doing this, necessarily casting off some of its more obviously crazy aspects and our terrestrial sentimentality. Projects such as Mars One, aiming for a human colony on Mars by 2027, rest on the irresistible excitement of space exploration. Not everyone shares this sense of excitement or accepts its associated economic priorities. Plans are going ahead in spite of the probability of pioneers not being able to return and a high risk of death. There is a sober recognition of the limitations of resources and life on Earth and the need, should we wish our species to survive, of settling at least some of us elsewhere.

The second set is an extension of Taylor's (2010) technological ape theory, in which artificial intelligence (AI) is lodged increasingly at the forefront of human progress. Currently, great strides are being made with robotic game players able to outwit human competitors, as well as robots designed to be human companions, assistants and substitutes in workplaces. But Kaku (2014), for one, envisages imminent advances in engineered telepathy, telekinesis, enhanced intelligence and changes to the structure of the brain itself. Doubted and feared by many, such advances are, however, no longer merely in the domain of science fiction or barred by ethical blocks. Much that is inconceivable to us now may alter dramatically within decades, so that, for example, neither pessimistic nor optimistic realism need survive if new forms of open-ended, technology-assisted reality-testing come to prominence. Whether robots designed by flawed humans can overcome endemic anthropic moral corruption (anthropathology) is open to question: must man hand on misery to robots?

But the third set is, I believe, even more intriguing. This is based on a scenario in which major catastrophes have been improbably avoided. Here we see humanity struggling on with its resistance to truth, or at least enduring its tensions between traditional illusions and inevitable scientific confirmation of hard unglamorous truths. What we might call the suicide wing of the DR movement will by definition have no future, except perhaps as mournful data for social historians. If the antinatalists had their way, there would be no human future within decades. Even some sober climate scientists now predict disastrous rising ocean levels of three metres (Hansen et al., 2016). If the near-term human extinction lobby (McPherson & Baker, 2014) are correct, none of us has any future, regardless of any actions we now take. The latter view holds that even those of us old enough to die soon within a natural life expectancy will be depressed at the utterly hopeless prospects for our descendants (Scheffler, 2013). Pessimists and optimists have to line up according to belief in the imminent or gradual endtimes, with the interim being anything but rosy; or in climate scientists being wrong, unforeseen positive events happening or humanity demonstrating last minute ingenuity and commitment and pulling us out of our nosedive.

In the long run, it seems, we are certainly all dead. Analyses of the very nature of matter, energy and human existence point to an inevitable end in which is combined some anthropogenic negative factors and natural disasters (Svensen, 2009). These latter are disasters only in our terms, otherwise they are mere events. All this could come about within centuries. Entropically, in what some call the 'long emergency', we will experience and unintentionally create more and more disorder in, or acceleration of population, urbanisation, information overload and desperate remedies for our malaise (Swenson, 1999; Spier, 2011; Ophuls, 2012), which may feel to us subjectively and self-deceptively like valiant, incremental progress courtesy of STEM activity. Although impossible to envisage with any accuracy, the transitional period to a declining posthuman future will contain some life forms (Garreau, 2005; Weisman, 2008; Tennesen, 2015) until eventually, over millennia, entropy prevails and everything returns to the nothingness from which it first emanated (Impey, 2010; Krauss, 2012). 'Life had a good run,' people would agree, says Impey (2010, p. 290) but by then the party would be over. Meanwhile, such is our predominantly positive, problem-solving, thanatophobic nature, this is not something we can focus on for very long.

References

Banville, J. (1999) *The Newton Letter*. London: Picador.

Baron-Cohen, S., Wheelwright, S., Skinner, R., Martin, J. & Clubley, E. (2001) The autism-spectrum quotient (AQ): Evidence from asperger syndrome/high-functioning autism, males and females, scientists and mathematicians. *Journal of Autism and Developmental Disorders*, 31, 5–17.

Bennett, O. (2001) *Cultural Pessimism: Narrative of Decline in the Postmodern World*. Edinburgh: Edinburgh University Press.

Clegg, B. (2010) *Armageddon Science: The Science of Mass Destruction*. New York: St Martin's Griffin.

Crawford, J. (2010) *Confessions of an Antinatalist*. Charleston, WV: Nine-Banded Books.

Dawkins, R. (1978) *The Selfish Gene*. London: Flamingo.

De Jong-Lambert, W. (2012) *The Cold War Politics of Genetics Research: An Introduction to the Lysenko Affair*. New York: Springer.

Diamond, J. (1998) *Guns, Germs and Steel: A Short History of Everybody for the Last 13,000 Years*. London: Vintage.

Feltham, C. (2015) *Keeping Ourselves in the Dark*. Charleston, WV: Nine-Banded Books.

Garreau, J. (2005) *Radical Evolution*. New York: Broadway.

Hansen, J. et al. (2016) Ice melt, sea level rise, and superstorms: Evidence from paleoclimate data, climate modeling, and modern observations that 2° global warming could be dangerous. *Atmospheric Chemistry and Physics*, 16, 3761–3812.

Impey, C. (2010) *How It Ends: From You to the Universe*. New York: Norton.

Kaku, M. (2014) *The Future of the Mind: The Scientific Quest to Understand, Enhance and Empower the Mind*. London: Penguin.

Koslofsky, C. (2011) *Evening's Empire: A History of the Night in Early Modern Europe*. Cambridge: Cambridge University Press.

Krauss, L. (2012) *A Universe from Nothing: Why There Is Something Rather Than Nothing*. New York: Simon & Schuster.

Levine, G. (2006) *Darwin Loves You: Natural Selection and the Re-Enchantment of the World*. Princeton, NJ: Princeton University Press.

Ligotti, T. (2010) *The Conspiracy against the Human Race*. New York: Hippocampus.

Lynas, M. (2008) *Six Degrees: Our Future on a Hotter Planet*. London: Harper Perennial.

Maxwell, N. (2004) *Is Science Neurotic?* London: Imperial College Press.

McClellan, J.E. & Dorn, H. (2006) *Science and Technology in World History: An Introduction*. Baltimore, MD: Johns Hopkins University Press.

McGilchrist, I. (2009) *The Master and the Emissary: The Divided Brain and the Making of the Western World*. New Haven, CT: Yale University Press.

McPherson, G. & Baker, C. (2014) *Extinction Dialogs: How to Live with Death in Mind*. San Francisco, CA: Taylen Lane.

Nöe, A. (ed) (2002) *Is the Visual World a Grand Illusion?* Exeter: Imprint Academic.

Ophuls, W. (2012) *Immoderate Greatness: Why Civilizations Fail*. North Charleston, SC: CreateSpace.

Oreskes, N. & Conway, E.M. (2014) *The Collapse of Western Civilization: A View from the Future*. New York: Columbia University Press.

Rees, M. (2004) *Our Final Century: Will Civilization Survive the Twenty First Century?* London: Arrow.

Rose, G. (2014) *The Melancholy Science: An Introduction to the Thought of Theodor W. Adorno*. London: Verso.

Rosenberg, A. (2011) *The Atheist's Guide to Reality: Enjoying Life without Illusions*. New York: Norton.

Scheffler, S. (2013) *Death and the Afterlife*. New York: Oxford University Press.

Spier, F. (2011) *Big History and the Future of Humanity*. Chichester: Wiley-Blackwell.

Stone, J.R. (ed) (2000) *Expecting Armageddon: Essential Readings in Failed Prophecy*. London: Routledge.

Svensen, H. (2009) *The End is Nigh: A History of Natural Disasters*. London: Reaktion.

Swenson, R.A. (1999) *Hurtling toward Oblivion: A Logical Argument for the End of the Age*. Colorado Springs, CO: Navpress.

Szent-Györgyi, A. (1970) *The Crazy Ape*. New York: Philosophical Library.

Tallis, R. (2011) *Aping Mankind: Neuromania, Darwinitis and the Misrepresentation of Humanity*. Durham: Acumen.

Taylor, T. (2010) *The Artificial Ape: How Technology Changed the Course of Human Evolution*. New York: Palgrave Macmillan.

Tennesen, M. (2015) *The Next Species: The Future of Evolution in the Aftermath of Man.* New York: Simon & Schuster.

Weisman, A. (2008) *The World without Us.* London: Virgin.

Zerzan, J. (2002) *Running on Emptiness: The Pathology of Civilization.* Los Angeles, CA: Feral House.

Zhavoronkov, A. (2013) *The Ageless Generation: How Advances in Biomedicine Will Transform the Global Economy.* New York: Palgrave Macmillan.

Chapter 9

The lifespan, everyday life and depressive realism

As Schopenhauer mercilessly put it, 'We begin in the madness of carnal desire and the transport of voluptuousness, we end in the dissolution of all our parts and the musty stench of corpses. And the road from the one to the other goes, in regard to our well-being and enjoyment of life, steadily downhill' (1851/1970, p. 54). We live in the domain of the bodily, in family and friendship networks, in schools, jobs and personal interests or varieties of inactivity and retirement, and in thoughts, feelings and conversations about experiences, tasks and prospects. The discourses of media and academic analysis have some validity but also distort common and idiosyncratic experience and introspection. Academics have the task of balancing apparent expertise against tentativeness on matters such as developmental knowledge (see, for example, Abela et al., 2008). Neither research that triumphantly declares a certain age group to be happiest, nor a biased book on depressive realism can correspond with the unique phenomenological worlds of over seven billion human beings. Neither academic accounts of the *lifeworld, paramount reality* or *narrative*, nor popular mythologies of individual life *journeys* can provide the last word on actual lives. Psychological surveys tend to ask crude, positively toned questions that do not recognise the great difficulty many people have in confessing to (or even recognising) dark thoughts and experiences. Perhaps a few questions probing nuances of marital dissatisfaction, career dysphoria, health and death preoccupations and suicidal flickers, while the interviewee is linked to a lie detector, or administered sodium pentothal, might unearth quite different results.

A central irony in this chapter concerns the importance given to the self. As Cioran puts it: 'Not a day, not an hour, not even a minute without falling into what Shandrakirti, the Buddhist dialectician, calls the *"abyss of the heresy of self"*' (1971, p. 109, italics in original). A radically pre-anthropathological account would regard us as primarily bodies moving a-biographically through existence, free of our fuss over the illusory 'I' and 'me' at the centre of his or her own drama. But now we are helplessly lumbered with our thought-saturated selves.

Even disregarding major personal crises (job loss, insolvency, divorce, bereavement, road accident, cancer) any of us is vulnerable to the occasional sub-critical perfect storm: a few days of domestic rows alongside work stress, insomnia, *wondering what it's all about,* seeing death grinning at the end of the ever closer cul de sac and occasionally wondering what it takes to throw oneself under a train. Wishing for death's delivery from suffering, yet simultaneously being terrified of death. Most of us pass through such crises without a breakdown, counselling or suicide attempt, and outwardly we may still appear 'normal', still repeating the obligatory 'Fine thanks' or responding positively to a telephone happiness survey. False positivity is, I suggest, much more common than false negativity. We will certainly disagree on whether any view on average life experience is tenable but let me insert here Thoreau's 'most men lead lives of quiet desperation' as a counterpoint to the image of the heart-breakingly beautiful new-born baby. Every fresh new-born who survives later accidents, violence and diseases will probably end her or his days frail, in some pain and finally lifeless. Bourdieu's (1999) sociological slices of damaged life and many of Ken Loach's and Mike Leigh's films capture the impoverishment, desperation, banality and tenderness of ordinary lives much more vividly than standard academic and statistically-based texts.

In this chapter I make some comments on the average lifespan, on typical experiences and subjective assessments, while appreciating that our lives can vary considerably. I have used a fairly conventional schema of life stages from conception to death, although this can be contested. An aphorism attributed to Russian actress Faina Ranevskaya – 'life is a sky-dive: out of a cunt, into the grave' – offers one of many grim assessments of the brevity and meaninglessness of individual life. The traditional British nursery rhyme *Solomon Grundy* (1842) also minces no words about the brevity of life. When sperm meets egg, aeons of genetic information are already prepared before the embryo appears; and when we die the corpse quickly enters its various stages of decomposition and the release of atoms back into the atmosphere follows. Since my perspective is that of depressive realism, I take the liberty of emphasising those negative aspects of our daily lives that are often neglected, minimised or censored elsewhere.

From conception to birth

Most psychology has traditionally neglected or minimised these earliest stages of individual lives, while many psychotherapy theories emphasise them. It should be clear, however, that your biological parents' decision, passion or thoughtlessness involved in conception is the first step towards your existence and your peculiar identity. None of us has any say in whether we are born (contrary to karmic, and some fanciful humanistic psychology theories of choosing our parents). We are not, contra existentialists' poetic phraseology, 'thrown into existence'. We are each a result of ontic aeons, evolution, genetic reproduction, sexual selection, the intrauterine environment and the birth experience itself, before we get anywhere near becoming a so-called person: phylogeny + ontogeny + the rest. I have suggested elsewhere that we would need a word like *biolography* to capture all that goes, micro-deterministically, into our making, and even that term does not honour our cosmic and atomic ingredients (Feltham, 2015). Already we would have to make many qualifications here to appease religious and other objectors. A non-existent God has no purpose or use for you, and many of us are so flawed that any mooted meta-designer would have to be regarded as culpably incompetent. Even if your parents wanted you and did their best to love you, this does not spare you the 'faults they had' (Larkin), nor the ensuing 'slings and arrows of outrageous fortune' (Shakespeare).

It isn't possible to know how many babies are wanted and planned as opposed to resulting from unwanted pregnancies, including those resulting from tawdry casual sex and rape. But even among those wanted, we know that a proportion have genetic defects or are damaged by intrauterine events, or the birth process itself, whether unavoidably or involving technologically induced trauma and medical negligence. We know that many foetuses are damaged by the mother's smoking, drug taking and alcohol consumption, as well as depression and other biopsychological problems during pregnancy. We know that each baby's genetic make-up depends on the parents' genotypes, and that physical appearance is largely determined by these. Future health and attractiveness are partly determined by culture and individual actions, but the foundations are genetically prefabricated. Propensities to certain body types – healthy, strong, sporty, attractive and their opposites – are strongly suggestive of life chances (Hakim, 2012), and the embittered battle concerning innate versus learned intelligence is by no means resolved.

Leboyer (2011) has said that hell begins at birth, or rather at birth by traditional, violently technological means, rather than at death (see also Kitzinger, 2006). Cioran (1998) puts it simply: 'fear of death is merely the projection into the future of a fear which dates back to our first moments of life' (p. 4). Some psychotherapy and obstetric theory insists that intrauterine trauma negatively affects the entire lifespan (Odent, 2006), possibly carrying a sense of hopelessness from before birth itself, a notion that contradicts the dogma of learned helplessness. Miscarriage and stillbirth are tragic experiences for the women concerned and abortion is a mixed experience of relief and sadness for many. Postnatal depression – both mild baby blues and postpartum depressive psychosis – are not well understood but one explanation is that some women instinctively realise the enormity of what it means to bring a new mortal into this world. Whether this enormity is persuasive as a cause of anxiety and depression, it is not one that gets investigated by much formal research. Live healthy babies usually bring joy to most (but not all) parents and are a universal symbol of hope, but it is unfortunately not the case that such births necessarily translate into future happy lives: at best this is a gamble for the new human being.

Infancy and childhood

The helpless and cute baby becomes a toddler, gradually talking, crawling and walking. Its every sign of meeting normal expectations of development is eagerly

The lifespan, everyday life and depressive realism   135

awaited, since failure to thrive and develop normatively can signify autism and other disabilities, health problems and social failure. The baby is slowly transformed from a gurgling, incontinent, laughing and crying, innocent and appealing little being into a proto-adult. This involves not only sphincter and bladder control but emotional self-containment, learning industrial sleep patterns, language and polite and safe behaviour. Human babies have a lengthy period of post-natal development during which their brains are still maturing and they are completely dependent. Although we are accustomed to speak in terms of child-centred upbringing, a great deal of babies' development is dictated by its society, whose agents are the unwitting parents. If the culture demands circumcision, for example, or female genital mutilation, swaddling or early intensive schooling, the baby or infant has no voice in this matter, and consensus grows that such practices are damaging.

Even regarding so-called normal development we should pause for thought. One of the longstanding, often bitter and still unresolved battles of the social sciences has taken place on the question of nature versus nurture, or genes versus culture. This debate has large implications for politics and social policy, as well as for optimism or pessimism as to personal development and equal opportunities. Kagan and Snidman's (2004) 25-year study of babies from the age of four months compared low-reactive with high-reactive individuals and found that innate traits of introversion and extraversion, and dispositional happiness, persisted across decades. This American study, while not ruling out possibilities of some changes via learning, runs somewhat counter to the expectations of positive psychologists, neuroplasticity enthusiasts and left-wingers. Even if significant changes in temperament and behaviour are possible, they seem unlikely. It is acknowledged and evidenced that extraverts have higher levels of lifelong wellbeing (Tantam, 2014), and it may be that personality dependent realism begins at birth (if not before), with DRs being a distinct breed.

We do not seriously question the restraints and behaviours outlined above because they become commonsense or even invisible to us, but I will just highlight one area in which our expectations are in conflict. This relates to speech, honesty and lies. Most children are taught to speak the truth and to observe the culture's moral and legal norms. Yet in a common double-bind situation, the actual expectation is that young children learn to suppress their spontaneity, to look and sound truthful and sincere while often withholding certain thoughts and embellishing or distorting others. Evans et al. (2011) claim to pinpoint lying beginning at about the age of 42 months. In other words, lying is learnt as a key social skill, perhaps not explicitly but in no uncertain terms; yet we see no fashionable concept of *learned untruthfulness* addressing the topic. Politeness is the most obvious example of this but deferring to elders and authorities is also part of this repertoire. 'Be honest but know when not to be honest' is a universal component of development. 'Know which subjects you may and may not talk about openly' is another key social skill; in other words, steer clear of taboos. But 'don't be a hypocrite' is also one of our common moral injunctions. This is all depressing, insofar as we have created and we live in a world that necessitates such doublethink, and doubly depressing in that we are each obliged constantly to monitor ourselves to ensure we fit in and do not offend. Try as we might to master this doublethink so that we even believe it ourselves (Smith, 2007), it is not surprising that some of us become neurotic or have breakdowns under the weight of such inner conflicts.

Children are discouraged from asking about and knowing the grimmer facts of life but their nightmares are telling, and Becker (1973) is not alone in arguing that they sense annihilation in experiences of their parents' absences. Euphemisms and evasions remain rife: babies are not delivered by storks any longer but come from 'mummy's tummy' until children are considered old enough to need sex education. Most children are still likely to be told that God looks after them and protects them, Father Christmas (until a certain age) rewards them, Mummy and Daddy will always be there; and when children die they will go to heaven, which is a nice place where your lovely parents will be waiting. Some believe children begin to think about death from about the age of five (Griffiths, 2007). Nagy (1959) had described children's death awareness as falling into three phases: denial (ages 3–5); acknowledgement but distancing, 'it happens to some but not me' (ages 5–9); dying as universal and inescapable (from age 10). The literature remains limited on the dawning of children's knowledge that their lifespan will probably stop at about 80 years or so, when they will quite likely be sick and frail (although see Solomon et al., 2015). One only has to observe the common reaction of small children to the sight of a dead bird, goldfish or cat to know that it can evoke a sense of horror. For those reared in God-fearing households, it can remain a terrifying expectation that only impossibly pure human lives will escape the horrors of death and eternal punishment.

Despite common troubles and anxieties, everything will be alright, most children are assured. Some aspects of this happy picture quickly dissolve for many children in the face of reality. If you have the bad luck to have abusive parents, divorcing parents, parents who die when you are young, growing up in an unreliable children's home, suboptimal adoption or fostering situations or in other troublesome or violent circumstances like war, disease epidemic or famine, you learn early on that life isn't good. But don't worry, the nice social worker or psychotherapist who has had a more privileged childhood than you will reverse or soften all that suffering for you later.

Compulsory mass schooling has been provided to educate you and prepare you for later life. This part of life works well for those who are able to sit still, conform and compete in exams. But if you are unlucky, you may be afraid of or be misunderstood by your teachers, bullied by other children or you may learn that you are one of the less clever. If you are very restless or inconveniently curious, you may be labelled problematic. If you are shy and not one of the brightest, you receive less attention. If you work hard, the story goes (and you can always work harder), you will leave school with good qualifications, go to university and proceed to a well-paid and satisfying career with high status.

The lifespan, everyday life and depressive realism   137

Modernity is about mass, and the majority of children must endure years of mass education that is poorly equipped in spite of promotional rhetoric to cater for individual differences. It is also poorly oriented towards actual future job opportunities, usually teaching subjects that are traditional, or sometimes fashionable or dictated by current educational policy. The school appears to suit some (and currently girls perform better than boys) but is experienced as a waste of time, boring, punitive or traumatic by others: 'just another brick in the wall'.

But, the protest comes, children are saved from child labour or abusive homes, are exposed to stimulation they might not get at home, their parents are freed to work and what else would be put in the place of school anyway? This is a key point. Once the oxytocin-fuelled days of idealised babyhood have passed and children are experienced as often more demanding than cute and rewarding, what are they for? To meet the parents' desire for the status of normality, to carry on the family genes and name, to compensate for parents' inadequacies or to honour God (Taylor & Taylor, 2003)? Most parents are perhaps sufficiently loving, responsible and resilient to endure the stresses of juggling parenting with the onerous demands of work, money management and other chores. But I doubt whether my own mother, for example, a stay-at-home 1950s mother and housewife, was unique in her exasperated cry of 'I wish I'd never had kids'. In childhood subjectivity Hardy's young Jude Fawley (or 'Little Father Time'), I and many others must have wondered about the pointlessness of a life dominated by desultory parenting, anxiety-filled schooldays, the uptight suburban nuclear family, work and death (see Cavan, 1932). Of course, psychotherapists feel sure that they understand and can remedy this early painful disconnection between the love-needing child and the inadequate parent, and this throws up the charge that depression and alleged depressive realism mainly results from negative childhood experiences. Well-documented mother-son conflicts certainly exist in relation to Schopenhauer, Beckett, Larkin, Cioran and Houellebecq. In Chapter 6 I considered the faith of psychotherapists in their own product to be misplaced, and the scale of negativity of the human condition to go far beyond the problems of childhood.

The parent-child or adult-child interstice is interpreted by psychotherapists mainly in terms of power, intergenerational parenting deficits and the unique relationship between each parent-child pairing. Much more rarely is attention given to the relevant themes of evolutionary psychology, transgenerational effects and parental helplessness in a socio-economic context. Most parents do not consciously abuse their children, provide them with substandard care or fail to equip them optimally for adult life out of deliberate malice. Rather, they may unintentionally repeat patterns of behaviour they learned themselves, which their grandparents passed on and so on, *ad infinitum*. Or, contrary to progressive assumptions, we see patterns of tyrannical parenting reacted against with permissive, child-centred parenting, both of which produce problems. But this is combined with the specific circumstances and limitations of the home, the couple, cultural and socio-economic realities and prevailing conditions.

138 The lifespan, everyday life and depressive realism

Even professors of child development and child psychotherapists are unlikely to escape the malign influences of this complex mix of forces. (Melanie Klein certainly didn't.)

In all likelihood most parents muddle through, doing their tired best. In the process they helplessly transmit the values, anxieties and pressures they themselves experience. For example, parental pressure for the child to perform well at school comes not only from the controlling superego or Parent ego state (of transactional analysis fame), or from parents' anxiety about how they may be perceived by their own peers, but from an awareness of how competitive the job market is. Indeed, another level of pressure on many (middle class) parents is worrying about whether they are 'doing it right' according to the latest parenting manual author, or the latest academic research. The sheer busyness and complexity of modern life makes parenting, and hence childhood, difficult in ways we may not yet appreciate.

Adolescence

The child begins the stormy passage from responsibility-lite and dreamy childhood to task-filled and responsible, independent adulthood. The torments of puberty are very well-known. Sex is not the taboo topic or religion-controlled, guilt-inducing experience it once was and sex education has improved, but sex is still learned as a private matter of experimentation and uncertainty. Is frequent masturbation OK? How does one initiate sex? Am I doing it right? Am I straight or gay? Is this real love? What degree of explicit mutual permission is needed before sex commences? Self-consciousness about appearance and awareness of the competitive nature of the sexual marketplace make for unease.

One of the greatest sorrows of adolescence – in addition to first experiences of love and its loss – is the conflict between biological urges and reproductive ability on the one hand, and socio-economic structures on the other. In other words, our biological nature compels or strongly encourages us to seek sexual pleasure but heterosexual sex is fraught with the potential problems of disease, pregnancy and premature long-term commitments. In the pathos-filled film *Splendour in the Grass*, the two main characters who are in love but from different social classes are deemed too young to commit to each other and eventually drift into more 'mature' but less passionate relationships. The conundrums and anxieties surrounding contraception, unwanted pregnancies and abortion, adoption and marriage put a crimp on sex as a biological drive and one of life's free pleasures. Writers like Tennessee Williams and Michel Houellebecq have commented that sex is for many depressively inclined people one of life's very few saving graces, and we may recall McMurphy's line to the young Billy in *One Flew Over the Cuckooo's Nest*: 'You oughta be out in a convertible, why – bird-doggin' chicks and bangin' beaver' (not hiding anxiously in a psychiatric hospital). Perhaps there is some wisdom in *Ecclesiastes* that everything has its season, and adolescence and early adulthood is not optimally dedicated to morbid introspection.

Although many adolescents pass quietly into an average adult narrative, many do not. This is the time when alcohol is discovered, cigarette smoking begins, drugs are experimented with and unprotected sex is sometimes engaged in. At this time peer norms often become more important than parental standards. Apart from the inherently pleasant stimulation of alcohol and 'uppers' or the pacification of some illegal drugs, there is an experience of pushing limits, living on the edge, snubbing mainstream society and exposing oneself to existential risk. According to Taubman Ben-Ari (2004) adolescent risk-taking, which includes these typical actions and also reckless driving and extreme sports, is a bid to resolve the existential fear of death.

Adolescence is, interestingly, also the time when many of us become acutely preoccupied with questions about religion, politics and meaning. Presumably the timing is due to a combination of cognitive and physical maturity, hormonal urgency and awareness of the realities of the adult world and its sad civilizational parameters. *Who am I, why am I here, what is the meaning of life, is there a God, why do we live the way we do, why are there wars, why do we have to die, is this all there is, what can I do?* These are the typical questions the agonising adolescent asks. Sometimes dismissed or humoured as teenage angst, this stage may in fact be the most powerful window most of us get on to acute existential awareness before succumbing to typical adult shutdown. I still recall how rare it was to find such matters discussed, openly or otherwise, in my own teenage years in the 1960s. It is into this questioning space that traditional religion often inserts itself, offering glib explanation and reassurance on metaphysical and moral matters. It is also a political space in which lifelong affiliations are often forged.

It is unsurprising that some teenage males are peculiarly susceptible to the extremes of religious fundamentalism, political idealism, violence, risk-taking (Peper et al., 2013), onset of serious mental health problems and suicidality (Kessler et al., 2008). Among homicidal and suicidal terrorists, relative youth and maleness correlate highly. Western civilisation requires compliant and productive citizens rather more than restless and agitated types, and young males are often at odds with this macro-ethos. While this mismatch is sometimes creative and humorous, it is frequently tragic, as in cases of psychotic breakdown, recruitment to terrorism, reckless lifestyles and actual suicide. Mass conformity and emphasis on safe, emasculated and predictable living do not suit everyone. It can be argued that vivid insight into what a typical life has to offer is at its most acute for young people who understand the constellation of relational risks, career limitations and existential demands facing them. Sadly, it is a stepping off point for those who decide the mismatch is too great (see the examples of Michelstaedter and Iacopponi, in Feltham, 2015, p. 69), the returns on effort are not worth the compromises required and suicide releases them. Civilisation is not about to be modified for the sake of a few anguished young people.

Adulthood

Already by this stage certain physical characteristics have peaked and mortality salience is evident (Shields, 2011). The main associations of adulthood are work, love and family and a home of one's own. We are expected to become financially independent of our parents and to know which career we wish to enter. While some traditional folklore and New Age prescriptions exist for 'knowing your vocation' and 'finding your passion', many of us have no such inner direction. We realise that some jobs have more status and higher salaries and we may have a shot at those, but equally we may realise that our temperament, abilities and interests are at odds with what society rewards. Crime, drug addiction, varieties of bohemian life and anarchism and homelessness are some of the desperate responses to the standard expectation. It may be seen as sad or depressing to have to resort to outsider identities and lifestyles with poor prospects, but there is also something depressing about the narrative of standardised lives according to which we should all become neatly obedient and successful cogs in the machine.

Who knows what proportion of us aim just to get by in life, to keep our heads above water, and how many are actively ambitious to achieve, to 'make a difference' or to stand out? For those who strive hard there must be some awareness, some occasional realisation that all that education, toil and sweat, planning and scheming, all the endurance of absurd jobs, all that accumulated knowledge and experience still leads to old age frailty, illness and death, with your worn-out carcass laid in a coffin and buried with maggots or burned to near-nothingness, and each of us is completely forgotten within decades. Even the most outstanding can only hope at best to earn a newspaper obituary, or become statues or references in books, and they will *experience* no adulation posthumously. The reality of our ultimate futility must flicker across the consciousness of most of us even if we manage to 'live in the present' somewhat or enjoy our worldly successes year by year. Suppression of awareness of ultimate futility is probably accomplished by most people automatically, somewhat like the negative automatic thoughts of Beck's cognitive behaviour therapy but in this case regarded as healthily suppressive automatic thoughts denoting normality. Interpretation of this experience as abnormal 'death awareness' or 'mortality salience' by clinicians and psychology academics implies that such thoughts belong to a minority and/or should be suppressed or cured. Normality and maturity demand they are banished. In the prime of life we are expected to be productive and hopeful, not morbidly preoccupied by our own annihilation decades hence.

The everlasting happy heterosexual marriage is no longer the sole kind of relationship to aspire to. About half of marriages end in divorce, gay marriage is accepted and some polyamorous, polygamous and other arrangements are available. But sexual and relational diversity does not equate to a utopia of coupling. An estimated 1% of adults count themselves as asexual. Serial or liquid relationships may now be the norm, and it is difficult to know whether the sums of happiness and unhappiness involved improve on the previous arrangements.

The lifespan, everyday life and depressive realism   141

Japan offers good examples of the breakdown of adult expectations. *Hikikomori* is a so-called condition of social isolation in which young people either never, or only after decades, make the expected transition from the parental home to independence. *Mendokusai* is a phenomenon characterised by people in their 20s and 30s showing no interest in intimate relationships, marriage and having children. Its rise to minor epidemic proportions is attributed to overpopulation, intense competition for jobs, and over-use of personal computers among other factors.

Romantic love makes life worth living, some of us find, or makes a satisfying life temporarily euphoric. From unexpected love at first sight to hard-won relationships that endure or come and go, love makes the world go round. Patterns change but the passion of love, of two people finding profound beauty, acceptance and excitement in each other's presence, has been in fashion for centuries[1]. It doesn't require belief or hard work, at least not in the beginning. Terror management theorists Mikulincer et al. (2004) argue that close relationships serve to 'deny the existential threat of one's finitude' (p. 287), that is, they banish the loneliness in which we are close to realising how death-prone we are. But love often becomes humdrum or sour, certainly moves through vicissitudes and often enough breaks down or fades to lukewarm companionship. The very person who once was the brightest light in your universe converts into the cause of boredom, conflict and cheating (Kultgen, 2013). We then create explanations for breakdown, couple counselling, marriage enrichment programmes or we come to accept that as lives get longer we must expect and enjoy the prospect of serial loves. Meanwhile, the emotional devastation of love gone awry is one of life's greatest disappointments, hurting lovers and their children and affecting attitudes deeply, sometimes also leading to suicide or murder. Underlying love's havoc, however, is the prior question of illusion: is love no more than a neurochemically-induced illusion?

Something like 80% of men and 90% of women have children worldwide and until quite recently almost 50% of American pregnancies were unplanned. Although some countries are currently seeing a slight decline in the birth rate, the majority of women have up to three children worldwide, except in Central Africa where the number goes up to between 4 and 7. About 130 million babies are born annually and the world population in 2014 was 7.25 billion and rising. Parenthood is, despite antinatalist cries, an ongoing enterprise and a huge part of the majority of adults' experience. It is not the biological near-inevitability it once was, with accessible contraception, bad experiences, cultural changes, statistical warnings about high costs and conscious evaluations of pros and cons still not offsetting the desire to have children. Childhood deaths aside, most committed parents spend many years caring for their children. Although impossible to calculate what proportion of them consciously think about their children's long-term future, some of us picture how our offspring will fare in the time after we are dead, what fortunes and misfortunes they will encounter and how and when the children-grown-old will die. The deaths of those who

142 The lifespan, everyday life and depressive realism

die before their parents usually trigger enormous sadness or depression. But even given the best prospects for them, we know our children will encounter the normal run of life's adversities before becoming old, enduring old age and dying. Such thoughts probably do not usually come until middle or old age but the very act of having children leads to additional gross suffering and mortality (Benatar, 2006; Perry, 2014). The most acute sense of cognitive dissonance is experienced by parents who both know they consciously brought children into this world *and* that this world is a vale of suffering.

Depressive attitudes to life are likely to be strongest among teenagers, single childless people and older people, partly due to a necessary suspension of negative thinking during the parenting years. As a parent of youngsters one is usually at one's busiest and often most stressed, life may be punctuated by real shared pleasures and tasks and the onus of sustaining positive morale obscures underlying negativity. Cognitive dissonance reduction may account for much suspended depressive antinatalism: 'I wanted children, so I can't complain now'. Or the rather artful 'I love my kids but if I had my life again I wouldn't have them'. Indeed, some evidence garnered from unusually candid mothers suggests that a proportion of them hate being a parent despite outwardly competent parenting (Senior, 2010). The juggernaut of reproductive expectations easily explains typical reluctance to confess to negative views of parenting. Pretending to children that their parents' marriage is happy and bound for eternity also often reinforces DR-denialism. Wayward or suffering children, divorces and witnessing one's adult children struggling unhappily and unsuccessfully with social and economic challenges can, however, tilt attitudes back towards a melancholy cast. But those who chose or by default slipped into childlessness (or as they like to recast it, a 'child-free' life) may also work hard at denying their loneliness or sense of something missing. Such are this life's odds stacked that perhaps you can't win either way.

Middle age

The meaning of midlife is changing with increasing longevity, and there must be some doubt about just what reality the term has; and certainly the so-called midlife crisis is probably now a redundant if poignant concept (Jacques, 1965). People in their 40s and 50s will experience quite different socio-economic circumstances, with some being in the doldrums of an unhappy marriage and some stuck in unfulfilling jobs but others remarrying in hope or energetically launching a second or third career or retiring early. The age of menopause and its precise symptoms vary from woman to woman but commonly include hot flushes, insomnia, mood swings, vaginal dryness, changes in body shape and intrafamilial problems. Some writers have put a brave, positive and often feminist spin on it – as a set of new freedoms from pregnancy, from sex itself, from inhibitions – but others reveal frankly the miseries of post-fertility, declining attractiveness and raging negative emotions affecting loved-ones. Some talk

The lifespan, everyday life and depressive realism 143

about this openly but many conceal it. Many medical and herbal remedies are touted, and couple counselling is often suggested, sometimes proving helpful and sometimes not. Becker (1973, p. 215) refers to menopause as an 'animal holiday' signifying a kind of death.

A male menopause is claimed to exist but if it does it is hard to pin down temporally as the baldness, greyness and pot belly increase so gradually over many years. While men remain sexually fertile for much longer than women, and much feminist resentment argues that older men still find younger women and successful careers, the norm for many is, like women, a decline in attractiveness and energy. More men find themselves divorced, struggling financially and figures for midlife suicide have risen in recent years (Shiner et al., 2009). Midlife signifies aspects of anatomical wilting and drooping that reflect the not infrequent mild to moderate depression that accompanies them, with pharmaceuticals being used hopefully to delay or reverse these sad features of ageing. Some resort to testosterone therapy and Viagra just as some women use hormone replacement therapy, even though by some accounts placebo factors may be at work here and negative side effects are common.

Relatively little is written about stalled lives but by midlife it becomes evident that some are by normal standards markedly off course. Disability and illness will visibly and understandably delay some in their maturation regarding social and sexual bonds and career progress. But a silent and lonely minority exist who have subthreshold problems (those, mainly male, who share features of Asperger-like traits, shyness and withdrawal) who are avolitional, anomic and unable to engage with others and with the world of work. Undiagnosed and unhelped, they may be the butt of jokes – the '40-year old virgin' and so on – and drift into atypical lives of illness, poverty, eccentricity and suicide. Social workers, psychiatrists, therapists, academics and careers advisers are ill-equipped and too impractical to offer any effective help. Similarly, by midlife many have found themselves labelled deviant as hardened criminals or addicts, and their prospects may turn from bad to worse.

Old age

Steadily downhill, as Schopenhauer put it. Shakespeare's *Seven Ages of Man* speech in *As You Like It* places the old in 'second childishness and mere oblivion, sans teeth, sans eyes, sans taste, sans everything.' There is no consensus on when old age begins but we do have various, often euphemistic terms such as late middle age, early old age, and so on. Avoiding the 'you're only as old as you feel' and 'it's only a number' clichés, and the fashionable form of denialism known as amortality, I shall pragmatically take retirement as the arbitrary point at which we may be deemed old. On retirement, which varies worldwide from the mid to late 50s for women (and some men) up to 68 for men (and some women), we may be deemed to deserve a rest, to be past our best, to be a liability in the workplace or to possess the human right to spend some years in leisure before dying.

While perceptions and realities of ageing are changing with increasing longevity, we have to recognise despite anti-ageist agendas that our bodies deteriorate inwardly and outwardly, our cognitive faculties often lose acuity and we are not usually reproductively or occupationally contributing members of society. Individual and national differences in how and when we age can vary significantly. Subjectively too, some of us feel old while others claim not to experience many of the typical features of ageing. Contrarily, some of us continue to feel 18 in our views and desires and forget that others see us as the worn 80-year old we are. Many experience an increase in illness, chronic pain, disability, loneliness, boredom and bereavement, as well as a reduction in income and access to escapes from tedium. Our precise circumstances in old age depend on biological factors and socio-economic perceptions and arrangements.

It is deemed impolite, ageist or inaccurate to speak of the ugliness of old age or of human decay in general. But compare pictures of the young Brigitte Bardot, say, with the 80-year old Bardot, of the achingly beautiful slim youth, with the weighty, wrinkled, heavily made-up old woman, and try to deny the sadness of ageing. Or consider Kirk Douglas, say. Older affluent men are sometimes resented for still being able to attract younger mates, yet many men as they age know just how ugly and miserable they feel, experiencing changes that are often attributed to loss of testosterone, accounting for the grumpy old man phenomenon (Diamond, 2004). Some would like disingenuously to claim a different *kind* of beauty for the old, but most of us have probably often looked in the mirror with some self-disgust.

Sometimes I look at my book collection and am struck with the sadness embodied in those tomes of younger-me aspirations to knowledge that is now passé and irrelevant. Everything fades and passes, our eyes see the examples of this, but our need for denial refuses to let us dwell for long on these sharp sadnesses. However, one highly technical study in Malaysia has it that 13% of the elderly are severely depressed (compared with only 2% of the general population) but nevertheless extraversion, social support, religious faith and acceptance of CBT can all be balancing factors (Loke et al., 2011). Not such good news for lonely old introverted atheists who are resistant to CBT.

It may be a blessing that most younger people regard old age as very far away for themselves, but it is certainly an illusion that it won't happen to them. The gradualness of time passing means that we can feel shocked to find ourselves 'suddenly' so old, with many of the above-listed unfortunate features. Time tricks us, passing slowly during empty days but seeming to rush by in annual terms. It is a commonplace to warn the young of the importance of saving and preparing for old age but it really hits home only when the time actually comes, when the wrinkles, liver spots, cataracts, sarcopenia, osteoporosis, Alzheimer's and other horrors are *theirs*. Only first-hand experience of the mixed difficulties of living and aversion to dying really cuts it. We now speak often of Holocaust denial and climate change denial but rarely do we speak openly of denial in regard to old age. But the young deny it in themselves, optimists often deny

The lifespan, everyday life and depressive realism 145

that it's really so bad when it happens (exceptional cases are always available) and the depressing nature of the topic is generally skirted around: it will happen to *you*, it *will* probably entail some increased misery, it *does* mean that most of your life is behind you and you *are* closer to your own complete extinction. It may not be exactly a taboo topic but it is avoided or minimised in conversation, and precisely because it is universal, inescapable and depressing.

Let me give a somewhat trivial personal example of a double sadness in regard to ageing. I was learning Danish in my 60s. I was well-intentioned when I began but as time went on I realised how little I retained and how poor my prospects were. I had only very rare opportunities, if any, to speak Danish, I am not an especially talented linguist, my idiosyncratic learning style means that I cannot master grammar in any explicit way and my age means that I often seem to forget almost as much as I learn. Although I persevered, the reality of my limits became clear to me. Although I was glad to be in a learning situation (and I succumbed to the superstition that such engagement wards off Alzheimer's), and I was fond of my classmates and the multilingual context, I sometimes confessed to them and to my teachers that I thought of dropping out because I felt a little depressed at my lack of progress. Invariably the responses were along the lines of 'You're not old, you can do it, you can do anything you put your mind to,' and so on. I did in fact drop out, finding it all unmanageable and sometimes humiliating. It is the denial of truth that is the second layer of sadness. The overwhelming cultural norm is optimistic, which includes a reflexive denial of ageing-associated perceived defeatism. It is saddening because one's reality is dismissed: you *must* stay positive and no-one wants to hear any negatives. Knowing viscerally your own mental tiredness parameters, you yet have to suppress all this, keep smiling, endure and mask the ongoing embarrassments of forgetfulness. We are strategically nudged into line with the hegemonic bolstering of shared positive illusions and away from the undesirable decline narrative (Overall, 2003; Erber & Szuchman, 2014).

The standard optimistic portrait of healthy and happy old age contains a great deal of advice about the importance of a healthy diet, exercise, hobbies, holidays and companionship, combined with the hope that we will remain disease-free and accident-free or only minimally affected by aches and pains well into our 80s or 90s, when we will die sweetly at home surrounded by loved ones. This ideal image of the last 20, say, years of life probably fits a minority of us. The habits of a lifetime are not easily changed, meagre pensions do not allow for holidays (many of the poor old have to choose between more food or heating, clothing, etc.), and friends and family are not always thrilled to spend much time with us. Some 376,250 elderly people lived in care homes in the UK in 2012, 40% of them with dementia. In the United States around 4 million over 65s are in care, and 25% of the elderly population can expect to be heading for such destinations. For many, with work routines and colleagues long gone, television is their main companion, or brief visits from dutiful family members or paid carers are eagerly awaited. Apart from those, acute loneliness can be biting: 'the experience of the pathos of disappearance' (Dumm, 2008, p. ix). Listen to Joan Baez's beautiful and sad song *Hello in There* about old age loneliness. Consider that solitary confinement is dreaded by most prisoners. Old, one recedes from relevance, and then from life itself. The quality of life's last years varies from reasonable to dreadful, but few of us wish to think about this and relatively few have much choice.

Much more negative attention has been given to death and dying than to ageing. But as Jean Améry (1994) claimed, old age may be worse than death itself, which is at least a release from suffering. Améry, a Holocaust survivor, dreaded old age so much that he killed himself at the age of 65. It is because old age has been intuited by some as so wretched that a minority have killed themselves rather than endure it. Although typical expectations now encourage us to think of long life as the desired norm, some young people who can see the imminent indignities, the pathetic clinging to even the most painful, disabled and disfigured lives that many endure, choose an early exit. Benatar (2006), as someone with a grim estimate of life's worthwhileness, neither advocates nor condemns suicide, but some will ridicule his argument that even minor discomforts like itches add to life's negatives. Quite clearly, however, the negatives that often tend to increase with age, such as dulled senses, high blood pressure, aching joints, insomnia and degenerative diseases, take their toll inwardly and outwardly, such as baldness, dry skin, skin blemishes, stray facial hairs, stooped posture and so on. Revulsion against ageing is not an exclusively modern reaction (Small, 2010). Gerontophobic suicide, as we might call it, includes the young who want no truck with ageing at all, the middle-aged who have had enough and the old who can bear no more.

One of the mundane realities of old age is that we have fewer positives to look forward to. In our earlier lives we can anticipate with some hope and pleasure achieving educational and professional goals, relational security and having children. However afflicted we are by disappointments, we can still expect further chances. In middle age we may begin to look forward longingly to retirement, especially when work is tiring or unpleasant. But unless on retirement we have amassed wealth and are able to travel extensively, engage in other new pursuits or have grandchildren, life is characterised by having less and less to look forward to. Life turns towards reminiscence even for many high achievers (Auster, 2013; Tallis, 2015). This is especially true for those on low incomes, who cannot even expect a modest annual holiday. The years from the 60s onwards, for many at least, have one dominant horizon: death. Things are not going to get better and we cannot even deceive ourselves that they will (Lang et al., 2013). Roisin et al. (2011) pose the question of 'Why do older people look so happy when they have nothing to look forward to?' After considering the traditional claims to elderly wisdom they conclude banally that we are all different in old age (after all, who would claim that even *most* old people look happy?); and strikingly, they make no reference to factors of poverty in a book that overall strives for an upbeat message. Trivers (2011), however, suggests that positivity in old age

The lifespan, everyday life and depressive realism   147

(from 60 up) can be accounted for in immunological terms. We feel better if we deceive ourselves positively and it does us little harm to deceive ourselves now, since 'it hardly matters what you learn' (p. 134), whereas learning for the young is crucial.

Death

Such is our fear of death that we delay it by medical means for as long as possible, even when quality of life is very poor. The average length of time people survive after an Alzheimer's diagnosis is 8 to 10 years. Some who are brain dead are kept alive for years, in one case up to 15 years. In the UK about 6,000 people are on life support systems at any one time and in the United States about 40,000. And there is fierce resistance to assisted suicide: healthy young women are currently gaining the right to go to war and kill and die, while unhealthy older people must often linger in pain and indignity. If we were brutally honest, we might describe many frail old people as the barely-walking almost-dead.

Death is not part of the lifespan but its end, the complete cessation of every individual life. We can include old age reminiscence, everyday experience in old age and end of life phenomena in lifespan accounts. But we can and we probably should include reports of how we die, that is, not only medical causes of death but any reported observations of the dying process. Indeed, we do have some such. Nuland (1997), for example, describes graphically and authoritatively many different kinds of death, denial of approaching and inevitable death, the malevolence of cancer, common pain and suffering and the futility of most attempts to lengthen life in its terminal stages. We also have some unusually honest observations of what happens to our corpses, none of which is at all cheering and for some is unbearable (Roach, 2004). But it would also be interesting to know what different feelings and thoughts we have about the anticipation of death (from any prior part of our lifespan). Commonly, we have those who claim to have no fear of death, based on machismo, stoicism, existential wisdom or mystical and religious beliefs; those who admit to varying degrees of anxiety and fear, including terror of being buried or cremated alive, 'fear of the unknown' or of being punished in hell; and those who feel that death is an affront. Kellehear (2014) optimistically believes that many of us in fact live our final days in experiences that are 'complex, surprising and wondrous' (p.xii) and undergo positive psychological transformations even in our last moments.

'Untimely' accidental deaths may reveal a great deal. Matthew O'Reilly (2014), a veteran emergency medical technician attended many accidents and agonised over the question put to him by dying people: 'Am I going to die?' Coming eventually to believe that truth is better than comforting lies, he found that almost everyone accepted his 'yes' without terror. He further observed that almost universally the dying expressed the wish to be forgiven for perceived wrongs; to be remembered by those who had known them; and to feel that their lives had some meaning. Coming in dramatic circumstances, one is inclined to

148 The lifespan, everyday life and depressive realism

attribute unquestioning authority to these 'universal human needs and truths': 'I'm sorry, please love me, please let me count.' These sentiments seem easily recognised and apparently cross the religious–unbelieving divide, sounding more authentic than last minute bargaining for divine favours. But they come from an emotional *in extremis* position. Perhaps we could all be kinder but some will barely be remembered or be considered to have led meaningful lives. What a meaningful life is exactly can be debated forever, and it is not a debate any terminally injured person has the appetite or time for.

Posthumanist believers openly state their case that we live in a death trance that we should confront and attempt to overcome by scientific and technological methods (de Grey, 2008). But consider another group, those of us who realise that death is a biological given that neither can nor should be overcome, and yet that cannot simply be accepted. Both biologically and attitudinally we are conditioned not to expect to die. All our wiring and social conditioning is oriented to survival. At the biological level this is readily understood. But as social entities, we are socialised to hope, to be educated, to strive, to acquire skills, build lives, behave honourably, assume meaningfulness. We are not educated to regard our lives as a few decades of existence that is to be abruptly terminated without remainder. Yet it is difficult to reflect on our imminent death without facing this futilitarian truth that everything we do eventually comes to nothing. We may buy into the idea typically urged upon us that our every small act, our individual ways of life, construct the civilisation around us and to come, and that we therefore have a responsibility always to act morally and with hope. Or more likely, we participate in the collective 'isolation' (to use the Zapffean term) of death thoughts from consciousness; that is, we do not think about death and we reinforce the social norm that it is morbid to think about it. It is certainly regarded as pathological to think excessively about death and to voice that fear.

Paradoxically, in this safe civilisation we have created, in which risks to life are minimised as far as possible, it seems we cannot take an honest view of the inevitable facts of biological deterioration and death. Nor can we incorporate this into collective open recognition and discussion. This may be partly due to religious tradition and the wariness of controversy and conflict that a secular discussion would initiate. But it is almost certainly due, too, to tacit agreement not to upset children and young people. The net effect of denial is that each of us feels somewhat lonely and weird with our own thoughts about our own imminent death, as if it is in any significant way different from others' fearful thoughts; and as if we could do anything at all to postpone it. But this is not only about fear of death. DRs may possess an instinctive actuarial awareness of what is in store, particularly as one gets older. Diminishing returns cannot be easily ignored, as all the efforts of self-maintenance are weighed against the dubious benefits of extra years of mere survival. We are encouraged to think of long life as desirable, indeed the longest possible life as desirable, but experience and observation tell us the negatives tend to stack up relentlessly and are capped off with nullification. The old autosuggestion 'day by day in every way I'm getting

The lifespan, everyday life and depressive realism 149

better and better' (the Coué method) cannot be sustained when the reality is quite the opposite. This is not then *fear* of old age and death but realism, truth rather than illusion.

Everyday life: How we spend our time

The majority of us spend our days in school or other educational settings, in jobs or unemployment, intimate and family relationships, personal interests, active or passive recreational pursuits and in idleness, sleep, illness and disability. Some are in institutions like prisons, or involved in extended travel or anomalous enterprises. Most of us are obliged to juggle money and fill in forms, trapped in monetary, capitalist and bureaucratic systems as we all are. Most of us are obliged to engage in some level of home maintenance and technological activity. On the one hand, you may be stressed by work demands, family conflicts, personal economics, tax forms and bureaucratic battles, but on the other by anything from moments and hours to days and weeks of boredom and loneliness. The quotidian demands and preoccupations of the everyday spare us awareness of emptiness and futility. These petty, daily miseries were well outlined in detail, almost comically, by James Beresford in his 1806 text *The Miseries of Human Life; An Old Friend in a New Dress*, in a dialogue between Messrs Testy and Sensitive.

We spend about a third of our lives asleep (much less for chronic insomniacs) and a third of our productive adult lives at work. Our hunter–gatherer days are long gone (and disputed as to the length of the typical 'working day'), via agriculture and industry, and we have come to dully accept the ritual of most of our daylight hours being consumed by some form of work. We must have unconsciously wanted to enslave ourselves, or we believed that the improvements foisted on the lower orders by the shrewd higher minority were worth the slavery involved. The Old Testament noted our characteristic toil and suffering, but thousands of years later life has changed mainly in its largely comfortable indoor nature. While many wild animals sleep, we practise our self-inculcated work ethic to earn our symbolic money which capitalism ensures is just enough to keep us on the edge of comfort but always needing or wanting more. We (or the majority) can barely imagine any other kind of life. Terkel (1972) famously charted the miseries of the workplace as told to him by many candid Americans. We no longer stare upwards at ecclesiastical architecture for our assurances that it is all worth it, but at indispensable individual computer screens that mesmerise us. Some are so closely identified with and locked into their institutions that they fully believe in and depend on them as they would a God. Work, often tedious and pointless, is the opium of the masses: we are all dopeheads in the radical DR vision.

We can lament the way we spend or 'fritter away' our precious time but what else would we do with it? The growing realisation that we have only one life and limited choices means that pressure to *live a more meaningful life* increases. Many feel pushed towards greater neophilia, committed altruism, spiritual aspirations

150   The lifespan, everyday life and depressive realism

or autobiographical bulking up generally. In the 2005 film *The Weather Man* David Spritz is disappointed that his TV job is no match for his father's Pulitzer Prize-winning status, that his marriage has ended and he is alienated from his children. In spite of his best efforts to write a decent novel, reunite his family and make a better life, his success is limited to a new $1million weatherman job with *Hello America*. We distinguish between empty celebrity culture and the great and the good, the latter deemed to have made a significant contribution to society; they have worked tirelessly, made a difference, pushed the limits, been pioneers in their fields (entertainment, the arts, sport, industry, academia, philanthropy, etc.) and are much-loved national treasures. But behind the honours, awards, titles, prizes, festschrifts, Oscars, biographies, waxworks, obituaries, canonisation and statues, we can usually see they are made of the same mortal stuff as the rest of us and are sometimes even greedier, vainer and more ridiculous. We can often see that their achievements are exaggerated, self-serving and illusory, above all dedicated to boosting self-esteem (Harmon-Jones et al., 1997). But we appear to need our Maslovian high achievers in order to deceive ourselves: *some* make it to the finishing line *and beyond* in glory; *some* have discovered meaning, we tell ourselves. The lowly remainder can admire them from afar and regret that we didn't try hard enough. Existence itself is fine, it is teeming with possibility – *we* are to blame for not making the most of it.

We face constant choices – between committed relationships or loneliness; remaining in a troubled relationship and seeking to repair it (couple counselling is a form of institutionalised hope), or risking stigma and insecurity; a secure but boring job or an insecure but potentially interesting vocation as an artist; staying in one place or moving to another city, rural area, or country. Existentialists regard these as exciting, bread and butter matters of courage-invitation and meaning-creation. Many of us stay in bad situations out of fear of change, while others frequently hop from one situation to another. The shibboleths of courage and wisdom are dangled before us: show you have what it takes. Choose from stoicism, heroic overcoming, outstanding altruism. Freedom is much vaunted, yet what we are free to choose between is relatively limited. Compromise is probably a more accurate concept for what actions we take and our greatest freedoms fall somewhere between childhood or adolescence and old age. Most of us do what most people do in a bovine fashion, with small gestures of quasi-individuality. Cohen and Taylor (1992) charted just such features of everyday life and its 'nightmare of repetition', in their classic sociology text, towards the end of which they confess to a certain 'nihilism and pessimism more profound than the mild scepticism' they began with, and they note 'the fundamental pessimism of the sociological tradition' (p. 233).

There is no linear, rational, happy life to be had – this is all mere pro-life propaganda. As he surveys his wife's latest moody reaction, he realises that no psychological contortion will ever satisfy her, and in feminist times he will always get the blame anyway. As she weighs up her options in the labyrinth of stoical commitment and heroic new starts in late patriarchy, she senses deep down that she can only really jump from frying pans to fires. Perhaps marriage has truly become 'the creepy cult of monogamy'. Whatever the magazines, self-help gurus and therapists say (and they certainly produce an unending stream of knowing injunctions and clichés), there is no mythical happier life out there. The often hinted at, magical therapeutic turning point rarely, if ever, materialises. Only compromise and hope exist. Sometimes it gets so bad that each unknown to the other occasionally wishes for passive delivery by death (of self or other), but meanwhile the show must go on, so go on it does, the charade of working-at-it, of rising-above-it-all or of sticking by that ultimatum. No linear rational happy life is hidden nearby, to hand or around the next decisional corner. Drift or apparent decisiveness, nothing changes anything. While not 'great literature', Chad Kultgen's (2013) *The Average American Marriage* charts the path from irresponsible early adulthood to ostensibly committed nuclear family status, with the male cheating, being caught, the divorce lawyer rubbing his hands together, the couple counsellor setting the clichéd therapeutic exercises and then a flaccid reconciliation taking place. The book ends with the narrator wishing he could tell his young son honestly what misery is in store for him when he grows up.

The everyday life of the depressive realist

Insofar as we can meaningfully say there is a personality type recognisable as a DR, who does not need to be persuaded about the tenets of DR and cannot be talked out of this worldview, how does he live his life? Suicide has always been an option, and always is the reserve option if things ever get too bad. I suspect that more perceptive people in their early to mid-teens glimpse the true nature of this life and its choices – conformity, suicide, utopian fantasy, metaphysical quest – and behave accordingly. But the young DR who passes through his early crisis of negative revelation must find a way of living and sustaining at least minimal morale. An infinitesimal minority of DRs may be lucky enough to be born into rich families or to have outstanding and marketable talent, and the arts clearly attract many of this minority. It would be interesting to know how many isolated intelligent DRs, especially those born into working class families without ready access to comforting books and friends, become 'clinically depressed' or resort to suicide, or drug-oriented, alcoholic and homeless or chaotic lives and outsider identities, in their loneliness. He or she is perhaps in a position analogous to that of the isolated young gay person many decades ago, with no ready community to join. Do we know if there is any relationship between DR and high intelligence? Perry (2014), on the basis of some available research, believes so, and some of those working with highly gifted young people concur (Webb, undated). To put this differently, is depressive realist awareness likely to be more common among certain middle class and/or unusually cerebral people? This may be so, the greater sense of material luxury, economic entitlement and educational opportunity bringing these DRs closer to reinforced depressive

152   The lifespan, everyday life and depressive realism

realism than the working class individual who must perhaps think primarily about economic hardship and survival.

Traditionally many DRs – if it is legitimate to anoint them as such retrospectively – would enter academia if possible, or perhaps dour forms of ecclesiastical work or the funeral industry. The university today is less friendly to odd personality types, however clever, thus closing some doors to economic survival. The street-smart DR may have decided early on in a 'cynical' estimate that certain careers simply pay the rent while leaving enough of one's time and mind free to battle dark thoughts, whether these careers be in dishwashing, games stores, offices, libraries or the financial sector. Some DRs are quite naturally at home in the mental health professions where their depressive sensibility can undergird empathy for others who suffer. Of more concern are those DRs who, sensing that life has no meaning or purpose other than everyday survival and pleasure, turn to crime or other predatory behaviours. However, I suspect most DRs are overthinking, scrupulous types with some natural tendency not to harm others.

Like all other life forms, the DR must seek Goldilocks conditions or adapt to challenging contexts. In his case, this means on the one hand avoiding situations that require too much inauthentic behaviour (call centres) and, on the other, circumstances that are not so low in stimulation that acute depression is triggered (museum attendant). The difficulty in finding a good occupational fit and tolerable life niche may be so challenging that many DRs become clinical depressives, living a pharmaceutically-supported life with or without periods of unemployment and psychotherapy. In periods of social crisis like war or mass unemployment DRs like everyone else may be swept into corresponding adaptive mental states. DRs in fortuitously affluent circumstances may be able to indulge themselves in esoteric DR-related reading habits, musical and other creative enthusiasms and decadent lifestyles that serve as defensive sublimation. Often enough the wily and resourceful subtype of DR may find effective social camouflage as a philosopher, poet, publisher or comedian. Always, however, the pull of nihilism and apathy threatens to undermine any career progression and stability: after all, what's the point of all that effort just to get to ugly and infirm old age, death and nothingness?

We do not know whether a majority of the DR minority live alone. The probability, given the DR's typically male identity, tendency towards poor career prospects, pessimistic personality, probable inability to compromise and antinatalist sensibilities, is that he may well live alone. Alternatively, the need for sex and companionship, and his thoughtful nature, may place him in relationships with likeminded women or men. One thinks of Cioran (living frugally) and Beckett (as a successful writer) both in long-term relationships, both ending their days in a nursing home. Schopenhauer regularly visited brothels (while having an independent income), Larkin (working as a librarian) in uncommitted and overlapping relationships. And, if they count as DRs, Kierkegaard (on an independent income) living alone, Kafka being a frequent brothel-visitor as well as having relationships with many women, Sartre and de Beauvoir in an unconventional long-term relationship and Foucault in multiple gay encounters. U.G. Krishnamurti lived a nomadic, or modestly globetrotting lifestyle, celibate after his 'mystical' experience. A friend of Beckett, the Dutch abstract painter Bram van Velde, lived alone all his life, in poverty, a monastic, artistic existence. But as for anonymous DRs, we do not know how they live and die, or indeed how many could be identified as DRs. The American cartoonist Harvey Pekar depicted and led a partly anonymous (and partly highly publicised) DR lifestyle, working as a hospital file clerk and married three times.

It seems reasonable to suppose that the majority of consciously depressive realists simply live lives of quiet desperation – simultaneously cursing the alarm clock that signals another day to get through, yet painfully aware of inching towards dreaded oblivion – alternating with moments of distracting humour, pleasure and short-term purposes, while realistically awaiting the grim reaper's mercy.

Note

1 Stone (1979) shows that mortality rates have historically limited the depth of intimate relationships as people intuited the psychological pain that would ensue when the early oxytocin-fuelled years of impassioned bonding passed.

References

Abela, J.R., Auerbach, R. & Seligman, M. (2008) Dispositional pessimism across the lifespan. In K. Dobson & D. Dozois (eds). *Risk Factors in Depression.* San Diego, CA: Academic Press.

Améry, J. (1994) *On Aging: Revolt and Resignation.* Bloomington, IN: Indiana University Press.

Auster, P. (2013) *Winter Journal.* New York: Faber & Faber.

Becker, E. (1973) *The Denial of Death.* New York: Free Press.

Benatar, D. (2006) *Better Never to Have Been: The Harm of Coming into Existence.* Oxford: Oxford University Press.

Bourdieu, P. (1999) *The Weight of the World: Social Suffering in Contemporary Society.* London: Polity.

Cavan, R.S. (1932) The wish never to have been born. *American Journal of Sociology,* 37 (4), 547–549.

Cioran, E.M. (1971) *Drawn and Quartered.* New York: Arcade.

Cioran, E.M. (1998) *The Trouble with Being Born.* New York: Arcade.

Cohen, S. & Taylor, L. (1992) *Escape Attempts: The Theory and Practice of Resistance to Everyday Life (2nd edn.).* London: Routledge.

De Grey, A. (2008) *Ending Aging.* London: St Martins Press.

Diamond, R. (2004) *The Irritable Male Syndrome.* London: Rodale.

Dumm, T. (2008) *Loneliness as a Way of Life.* Cambridge, MA: Harvard University Press.

Erber, J. & Szuchman, L.T. (2014) *Great Myths of Aging.* Chichester: Wiley.

Evans, A.D., Xu, F. & Kang, L. (2011) When all signs point to you: Lies told in the face of evidence. *Developmental Psychology,* 47 (1), 39–49.

Feltham, C. (2015) *Keeping Ourselves in the Dark.* Charleston, WV: Nine-Banded Books.

Griffiths, M. (2007) Death understanding and fear of death in young children. *Journal of Clinical Child Psychology & Psychiatry,* 12 (4), 525–535.

154 The lifespan, everyday life and depressive realism

Hakim, K. (2012) *Honey Money: Why Attractiveness Is the Key to Success*. London: Penguin.

Harmon-Jones, E., Simon, L., Greenberg, L., Pyszczynski, T., Solomon, S. & McGregor, H. (1997) Terror management theory and self-esteem: Evidence that increased self-esteem reduces mortality salience effects. *Journal of Personality and Social Psychology*, 72 (1), 24–36.

Jacques, E. (1965) Death and the mid-life crisis. *International Journal of Psychoanalysis*, 46 (4), 502–512.

Kagan, J. & Snidman, N. (2004) *The Long Shadow of Temperament*. Cambridge, MA: Belknap.

Kellehear, A. (2014) *The Inner Life of the Dying Person*. New York: Columbia University Press.

Kessler, R.C., Amminger, G.P., Aguilar-Gaxiola, S., Alonso, J., Lee, S. & Ustun, T.B. (2008) Age of onset of mental disorders: A review of recent literature. *Current Opinion in Psychiatry*, 20 (4), 359–364.

Kitzinger, C. (2006) *Birth Crisis*. London: Taylor & Francis.

Kultgen, C. (2013) *The Average American Marriage*. New York: Harper Perennial.

Lang, F.R., Weiss, D., Gerstorf, D. & Wagner, G.G. (2013) Forecasting life satisfaction across adulthood: Benefits of seeing a dark future? *Psychology and Aging*, 28 (1), 249–261.

Leboyer, F. (2011) *Birth without Violence*. London: Pinter & Martin.

Loke, S.C., Abdullah, S.S., Chai, S.T., Hamid, T.A. & Yahaya, N. (2011) Assessment of factors influencing morale in the elderly. *PLoS One*, (6), e16490. Doi: 10.1371/journal. pone.0016490.

Mikulincer, M., Florian, V. & Hirschberger, G. (2004) The terror of death and the quest for love: An existential perspective on close relationships. In J. Greenberg, S.L. Koole & T. Pyszczynski (eds). *Handbook of Experimental Existential Psychology*, pp 287–304. New York: Guilford.

Nagy, M.H. (1959) The child's view of death. In H. Feifel (ed). *The Meaning of Death*, pp 79–98. New York: McGraw-Hill.

Nuland, S. (1997) *How We Die*. London: Vintage.

Odent, M. (2006) The long-term effects of how we are born. *Journal of Prenatal and Perinatal Psychology and Health*, 21 (2), 179.

O'Reilly, M. (2014) 'Am I dying?': The honest answer. *TED Talk*, 27 September.

Overall, C. (2003) *Aging, Death, and Human Longevity*. University of California Press.

Peper, J.S., Koolschijn, C.M.P. & Crone, E.A. (2013) Development of risk-taking: Contributions from adolescent testosterone and the orbito-frontal cortex. *Cognitive Neuroscience*, 25 (12), 2141–2150.

Perry, S. (2014) *Every Cradle Is a Grave: Rethinking the Ethics of Birth and Suicide*. Charleston, WV: Nine-Banded Books.

Roach, M. (2004) *Stiff: The Curious Lives of Human Cadavers*. London: Penguin.

Roisin, J., Ryan, P. & Aherne, C. (2011) The paradox of ageing: Why do older people look so happy when they have nothing to look forward to? In P. Ryan & B.J. Coughlan (eds). *Ageing and Older Adult Mental Health: Issues and Implications for Practice*, pp 230–247. Hove: Routledge.

Schopenhauer, A. (1851/1970) *Essays and Aphorisms*. London: Penguin.

Senior, J. (2010) All joy and no fun: Why parents hate parenting. *New York News and Politics*, 4 July.

Shields, D. (2011) *The Thing about Life Is That One Day You'll Be Dead*. London: Penguin.

Shiner, M., Scourfield, J., Fincham, B. & Langer, S. (2009) When things fall apart: Gender and suicide across the life course. *Social Science and Medicine*, 69 (5), 738–746.

Small, H. (2010) *The Long Life*. Oxford: Oxford University Press.

Smith, D.L. (2007) *Why We Lie: The Evolutionary Roots of Deception and the Unconscious Mind.* New York: St Martins Press.

Solomon, S., Greenberg, J. & Pyszczynski, T. (2015) *The Worm at the Core: On the Role of Death in Life.* New York: Allen Lane.

Stone, L. (1979) *The Family, Sex and Marriage in England 1500–1800.* London: Penguin.

Tallis, R. (2015) *The Black Mirror: Fragments of an Obituary for Life.* London: Atlantic.

Tantam, D. (2014) *Emotional Well-Being and Mental Health: A Guide for Counsellors and Psychotherapists.* London: Sage.

Taubman Ben-Ari, O. (2004) Risk taking in adolescence: "To be or not to be" is not really the question. In J. Greenberg, S.L. Koole & T. Pyszczynski (eds). *Handbook of Experimental Existential Psychology*, pp 104–121. New York: Guilford.

Taylor, M. & Taylor, L. (2003) *What Are Children For?* London: Short Books.

Terkel, S. (1972) *Working: People Talk about What They Do All Day and How They Feel about It.* New York: The New Press.

Trivers, R. (2011) *Deceit and Self-Deception.* London: Allen Lane.

Webb, J. (undated) *Existential Depression in Gifted Individuals.* Reno, NV: Davidson Institute. Davidsongifted.org/db/Articles_id_10269.aspx

Chapter 10

Arguments against depressive realism

In this chapter I want to look concisely at typical objections to depressive realism before going on to examine in a little more depth the arguments put forward by some positive psychologists and rational optimists. We might say it is in the nature of universal assumptions that anyone could potentially be wholly or partly right or wrong. Let me follow the terms suggested by Burton (2014) when he speaks of dogmatic and undogmatic global scepticism. In the first case, one is certain in DR terms that everything is painfully meaningless, or empty; in the second case, one does not know whether everything is meaningless or empty and does not know if one can *ever* really know. In my own experience, an affective swing is in operation between dogmatic and undogmatic DR. Sometimes I seem able to be certain about (or unable to doubt) my own knowledge that all reality is quite depressing. But at other times I am uncertain, even to the point of suspecting I may be wholly incorrect. I would not, however, call this global agnosticism but rather a bipolar dogmatism-nondogmatism.

1 One of the strongest or most directly troubling objections to DR comes from within the person of the DR himself. In the opening scene of the 1980 Woody Allen film *Stardust Memories* the lead character Sandy Bates is sitting in a train carriage full of miserable-looking people, all shot in black and white, while at the next platform another train contains a scene of people looking happy and having a party. Bates's face says it all. One is on the wrong train, one has backed the wrong horse and the fault is in oneself. If only one could change trains, as Bates tries to do, but it is too late. In this view, DR is perhaps a piece of bad luck of genetic or familial origin. The 'objective world' is not at all depressing but somehow you are permanently fixed with the certainty that it is. A painful cleft stick to the genuine DR, this will be taken by the opposition as evidence that depressive realism is wrongheaded and can be overturned by changing trains – change your mind, make an effort, stop feeling sorry for yourself, take a course in logic, see a therapist and so on. We can insert here Turgenev's character Bazarov from *Fathers and Sons*, who as a young man has a kind of psychological swagger of cynical nihilism that he relinquishes only as he falls in love just

before dying. In this scenario the DR position is always personalised and pathologised. The DR himself may feel the counter-DR accusation nagging at him, adding all the more to the sense that life is bitterly conflicted.

2   Depressive realism is a serious misreading or misrepresentation of reality. This statement then has to be unpacked as referring to unintentional intellectual error; subjectively shaded, self-pitying, semi-wilful bias; or determined, totalising bleakness-projection. DRs are commonly condemned as irresponsible, basking in subjective gloom and lacking evidence for their claims. Critics of DR are often unclear about whether they consider it to result from epistemological error or clinical psychopathology. From where does such misanthropy and nihilism arise? Are some born sour, or do they have terrible experiences with parents that turn them against living a satisfied life? Or are they poor reasoners who infer far too much negativity from scant evidence of local conditions, transient and personal bad luck? Thacker (2015), for example, suggests that pessimists suffer from spite: 'for the pessimist, the smallest detail can be an indication of a metaphysical futility so vast and funereal that it eclipses pessimism itself' (p. 22).

Are eminent DRs, the common targets of the wrath of Tallis (1992, 2011), wilful and perverse twisters of abundant evidence of post-Enlightenment progress, or stupid in spite of their vaunted reputations? By some accounts, it is simply perverse not to recognise that you are better off than human beings in former times that died young or after years of terrible toothache and disease, or than your contemporaries who are disabled, homeless and lonely. (Recall Ralph McTell's, 1969 guilt-tripping song *Streets of London*). An associated response to DR was brought home to me when a female colleague read some DR material: she thought it was a joke, she just could not believe that anyone actually felt this way about life, it just didn't seem *possible!*

3   Then there are those who regard all DR-oriented discourse as akin to evil, or as a form of misanthropy or 'antihumanism'. Such criticism can come from different political angles. Zubrin (2012), for example, cites the supposedly Darwinian-inspired eugenics movement of the late 19th and early 20th century as evidence of antihumanism. In his trawl of whom he outs as antihumanists he includes Rachel Carson for opposing DDT, 'defending malaria' and unleashing 'a crusading liberal mass movement'; Aldous Huxley for supposedly pro-eugenics sympathies; Thomas Malthus, Paul Ehrlich and other population control prophets for ushering in a 'doom cult'; the 'anti-nuclear [power] crusade'; the green movement; and pushers of climate change hysteria for 'quenching humanity's fire'. In this view, we live in a world of plenty where science and invention are our liberators and allies, and doomsayers and controllers are antihuman. Zubrin is an ardent, right-wing advocate for space exploration among other projects. His plea that 'the world needs more children' (p. 25) flatly confronts the antinatalist aspirations of many DRs. But there are many left-wing opponents of DR too, most of them identifying loss of enchantment – due to industry,

158 Arguments against depressive realism

late capitalism, technical-rational patriarchy, left-hemispherical dominance and so on – as responsible for our malaise and seeing the cure in infinite multiculturalism, the green movement, feminism and animist spirituality. Bookchin (1995) offers a leftist critique of his take on antihumanism that is also critical of many of the movements mentioned above. For this loose but largely left-wing collective, DR in its hopelessness is pure and dreadful 'cynicism' or, in more romantic terms, a symptom of the need for change. Yet another group of opponents is found in the Catholic subgroup that labels as 'subhumanism' the trend towards atheism, nihilism and dangerously relaxed, sinful morality that is regarded as inevitably accompanying atheism. Opposing the encroachment of scientific values ('scientocracy') and the environmental movement, the religiously backed human exceptionalist Wesley J. Smith (2014) argues that human beings are being downgraded and cast as villains to be vastly reduced in number.

4 Another way of reading DR as an error is through the lens of Buddhism. Depressive realism and Buddhism have in common the perception that all life is suffering, based on illusion. But Buddhism claims to have a path out of suffering and illusion, and it might interpret DR as falling prey to the classic dualist illusion that pushes it into pessimism. Buddhists may say that both pessimism and optimism are illusions that are overcome only by staying on the mindful path beyond all illusions. The DR, of course, (usually) sees nothing ahead other than further illusions and suffering. Enter another quadrilemma: (1) DR is wrong; (2) Buddhism is wrong; (3) both are right; (4) both are wrong. (This is to avoid the objections that both right and wrong are meaningless, and language is severely limited.) Entrenched DRs know they are right, and Buddhist devotees must presume they are right since Buddha himself (we are told) found the way out and embodied nondualism. DRs observe that although this way beyond all illusions sounds good, one has only to speak to or observe a few Buddhists to discover that their transcendental aspirations have not been met, and probably never will be. The second coming of Jesus never comes, and mass enlightenment never comes; only hope endures. So the DR feels justified in his gloomy assessment, while the Buddhist carries on confidently expecting liberation, or claiming not to expect anything other than what is. All, or almost all (allowing for unknown private enlightenment experiences) human beings remain mired in illusion until they die. And DRs, while sometimes hankering for the promised transcendence, have to live on with gloom-as-usual. Even the realisation that your own imagined death and the future demise of the species are figments of your painful imagination (they are inevitable but their reality will not be as you imagine them) does not burst your illusions.

5 DR is a pose. Anyone stricken with authentic, radical depression either kills himself or is clinically depressed. There are seeming ultra-DRs who turn out to have adopted the dark mantle to impress others. As Wilson puts it, 'we must question the glib irony that rules our culture, for it too,

like addiction to happiness, divorces one from the real. The ironic poseur, despite all his edginess and neurosis, is entirely detached, unmoored, a denier of blood and guts . . . a pseudocool faker' (2008, p. 134). Some romantic poets and contemporary singers have excelled at this attitude, which sometimes hangs midway between pose, accidental early death and suicidality. Lana Del Rey, for example, singing *Born to Die* or *Summertime Sadness* is a key, enigmatic player today, whose music is referred to as Hollywood sadcore. Captain Kirk's 1989 morbid-bravado track *Your Son is Dead* takes the form of a death message: 'Your son is dead; he died of an overdose', and the word overdose is repeated against monotonous techno-drug-and-dance music. Bowring (2008) speaks of the fetishisation of depression popular among so-called Emos who dress in melodramatic black. Such 'affectation of melancholy' Bowring links with 17th and 18th century styles in which genius was sometimes associated with melancholy. It is not credible, runs this argument, for DRs to articulate dark views while engaging in normal social activities and defending themselves against threats, for example, in the case of the deeply pessimistic DR whose hypochondriasis nonetheless takes him to many medical appointments (see Woody Allen's *Hannah and Her Sisters*).

6   It's a new day, the sun is shining, birds are singing, maybe you're on holiday, or in love, your football team has won or your baby has just been born. Life is good. How could you possibly call this depressing? Perhaps there is some progress with a cure for cancer, or an end to yesterday's war. There is undeniable pleasure in the present and hope for the future. The DR view seems perverse to optimists and hedonists. You're a young professional with a decent income, a great apartment and much to look forward to. But even if you're young and unemployed you can hope for a job soon, a lottery win or a parent dying and leaving you money. You sit in The Bank pub in Dublin, admiring the opulent décor and the piano player, bathing in the happy buzz; you look out on the dense city of London from the Shard or the Sky Garden at 20 Fenchurch Street and marvel at man's architectural achievements; or your heart soars and you cry as you listen to an orchestra playing *The Lark Ascending* or Black's *Wonderful Life*, or perhaps you melt at the conclusive joy in the film *Dirty Dancing*. Sloterdijk suggests that 'much stupid nihilistic prattle' ignores the preciousness of life, which can be celebrated (1987, p. 203). But transient exalted states pass, and as in drug aftermaths, you may feel even lower later, especially when your best years are clearly past. Good events are usually outnumbered and put in the shade by bad events (Baumeister et al., 2001). This is probably why we are always looking for another buzz or restlessly creating another goal for ourselves.

7   We have an interesting philosophical conundrum: on the one hand is the Zapffean view that the accidental evolution of consciousness gave rise to a *surplus* of consciousness that has been our downfall, obliging us to want more from life than is available, to ask questions that have no answers and

160 Arguments against depressive realism

to suffer accordingly, a view that resonates with the Buddhist concept of *samsara*. We would do best to fully realise the tragedy that has occurred and abort the exercise of existence altogether. On the other hand, consider the biocentric view that human consciousness does not lie towards the causal end point of a linear cosmic and evolutionary process but itself 'creates' the universe (Lanza & Berman, 2010). In other words, until consciousness arose matter was undifferentiated; it takes consciousness to perceive, understand, analyse, appreciate and 'organise' the universe, which is otherwise a merely unreflective, dumb mass of phenomena. The universe cannot appreciate itself without human consciousness exploring, measuring, labelling and marvelling at its components. Human consciousness has determined that the universe is 13.7 billion years old, for example (if in anthropocentric terms), and continuing human science determines the details of the character of the universe. Anyone pondering this apparently irreconcilable polarity of views must also realise the short-term mundane irrelevance and ridiculousness of these questions insofar as the vast majority of lives are lived in indifference to big questions.

8 DR has nothing obvious to recommend it to the living as a guide to life, as a motivating force. It is an energy-sapping outlook. It may have some place in the ranks of ethical evaluations, for example, in deciding whether or to what extent it is justified that future lives are consciously created, or what to think about and how to approach death. But one cannot expect to see a DR worldview spawning dynamic and charismatic business leaders and educators, upbeat entertainers or moral exemplars. Interestingly, this in itself suggests a somewhat entropic herd mentality requiring the energetic input of outstandingly negentropic individuals. If the majority were naturally, consistently and highly energised, no significant DR tendencies or need for counter-DR arguments or exemplars would be necessary. We might then think of DR or some aspect of it as resulting simply from observation of the uninspired masses: most of us are probably energised by a particularly beautiful sunny day, yet few can sustain such a high. The success of Hollywood stems perhaps from the combination of consistent southern Californian sunshine and concentrated wealth beaming out entertainment to the rest of the sorry world. This also chimes with the wisdom cliché of 'better to light a candle than curse the darkness', and the remedy might be to call for the building of more Tinseltowns, more Las Vegases or Dubais. The more feelgood distractions we come up with, the better.

9 Curiously, it may be the case that DR themes are more widely acknowledged than supposed, but tacitly suppressed or edited for the sake of decency. In other words, while some sections of the population agree that ours is a sad, meaningless, tragic and godless existence in an absurd society, with death always in the wings, voicing this view is officially considered morbid and in bad taste. 'Man to man' it may sometimes be discussed over drinks but never shared with the children and probably very rarely with 'the ladies' (see

Fessler & Navarrete, 2005 for pertinent views on gender, age and culture). In other words, like many other topics (e.g. sexual fantasy, hatred and envy, politically incorrect views, terrifying phobias) it is taboo, or relatively taboo. It is not a fit subject for polite dinner party conversation, or indeed for most other social forums. I suspect that even in the average course of psychotherapy, dwelling on such themes would relatively quickly be pathologised and interpreted as neurotic death anxiety or projected disappointment, and/or subtly suppressed in favour of more upbeat, growthful, goal-oriented and certainly more *personal* topics. After all, DR themes are dark and most of us cannot bear very much of them.

If I am right about this (it is true in my experience, but I can cite no 'evidence'), then we have a cognitive dissonance scenario. I don't believe life has any meaning, I think death ends everything and I observe that most of our prized institutions are built on illusions, lies and denial; yet at the same time I need the comfort of a partner, a family and a job. I know well enough to keep my mouth shut most of the time but occasionally a dark thought slips out and I can see the disgust or fear my comments bring and my risk of losing my social supports. Consequently, I try to forget or suppress my own observations, or I raise them only in specific circumstances, perhaps with a trusted mate or even on an online forum (e.g. www.knust.com/planetzapffe; www.ligotti.net; http://antinatalism.blogspot; http://theviewfromhell.blogspot); and in the latter case I feel as if what I am doing is akin to watching and taking part in pornography.

10 The existentialists want to stress freedom. We are not significantly determined; we always have large areas of choice that require only courage to put into effect, after we sweep aside our disingenuous bad faith. Simone de Beauvoir (1986) argued as others have that nihilists are disappointed with the meaninglessness of life but incorrect to consider personal decisions futile. She accepted her freedom and used it to fight for feminist and socialist causes, as Sartre also fought temporarily for communism. Where (passive) nihilists usually look to the futility on the horizon, existentialists like these look at what calls to be done proximally to raise levels of justice. They dismiss (or don't even consider) arguments about evolutionary determinants and historical cycles, and create their own reality which they assume to be uncontaminated by the past. They have no truck with any myth of *akrasia* but act heroically to challenge historical baggage and social conventions. They are interpersonally and politically engaged, not detached and pessimistic in the manner of Schopenhauer, so that Yalom (2007), for example, can by fictional device place a contemporary Schopenhauerian character in an (essentially romantic) existentialist therapy group where he learns the values of therapeutic American intimacy, warmth and emotion. Frankl too stresses existential meaningfulness in the context of human atrocity, as if everyone is free to construct positive meaning or an end-goal – by mental self-trickery – that magically trumps any amount of

162 Arguments against depressive realism

terrible suffering. Freedom and meaning are existentialism's two central pillars of hope.

11 The DR argument turns on the observation that in the long run we are all dead. Not only individuals but the human species, all species, all life, the entire universe will be dead. As far as we know or can probabilistically assess, this is all true and it does seem depressing. But its long-run perspective overlooks the obvious counterpoint that in the immediate term we are alive, and life may be considered precious, if freakishly so. Most of us have eighty or so years of life and the universe has billions of years to run, and in that long interim almost anything can happen, including discoveries that extend the lifespan, postpone death indefinitely, and cancel out premature theories of cosmic annihilation. But even within the long-run endgame scenario our lives in the present may be considered fascinating and timeless. The closer one can live to the natural present, 'the now', the freer one is from dread of death (or indeed dread of and desire for *anything*). DRs mistakenly jump to the conclusion, the final curtain, instead of gracefully playing and relishing their parts on the stage of life. The DR rebuttal must be the observation that very few genuinely live in the present, most only aspiring to do so or mistaking trendy 'mindfulness' for the real thing; and that *mass presence* is a highly unlikely scenario without which, however, anthropathology will probably take us into an ever more unnatural and unhappy future. Enjoyment of the present doesn't pay attention to underlying and long-term climate problems, for example.

12 The untrue is true, the impossible is possible. Here is the argument that, for example, a personal God created the universe and watches over it; and biological beings like ourselves who die don't really die, or are counter-biologically resurrected after dying. Perhaps their cremated, rotted or mangled bodies are magically reassembled, or some form of extra-corporeal existence is meant. From a mainstream DR position the above assertions are contemptuous of the obvious facts of an accidental universe and subsequent biological imperative. But we can't deny that billions of human beings do believe them. From a theistic perspective the entire DR argument is built on sinful, arrogant errors. We are God's children and by believing in him we ensure ourselves an eternal life, since those are the terms he allegedly presents to us. We are eternal beings who simply shapeshift at the point of our earthly death, entering another existence, becoming another atomic arrangement or incarnation; those with the correct faith see this now and live accordingly. But this is either desperate fantasy or ignorance of the laws of biology.

13 It is not a strong argument but some hold that DRs are simply curmudgeonly personalities who project their own pessimism and negativity outwards. Whether we think here of Paul of Tarsus or Ebenezer Scrooge, or the recalcitrant patient in Kleinian therapy, the picture is of someone who has hardened his heart against the good news of Jesus, the innate goodness of his fellow human beings or trust in the therapeutic process and who

Arguments against depressive realism 163

stands in need of a change of heart. The scales do not, however, fall from the eyes of very many DRs, who therefore go on poisoning life for everyone else. 'Comprehensive pessimists' in Scruton's (2010) terms are 'unattractive characters'.

In an alternative view, the curmudgeonly DR like *Curb Your Enthusiasm's* Larry David (also evident in *Boris Yellnikoff*, in Woody Allen's film *Whatever Works*) is humoured and even found hilarious for the very outlandishness of his anti-social negativity. In the later film *Magic in the Moonlight* Allen's central character Stanley is a curmudgeonly rationalist who works as a very successful magician and loves to expose charlatans. On encountering a psychic, Sophie, he becomes entranced by her powers and briefly becomes a happy believer, before her psychic powers are shown to be fake, but nevertheless they fall in love and all is well. The film has multiple layers of illusion – the medium of film itself; spiritualism; the lure of money; the certitude of DR scepticism; love; the 'happy ever after' theme; and the question is posed whether illusion is really so bad if it brings comfort to the distressed.

Charlie Brown, the young loser of the *Peanuts* cartoon, is also well loved, especially for an American. Such characters are portrayed as oddities, yet they may each be regarded as an unrepressed everyman or universal inner curmudgeon (Ralkowski, 2012). Support for one aspect of DR (chronic ennui) as normative is given by Irvine (2000) who sees in much contemporary (post-World War 2) popular culture evidence of a common boredom that is beyond mere reaction to events.

Another good example here is the 2013 film *Saving Mr Banks* which tells the backstory of *Mary Poppins*. The author of the original text, Mrs P.L. Travers (born Helen Goff), is shown objecting to Walt Disney's upbeat adaptation of her script, but gradually becoming softened by her own memories and insights and by Disney's own persistent, intimate interventions and his creative team's sincerity. The film depicts Disney as an honourable seeker of truth and creative genius who wishes only to bring heart- warming entertainment to children. Travers is depicted as an uptight upper class Englishwoman who has repressed painful memories of her much loved but alcoholic father who died at the age of 43 in Australia. *Mary Poppins* as Disneyfied, and *Saving Mr Banks*, serve to recommend not only Disney himself, and Walt Disney Pictures, but Hollywood and American redemptive fantasy. But this treatment seriously distorts Travers' real story in the process. As one of Disney's team says pointedly to Travers' objections regarding accuracy, 'Does it matter?' Travers' own life had many tragic and fascinating elements but in *Saving Mr Banks* she is reduced to a somewhat curmudgeonly, in-need-of-therapy and ultimately impotent resistor of the Disney magic. Tellingly, Travers' father – probably a fun-loving if irresponsible London banker – pronounces the line 'This life is just an illusion', and it may be that the Disney message is 'therefore, choose a happy illusion rather than a sad one'.

164 Arguments against depressive realism

14 I have argued elsewhere for DRs to be treated respectfully as a minority group, but this can easily be turned upside down. There are probably many who are not hostile to the DR argument and its proponents but are completely unaware of them, and even if they become aware will remain indifferent. In this scenario DR is an irrelevant minority issue. People who are very high achievers and/or who embody joy are probably a minority, too, but they fascinate us and are sometimes studied as models to be emulated, whether in Maslovian or NLP terms. But people who suffer from mental illnesses may at best be pitied and more often avoided. Even in terms of health policies and expenditure we know that mental ill health is unjustifiably under-funded. This probably results from the association between physical illness, urgency of treatment and risk of death, which has always eclipsed the needs of the mentally ill. It is probably also related to the uncertain aetiologies surrounding mental illness and accompanying uncertainty of best treatments. Although some evidence-based psychological therapies are now recommended, far less credibility is given to them than to physical treatments for, say, cancer. Given that major depression is debilitating and painful for sufferers, and increasingly common, we might expect it to be far better addressed than it is. Depressive realism, as an attitude and worldview that may be accompanied by dysthymia, cannot command even the sympathy and resources for severe depression, nor do its representatives consider it a mental illness, so we should hardly expect DR to be noticed or acted upon in any way. Arguably, the majority are neither filled with joy nor significantly *consciously* distressed but coping sufficiently well most of the time, and are at worst sometimes fed up or bored. But few ask whether these fleeting emotional negative states correspond to an outer negative objective reality.

15 Some may readily concede that life contains negatives but believe these to be specific in kind, or specific to certain times. The DR worldview can be regarded as far too much of a generalisation unsupported by convincing aetiologies, evidence and suggested remedies. So, for example, the evidence-oriented will demand statistics on exactly what proportion of old people can be considered poor and regard themselves subjectively as depressed. Similarly, people can be asked for subjective estimates of how glad they are to have been born, and how satisfied they are with their lives, before allowing any discussion that existence might be worse than non-existence. Evidence can be cited that a majority have religious beliefs, that these beliefs safeguard them against unhappiness and boost their health. Statistics can always be found to support a case that CBT has worked, that social policies have effected improved morale, greater equality or whatever. Examples of dramatic life changes can be correlated with neuroplasticity. Blanket DR can be challenged for not lending itself to precise analysis or improvement, so intent is it on stressing perennial negativity. DR in its turn spurns statistics; after all, the *average* person necessarily has 1.9999 legs even if the median person has 2! The *realism wars* ultimately become absurd.

16 Some may fully concede to the DR view but rather than thereafter falling into lamentation adopt a position of what we might call maximum alleviation. In other words, let's agree that life is horrible when one really thinks about it, but since it is, and we are not about to kill ourselves, let us make things as bearable as possible. Here we have a strategy of conscious Zapffean distraction and, in a sense, of isolation. We need no anchoring, no illusions, accepting the meaninglessness of life. But human psychological frailty is acknowledged. In order to live with a DR worldview, we need as much hedonistic distraction as we can muster: humour, sex, drugs, the arts, sport, travel, whatever it takes to pass our time with minimal distress. How practical this is in the long-term it is hard to say. Addiction to hard drugs is an example of how this painkilling strategy can backfire when an understandable desire for relief is gradually converted into an added dimension of suffering. Perhaps drug addiction is no worse than nor different from religion, commencing with harmless pain relief but becoming all-encompassing, counterproductive and sometimes deadly.

17 Finally, we must reckon with the postmodern view that all such theories or ideologies are relative to each other, that DR is simply one of many, with no claim to be the true one or any truer than others. It is the complementary pole of optimistic realism, let us say. It stands at best alongside dozens or hundreds of other systems of thought. But this is a tough one to accept, and I imagine very few religious believers, for example, actually subscribe to it. Into this argument let us also place the view that depressive realism, like other worldviews and ideologies, is seen by many (particularly sceptical working class and/or anti-academic critics) as just another piece of faddish jargon. DR is a passing intellectual amusement that few will notice and none will recall in a few years from now. Or it will re-emerge renamed as another intellectual fashion, as with all other social and intellectual fads.

Ignorance of depressive realism

In a brief online discussion I had with a senior Jungian writer, he reacted with visceral distaste when I used the term depressive realism – 'what sort of jargon is *that*?' Putting aside the irony that someone from the jargon-saturated Jungian pot tradition would call my DR kettle black, this anecdote demonstrates the mundane difficulty of keeping step with intellectual fashions. We could certainly consign DR to a long and weary tradition of black-and-white ephemeral narratives, and there is no reason why anyone should feel compelled to be interested in it. Passive ignorance is nothing, however, compared with actively and hostilely ignoring something.

It is perhaps a small step forward for a publisher to show interest in or take a mild business risk with DR, but another matter to realise the depth of indifference among academic and professional peers. Quite understandably, it does not readily fit into existing psychology, psychotherapy or philosophy programmes of study. Even among theoretical advances rejecting majority traditions, DR is not very welcome. Critical psychologists want to reject standard apolitical psychology for something regarded as progressive, Lacanian analysts push a linguistic agenda and so on. These developments within their micro-worlds are welcomed by loyalists as logical and good for business. Existential therapy partly thrives on a programme of disillusionment but is seen as 'sexy' or meaningful compared with the nihilistic, unusable gloom of DR. Who wants to attend a workshop on DR? I know from various efforts to interest others that this apparent indifference is a stubborn reality. DR is irrelevant, pathological or eccentric: this is probably the dominant current perception. I have argued that DRs are an oppressed minority and that this represents a mental health injustice, but very few really believe this. DR has enough elements perceived as right-wing for it to be consigned by most academics to mockery or oblivion.

Positive psychology versus depressive realism

I have already raised many questions about positive psychology and its claims. Here I want to summarise how these impact on DR, and vice versa. The positive psychologists want to acknowledge but erode or overturn DR. For example, Fox (2013) is not a positive psychologist as such but her analysis of the neurology of pessimism and optimism, including a consideration of genetic factors, drifts inevitably towards an emphasis on the 'malleable mind' and 'new techniques to reshape our brains'. Building on the epigenetics story, Fox explains how the brain afflicted by post-traumatic stress disorder, for example, can be retrained by the techniques of cognitive bias modification to be pulled back from constant negative reinforcement towards happier outcomes. This happy-ever-after compulsion continues in the book's last chapter, with strong endorsement of CBT and the positive psychology movement. Oddly, CBT is described as 'the classic talking therapy' which is allegedly 'a highly complex psychological intervention' (p. 176). Most psychotherapists and counsellors would probably describe psychoanalysis not CBT as the classic talking therapy, and very few would deem CBT 'highly complex' but, rather, a somewhat simplistic and mechanistic approach compared with its subtler therapeutic siblings. *Flourishing*, that flavour-of-the-month upbeat concept, caps off Fox's positive ending with rave reviews of the work of Seligman, Csikszentmihalyi, Fredrickson and others, uncritically citing the latter's magical three-to-one recipe of positives to negatives (discussed earlier here, in Chapter 5). For such writers there has to be a positive outcome or happy ending. There can be no allowance that a DR view might be correct (or at least might stubbornly hold for DRs themselves), and evidence will always be created to show that the mis-wired *unhappitants of the earth* can yet be saved by a concoction of meditation and therapeutic techniques (Kabat-Zinn, 2013).

It is telling that positive psychology's two main ingredients are psychological and spiritual. First, this gives a boost to the otherwise sorry discipline of psychology that has relatively little of substance to offer the world. But secondly, it

Arguments against depressive realism

conscripts a ragbag of shallow versions of mindfulness, compassion, forgiveness, meaning, purpose, virtue and Dalai Lama-endorsed banalities so that millions can feel comforted by a combination of pseudo-scientific and thin religious concepts and practices. Illusions of the valiant psyche proliferate. In the 1960s humanistic psychology and the human growth movement offered similar illusions of infinite self-fulfilment which did not materialise. Seligman's (2003) popular positive psychology text, a New York Times bestseller, has as its sales-hook subtitle 'Using the new positive psychology to realize your potential for deep fulfilment'. It's *new*, *positive*, it shows you how to realise something as nebulous as your potential so that you will be forever positively transformed, and authentically so. It is difficult to write more hyperbolically and emptily unless you are an advertising copywriter. In the ways of positive psychology, we are spared from the need to look at insoluble socio-political problems and the underlying tragic phenomena of existence itself, which Seligman shrugs off as the 'rotten-to-the-core dogma' that dominated early 20th century psychology.

Raymond Tallis and the case against pessimism

In several texts (but primarily Tallis, 1997, 2011) Raymond Tallis has outlined his position as a certain kind of pro-humanist, pro-Enlightenment opponent of contemporary pessimism, and much of poststructuralist philosophy. He is an avowed atheist, and as much of his career was in geriatric medicine and neurology, he is certainly a scientist. His care for old people and his defence of the NHS speak of compassion and integrity. But he is a fierce adversary of those from the last two centuries, and especially today, who show 'hostility towards the idea of a human being as a conscious, rational agent and of human society as susceptible to progressive improvement' (1997, p. xiv). Tallis is right to counter complaints against modern alienation by citing our better physical conditions today, superior health care and longer lifespan: who besides John Zerzan and Derrick Jensen would want to reject all that and return to pre-industrial, indeed pre-agricultural conditions of periodic hunger, awful toothache, high infant mortality rates and terrible diseases? Tallis is probably right to anticipate further scientific improvements and long-term betterment generally. But in order to justify this he seems to feel a need to lash out at critics of modern life, at evolutionary psychology, neurophilosophy and at doubts about the reality of the self and free will.

What we find in Tallis is forceful argument that has the appearance of selfless logic. We all tend to present our arguments in this way – 'it's not *me* saying this, it's where all the evidence points'. If you have catholic taste in music you can find yourself emotionally swayed by different musical genres; to some, but a lesser extent this is also true of intellectual argument. One can succumb even to one's enemies' arguments when they are eloquent enough. So I can be swayed by Tallis's apparently consistent rationality, his passion for progress, his dislike of 'theorrhoea' and his mocking exposure of apparent nonsense (I am with him on his anti-Freudianism, his severe doubts about alternative medicines and his angry attack on Lacan, for example). I start to doubt myself and feel foolish. I cannot help wondering if Tallis isn't simply a more clear-sighted, honest and better man than me. Yet I suspect that Tallis must have witnessed a great deal of suffering when working with older people; as a scientist he must realise that evolutionary and historical time – and as yet unknown but not unknowable factors – fully account for our distinctiveness from animals. Indeed, he agrees with Dawkins that natural selection is futile, a 'mindless, pointless process' (2011, p. 211). Tallis denies, however, that we humans today are mindless and pointless, because we have transcended natural selection, we are 'sighted watchmakers', purposeful creatures, not Dawkins' blind watchmakers.

Perhaps I should concede:'yes, one can see the world in Tallis's way'. Yet why do we see the world so differently? Is one reasonable and clear-sighted while the other is irrational and prone to a distorted vision of life? The scientific, rational optimist here seems to have a sounder grasp of reality than those he quarrels with. I readily agree with Tallis's dismissive take on postmodern writers, on the right-wing agenda to dismantle the NHS and on God; we have some common enemies. But Tallis is an Oxford-educated polymath who enjoys a flamboyant dress sense (presumably an extravert), and he has great intellectual self-confidence. He doesn't feel self-deceived (ever?), appears to possess strong willpower (in all areas?) and in these ways demonstrates that he differs significantly from many others, certainly from me. Does Tallis believe he has created his own optimistic worldview or has he always seen the world in this way? Perhaps he does have superior insights in some domains (presumably in geriatric medicine) but not necessarily in all those areas of knowledge he tackles. He appears to believe that those who take a pessimistic view are largely very foolish, for example, to judge by his scathing criticism of John Gray (Tallis, 2011, pp. 1–13), whose popular works he refers to as self-indulgent and lacking merit. What is missing from Tallis's polemical account, I think, is any interest in what I have called personality-dependent realism (PDR), or the basis for each of us to hold our phenomenologically unique view. Why, for example, would a philosopher of science like Alex Rosenberg (2012) defend 'scientism' and material determinism while Tallis (2011), a scientist who philosophises, attacks such views? The vast majority of us know no better, we do not understand the technicalities of science or the nuances of philosophical logic. Most of us do not know how to adjudicate in such epistemological battles. We tend to rely on what Kahneman (2012) calls the 'affect heuristic', or what makes emotional sense to us, even when we disguise our emotional entrenchment as reasoned.

Meanwhile, whatever it is that informs my PDR and my affect heuristic, and pushes me towards a depressive realist view, is strongly at odds with whatever informs Tallis's PDR and affect heuristic. In other words, I claim that none of us is a blank slate awaiting timely rational fusion with ideas before we take up an intellectual position. Likewise for John Gray, Alex Rosenberg, me and you. Something inside us has already leaned in a certain direction, let us say, and this can only be our combination of phylogenetic and uniquely ontogenetic factors. This is not necessarily contentious, but it raises the problem of how and when the conscious rational agent comes into the picture. Is there a certain age at which we reach rational maturity, when we abandon any existing prejudices, identify and make good any areas of ignorance? Can we all expertly scan all relevant knowledge, evaluate it and constantly adjust our views towards greater veridicality? This cannot be true, since if it were, we would all be in constant epistemological synch. What accounts for our differences in judgement? Can we trace the origins of our differences or are they mysterious? If Tallis is correct in his evaluation and the pessimists are incorrect, how did this impasse occur? Is Tallis's rational agency superior or his commitment to a morality of optimism nobler, and if so where did those qualities come from? Tallis rejects the principles of genetic and neurological determinism but his 'conscious rational agent' is surely not *sui generis*. He doesn't say whether he believes his intellectual enemies are poor logicians, misinformed, under the sway of addictive ideologies, determined by their own PDR or simply stupid. But we must assume that he sees himself as free of those epistemological faults, again without explanation for his happy superiority.

'Contempt for the idea of progress has always been attractive to some because it justifies sparing yourself the effort of trying to leave the world a better place than you found it' (Tallis, 2011, p. 4). The compassionate doctor who brings you relief, and sometimes cure, trumps the contemptuous misanthrope who only shrugs his shoulders or brings you down, we might say. We might cleverly philosophise about medical research being ultimately little more than thanatophobia, and we might say that the surest way of reducing human suffering lies in having fewer children, for example, and there is some truth in this. But in proximal personal terms, no-one in pain is likely to turn away a doctor who can relieve that pain, and rely instead on cathartically cursing the universe. Tallis's medical work has brought relief but his polemics seem an indulgence. Old men arguing with each other in print and adding tomes of ideation to an already information-overloaded existence probably don't contribute much of any use to the world. A little rapprochement might be had in areas of agreed nonsense and agreed need for a compassionate agenda.

The 1984 award-winning film *Threads* depicted the result of a nuclear war between the United States and the USSR. In the harrowing detail of its aftermath we see the effects of fall-out in Sheffield, England, and are told of the uselessness of medical intervention. There are no medical supplies of any kind in this post-apocalyptic scenario ruled by martial law. Disease, starvation and violence are the norms. Thankfully, the historical nuclear threat has passed and most (but not all) of us assume it now to be an impossible or at least highly unlikely scenario. But we can deploy it as the psychological back-drop for the mentality of the extreme DR. In spite of periodic regional conventional wars, nobody expects anything of nuclear magnitude and horror, but the threat is always a little closer in some minds. Even without such threats, for

170 Arguments against depressive realism

some on the worst end of the DR spectrum, life *feels like* this; one can feel as if everyday life is a grim wasteland; the post-Biblical 'Fall' has already happened. Presumably for Tallis, everyday life is not and has never been like this. He has had many advantages in life, including a driven father and superior education, robust self-confidence, middle-class affluence and a freakishly powerful intellect not possessed by 99% of the population. Only if Tallis had the abrupt misfortune of Job might he know experientially what the depressive feels like. (In fact Tallis had an experience of deep despair at 15, from which it seems philosophy rescued him; and in his 60s appears to have turned darkly towards reminiscence, in Tallis, 2015.) 'Poverty of spirit and meanness of mind' (Tallis, 1992, p. 409) do not perversely invent themselves in otherwise tranquil lives, any more than Tallis woke from a nightmare and decided to invent robust and rational optimism.

Western debates about pessimism versus optimism also betray their cultural origins and bias. We seem to see matters helplessly in dualistic terms – reason and emotion, progress and stasis, Enlightenment and counter-Enlightenment and so on – and we are hooked on a belief in substance underpinning such terms. Tallis has nothing to say about Eastern philosophy, especially about Buddhist views on the impermanence (*anicca*) and unsatisfactoriness of life, or suffering (*dukkha*) and realisation of the non-self (*anatta*). Vipassana meditation has precisely these as the three marks of existence the meditator sees through. This tradition is much older than the pessimism Tallis attacks and has none of the arrogant dismissiveness he sees in modern pessimism. Yet, as I have argued in Chapter 2, many original religious insights were probably based on stark awareness of these existential truths.

A sad indictment of contemporary socio-political discourse is its interminably egocentric and patriarchal quality of intellectual jousting. We all know best. Exactly like tribalistic epistemologists, we think alone, work out arguments solipsistically and often we savagely 'shoot down' our opponents. Rarely is the alternative explored, which would be dialogue with the genuine intention of understanding differences and approaching consilience (Bohm, 2004). Concepts like *hope* have about them an aura of the sacred: who could possibly argue against hope? Well, DeCasseres could, speaking of 'the old whore Hope' and its 'paid pimps' (2014, p. 21) and the much more courteous Jiddu Krishnamurti often spoke of the insignificance and illusory operation of hope. A mature dialogue almost certainly has to build in an examination of life with the possibility of little or no hope, evil-countering arguments like those of Matuštík (2008) notwithstanding. We can easily agree on almost any hypothesis within a scenario of vague and infinite hope; it is true that looking ahead for thousands of years and assuming an inevitable degree of progress, we are bound to concede to modest optimism. But we should also look at the scenario wherein things can not only get better but worse, and on a timescale that may not be either indefinite or millennially generous but seriously foreshortened (Scheffler, 2013).

References

Baumeister, R.F., Bratslavsky, E., Finkenauer, C. & Vohs, K.D. (2001) Bad is stronger than good. *Review of General Psychology*, 5 (4), 323–370.

Bohm, D. (2004) *On Dialogue*. London: Routledge.

Bookchin, M. (1995) *Re-Enchanting Humanity: A Defence of the Human Spirit against Antihumanism, Misanthropy, Mysticism and Primitivism*. London: Continuum.

Bowring, J. (2008) *A Field Guide to Melancholy*. Harpenden: Oldcastle Books.

Burton, D. (2014) *Emptiness Appraised: A Critical Study of Nāgārjuna's Philosophy*. London: Routledge.

De Beauvoir, S. (1986) *The Ethics of Ambiguity*. New York: Citadel.

DeCasseres, B. (2014) *Anathema! Litanies of Negation*. Baltimore, MA: Underworld.

Fessler, D.T. & Navarrete, C.D. (2005) The effects of age on death disgust: Challenges to terror management theory. *Evolutionary Psychology*, 3, 279–296.

Fox, E. (2013) *Rainy Brain, Sunny Brain: The New Science of Optimism and Pessimism*. London: Arrow.

Irvine, I. (2000) *The Angel of Luxury and Sadness (Vol. 1): The Emergence of the Normative*. www.greatunpublished.com

Kabat-Zinn, J. (2013) *Full Catastrophe Living (Rev. edn.)*. London: Piatkus.

Kahneman, D. (2012*) Thinking, Fast and Slow*. New York: Penguin.

Lanza, R. & Berman, B. (2010) *Biocentrism*. Dallas, TX: Ben Bella.

Matuštík, M.B. (2008) *Radical Evil and the Scarcity of Hope: Postsecular Meditations*. Bloomington, IN: Indiana University Press.

Ralkowski, M. (2012) Deep inside you know you're him. In M. Ralkowski (ed). *Curb Your Enthusiasm and Philosophy*. Chicago, IL: Open Court.

Rosenberg, A. (2012) *The Atheist's Guide to Reality: Enjoying Life without Illusions*. New York: Norton.

Scheffler, S. (2013) *Death and the Afterlife*. New York: Oxford University Press.

Scruton, R. (2010) *The Uses of Pessimism and the Dangers of False Hope*. London: Atlantic.

Seligman, M.E.P. (2003) *Authentic Happiness: Using the New Positive Psychology to Realize Your Potential for Lasting Fulfilment*. London: Nicholas Brealey.

Sloetrdijk, P. (1987) *Critique of Cynical Reason*. Minneapolis, MN: University of Minnesota Press.

Smith, W.J. (2014) *The War on Humans*. Seattle, WA: Discovery Institute.

Tallis, R. (1992) *Enemies of Hope: A Critique of Contemporary Pessimism*. Houndmills: Macmillan.

Tallis, R. (1997) *Enemies of Hope: A Critique of Contemporary Pessimism, Irrationalism, Antihumanism, and the Counter-Enlightenment*. Houndmills: Palgrave Macmillan.

Tallis, R. (2011) *Aping Mankind: Neuromania, Darwinitis and the Misrepresentation of Mankind*. Durham: Acumen.

Tallis, R. (2015) *The Black Mirror: Fragments of an Obituary for Life*. London: Atlantic.

Thacker, E. (2015) *Cosmic Pessimism*. Minneapolis, MN: Univocal.

Wilson, E.G. (2008) *Against Happiness*. New York: Sarah Crichton.

Yalom, I. (2007) *The Schopenhauer Cure*. New York: Harper Perennial.

Zubrin, R. (2012) *Merchants of Despair: Radical Environmentalists, Criminal Pseudo-Scientists, and the Fatal Cult of Antihumanism*. New York: New Atlantis.

Chapter 11

Lessons and possibilities for individuals and society

This bulk of chapter is in a sense a disingenuous appeal to the utility of depressive realism. We might say that it breaks off sharply from the dark radical honesty of Ligottian DR and offers instead a somewhat fainthearted, wistful version of DR. Anyone who agrees that humanity faces massive and systemic problems must choose between some form of personal exit, radical solution, passive nihilism or piecemeal reforms. For the anarcho-primitivist Zerzan there is no possible compromise: only a return to pre-agricultural conditions will do (or *would do*, since it can never happen). Implied in and sometimes practised from the depths of DR analysis are radical honesty, silence, stillness, antinatalism and *hikikomori*. These are all in themselves fairly harmless behaviours presenting no significant threat to mainstream society, yet most of them are taken as signs of rudeness or mental illness and, were they to spread, they would in fact become a threat to functional society. They are refusals to conform. Ligottian nihilism (Ligotti himself eschews the term nihilism) has an integrity that offers no solutions. Going further than Zerzan, Ligotti and his ilk identify existence itself as malignantly useless and make it plain that nothing can ameliorate it. Benatar, Ligotti and Zapffe must all be considered advocates of voluntary human extinction (if not also Beckett, Cioran and others). By contrast Zerzan calls for action and implies a romantic vision of (a reduced number of) good humans returning home to the bountiful earth. Zerzan has an agenda; Ligotti does not, unless it is passively wishful antinatalism and annihilation.

The most extreme form of DR leans into nihilism, and nihilism's most extreme manifestations are transgressions, suicide, murder and terror. If DR is a mindset that compulsively sees through untruths and illusions, it cannot help but challenge the social contract. The demise of moralistic religion has already led to a profound relaxation of sexual mores, so that few are any longer shocked by and many welcome casual sex, adultery and easy divorce, homosexuality, kink and indeed any kind of individualistic expression that intends no harm to others. Psychotherapy is no longer considered stigmatic, infants and old people are often put into care institutions rather than cared for by families and mass tattooing is normalised. The waves of liberation movements from the 1960s have disenchanted us vis à vis 'old-fashioned' restrictive values but have also forced upon us new codes of thought and behaviour, summarised in the clumsy phrase 'political correctness' and the morality of uncritical respect for difference and diversity. (I lazily say 'us' and, of course, this is not true for everyone.) We have learned from psychoanalysis that whatever is repressed will emerge projectively later or elsewhere, often in even more virulent forms. Hence, in recent years we have seen waves of paedophile scandals, celebrated cannibal cases, serial murders, school shootings and mass murders committed by terrorists. The naivety of the nice peaceful Left runs parallel to the converse unbridled greed of bankers, internet criminals, drug dealers and pornographers. These trends might scotch any illusions of linear and easy progress but they do not. If Dostoevsky's over-quoted 'If God does not exist, everything is permitted' is true, nihilism steps into the vacuum, and subsequently moralistic alarm steps in to call for a return to traditional values. But Pandora's box will not close, every demon is now loose.

DR fits into this scenario thus – suicide becomes more thinkable, as does antinatalism; if I feel oppressed by monogamous boredom, I can get divorced or cheat. If relationships are too difficult and restrictive I can avoid them altogether *mendokusai*-style. If I have no sense of belonging or hope, no real job satisfaction and no commitment, I may be seduced by fundamentalist religion or cults within them that permit me to fantasise martyrdom and get high on killing in their name (group psychopathy escapes clinical diagnosis). If I feel affronted by mass immigration in my homeland, I can kill dozens of young people in protest. If there are no real rules from above (and there are not), then why should I not make as much money as possible in order to gain as much distracting pleasure as I can? I am not at all suggesting that most people with a depressive outlook commit heinous crimes (they are too apathetic to) or that they necessarily act selfishly, but the link between disenchanted DR and amoral nihilism is there. Rosenberg (2012) argues that we are guided by a form of 'nice nihilism' that suits our species as fitness-maximising, but he doesn't convincingly reckon with the many anchors that resist nihilism, or with the gravity of cryptic nastiness. It is arguable that the widespread social denial of DR conceals an epidemic of unrecognised nihilism that expresses itself variously in the behaviours I have just outlined: denying our terrifying underlying nothingness, we desperately resort to every kind of morality, immorality and amorality available. We cloak our actions in the religious, political and human rights rhetoric of the right and the left. But we know not what we do – these are all futile terror management actions.

On the face of it, society has little use for depressive realism or indeed for any significant negativity, and certainly spurns any Zerzanian agenda. DR's evangelism of bleakness is not wanted here. However, a large literature exists arguing for the benefits of learning from negativity and failure (e.g. Ormerod, 2005; Feltham, 2012). Much of this is disingenuous platitude and management hype, but some of it concentrates on the importance of failure in specific, critical circumstances. Insurance professionals must calculate risk, and accident investigators have to learn from black boxes the causes of airplane crashes. In

174 Lessons and possibilities for individuals and society

more philosophical terms, Scruton (2010) draws on Schopenhauer's concept of 'unscrupulous optimism' to identify its various fallacies. He argues that we should 'look with irony and detachment on our *actual condition*' (p. 232, italics added), instead of succumbing to the lure of Leftist 'junk thought.' Everyone claims to learn something from negatives and DR 'prophets' are those most likely to speak the unpopular negatives.

Changes to clinical definitions

In light of psychologists' discussions of DR and the possibility of agreeing, how-ever perversely, that people with chronic mild depression may see the world more accurately than those who are non-depressed, perhaps we should use this as the basis for a bid for redefining at least one area of depression. Most psychiat-ric and psychological texts agree that no single 'cause' of dysthymia can be iden-tified but equally, few if any include a discussion of DR, that is, of the possibility that the inherent sadness of life itself is a (or *the*) cause of dysthymia. Neither do such texts ever include discussions on the possibility that illusion-based, non-depressed 'normality' is a kind of mass sickness of misperception or deceit. Much of psychoanalysis and humanistic therapy theory, for example, states or implies that so-called average or normal functioning is either somewhat pathological or suboptimal. However, therapeutic texts invariably point towards therapy as lifting the individual to less self-deceived or greater self-actualised functioning.

The argument that normal adaptive functioning in a sick world can itself be considered pathological is an old one (Fromm, 2001), but not well made and still not taken seriously. We do not have a good antonym for depression, *mania* being one of the closest but not conveying any sense that a widespread upbeat mentality might be considered pathological; or that *delusional denial* of wide-spread malaise might be taken as something less jocular than Pollyannaism. It is inconceivable that the psychotherapy and psychiatric professionals themselves would in effect declare, 'the baseline for human beings including ourselves is one of pathological self-deceit and illusion serving to keep us functional in an insane world'. Nor are we likely to read the corollary of this – 'individuals experienc-ing chronic dysthymia who hold a negative worldview and who are known as depressive realists, might be considered less pathological and more mentally healthy than others'. What we could push for, however, is some recognition that in the markedly non-consensual field of mental health aetiologies and defini-tions we include reference to DR as a legitimate argument and a candidate for a reasonable explanation for depression. Some forms of severe depression, too, can be reformulated as pathologised DR that has tipped over into a level of despair that renders the individual altogether dysfunctional. This is not to romanticise horrible depression or to fetishise those with severely distressing mental illnesses but rather to put forward an alternative aetiological theory. Along with this, we might experiment with the unashamed expression of DR views in ways that could be measured for improved mood. In other words, would respected and non-stigmatic depressive publications or forums relieve some DRs of some of their dysthymia?

Education and depressive realism

Cioran puts it this way: 'The only thing the young should be taught is that there is virtually nothing to be hoped for from life. One dreams of a *Catalogue of Disappointments* which would include all the disillusionments reserved for each and every one of us, to be posted in the schools' (1998, p. 127). Such a darkly tongue-in-cheek proposition is on the face of it highly unlikely ever to be realised. However, consider that in most schools there are lessons in religion or social studies in which the pre-scientific beliefs of at least one or two major religions are studied. In faith schools a single religion will be taught, and all religions have some sort of philosophical anthropology to propound, with a view of the good life and an implied view of the bad life, of sin and evil. Some schools already teach atheism, or at least give it some airspace (Shaha, 2014), and the pedagogic use of the theme of suffering has been commended (Jardine et al., 2014). French schools teach philosophy quite extensively, and it makes a small appearance in some UK schools, with a tame version of critical thinking slowly increasing. And in many subjects there are topics implicitly related to DR themes, for example, in literature (tragic and absurd themes), biology (purposeless evolution, clinical death and animal decomposition after death), history (wars, the Holocaust) and sociology (crime, mental illness, injustice). Where philosophy is taught, existentialism may receive some attention, and DR is an implicit component of that.

The difficult question is at what age, if at all, should young people be exposed to the bleakest of DR ideas? Would it be possible for a school curriculum to include lessons on atheism, suicide, on death as final, on the infirmities of old age, on the bleaker realities of the employment market and workplace, the absurdities of society, antinatalism and so on? One can imagine a carefully edited version of these topics being taught to older teenagers perhaps, but educational authorities and parents' committees, not to mention governors of faith schools, would baulk at the notion of young children having to take in such bleak and pessimistic ideas. Once, drunk at a party, I held forth to several 19-year-olds on DR themes – dismal career prospects, unhappy marriage and divorce statistics, death, having death-bound children who will go on to repeat the same pattern – and the feedback I received the following day did not commend my chances of being invited back. Most of the young are made for hedonism and hope. But a significant, hidden minority may develop depressive and suicidal symptoms precisely because these topics remain taboo (Jackson & Peterson, 2004; Bloom, 2015).

Higher education remains the embodiment of aspirations towards scientific progress, the scholarly pursuit of truth and justice and the centre of professional training. Universities' identity and mission are no longer clear, however.

176 Lessons and possibilities for individuals and society

Standards have almost certainly dropped, and universities are often torn between serving capitalist masters on the one hand and uncritical left-wing ideologies on the other. They are not places where one can expect to find much passionate enquiry about existential matters, nor do they entertain the full spectrum of possible debates about the ethics of reproduction, suicide, death, atheism and associated DR themes. A radical DR analysis of the university system sees it as in entropic decline, propped up by an awkward mix of tradition and conveyor belt accommodation to prevailing economic pressures. Some academics struggle to retain and re-stimulate radical, critical thinking and personally engaging topics, but their efforts are against the grain and likely doomed to failure (Davies & Barnett, 2015). It is worrying to speculate that academic entropy combined with commercial and governmental over-control, and erosion of free speech, may be responsible for our current, dumbed-down intellectual culture. Or it may be that intellectual traditions going back to Chinese learning centres over 4,000 years ago, Plato's Academy and medieval universities have run their course and are succumbing to the wider death throes of civilizational decay.

Depressive realists as a minority group

Let us reinforce the point that DR and clinical depression are not identical. Among famous depressives, for example, we can list John Adams, Woody Allen, David Bohm, Winston Churchill, Calvin Coolidge, Charles Darwin, Charles Dickens, Isaac Newton, Abraham Lincoln, John D. Rockefeller, Leo Tolstoy, Queen Victoria and Boris Yeltsin. In other words, not only creative people but some famous high-functioning scientists and political leaders. Depression does not condemn all its sufferers to awful, marginal lives but neither do all depressives hold DR views or are remembered as dysfunctional pessimists. Jeffreys (2010) pointedly contrasts the cynical DR of Houellebecq, for example, with the warmer and wiser writings of David Foster Wallace, whose clinical depression resulted in his suicide. One of the problems of coming out as a depressive realist is that, given our species' propensity to labelling and judging, the DR becomes permanently fixed as a DR, with no allowance for nuance, mood or *volte-face*. The phrase 'pessimist of the intellect, optimist of the will', attributed to Gramsci, shows at least some wiggle room. Any DR's pessimism, and DRs in their differences, may vary in shade with mood, topic, period, weather, place, age, personality, gender, culture and so on. 'Humankind cannot bear very much reality', T.S. Eliot averred. This is clearly true of the majority from a DR perspective but it also has a message for the DR minority. Very few of us can bear constant awareness of life's negatives – especially old age and death – and it is likely that the majority of the minority who are diehard DRs have to seek some periodic denial or solace and distraction. We might say 'I am a depressive realist when I cognitively weigh up the human condition, my personal prospects and that of the species' but at other times 'I am a regular biologically and socially functioning human being with cryptic or fluctuating DR views'. The chronic

Lessons and possibilities for individuals and society 177

clinical depressive might be considered not to fit this latter description and see only bleakness in life, but even he or she probably has some periods of remission.

However, I think we must acknowledge the significance of DR having a minority and stigmatic status before unravelling its position further (Case & Williams, 2004; Williams et al., 2005). It has long had an honoured place in the arts and humanities, and latterly in popular culture (in pop music, soap operas, etc.), although not explicitly as DR but as entertainment and fascination by misery and drama. Depression has recently, in the form of *mental health concern* and *difference,* been included in appeals to equal opportunities in the workplace. But given late capitalism's stress on occupational enthusiasm, dynamism, 'passion for innovation', excellence and other hyperboles, DRs will clearly never be frontrunners at most job interviews. ('Why do you want this job?' 'Well, one has to do something to make money in this fucked-up world' – this is not going to turn out well.) Nor can anyone legislate for positive discrimination in terms of social popularity.

Occasionally, I have asked large groups of students who among them are interested in considering questions about the meaning of life and death, and the human condition generally, and the muted response usually highlights the minority character of such interests even before focusing specifically on the darkest side. It has to be noted that most of my students have been mature women studying counselling, and/or in people in their 20s and that students generally have some sense of optimistic investment, of anchoring in Zapffe's terms, which will predetermine an aversion to strongly dismal topics. At first consideration, then, it seems that DR has nowhere much to go beyond being a minority personality type and interest group. But this need not stop its promotion and we might remember that size and popularity do not necessarily equal truth or significance. Plutocrats, Jews, gays and geniuses are all minority groups but hardly insignificant or lacking influence. Atheists have been a tiny minority for millennia but their ranks are now swelling. A small international franchise of 'death cafés' started in 2011 to host non-stigmatic meetings for like-minded people wishing to discuss death and human finiteness frankly. Non-religious, non-profit and unceremonious arrangements for disposal of corpses are increasing. If World Health Organisation figures are to be believed, depression is becoming the number one health concern worldwide, and dysthymic DRs might well be part of those decidedly non-minority figures. Another suggestive lead here is the view that introverts, highly gifted and 'highly sensitive people' find the majority assumptive view of optimism difficult and suffer from discrimination in the job market; and may be considered to be in the disadvantaged position women in the West were in fifty years ago (Cain, 2013).

Depressive realism has something in common with anti-psychiatry, queer theory and affect studies insofar as it offers an intellectual challenge and an implicit call for certain injustices to be addressed. The anti-psychiatry of R.D. Laing and his colleagues was a historical movement of the 1960s and 1970s. It continues and has morphed into different forms of anti-medicalisation, anti-pharmaceutical protest and mental health services users' rights but is somewhat limited in its scope. Queer theory, gaining traction from gay liberation, has attempted to subvert accepted views of sexuality and social attitudes but is largely confined to liberal academia. Affect studies too, while critiquing the privatisation of depression and other mood states, is mainly an academic experiment rather than a significant social movement (Cvetkovich, 2012). Depressive realism may simply go the way of all minority eccentric groups, DRs enjoying their own sublimation efforts but never seeing their ripples affecting mainstream society significantly.

Depressive realism and radical honesty

It could be said that the roots and reinforcers of DR lie in DRs being primarily truth-tellers who have found that their truth is not welcome anywhere. If you think life sucks and/or your fellow human beings' lives are a lie, and you tell them, you're quite likely to be rejected, ridiculed and isolated. DR is in this sense a retreat into self-defensive defeat. It may be that some, like Diogenes or Jesus (assuming the stories about them are true) were heroic truth-tellers willing to take the consequences of what they said and did. These consequences are, of course, rejection, poverty, sickness, homelessness, loneliness, death. Tallis (1997), however, has not been slow to deride contemporary pessimistic critics of progress who nevertheless enjoy affluent living conditions. I observe that an otherwise sensitive friend (steeped in religious, socialist and feminist thought) has no qualms about asking me, 'Are you still writing all that negative stuff?' while I politely but dishonestly refrain from asking her 'Are you still involved in all that religious mumbo jumbo?'

Blanton's (2005) concept of radical honesty has grown from a Gestalt therapy technique into a novel (or, rather, re-heated) concept, into an incipient social and political movement. If its premises are to be believed, you could express your bleakest DR sentiments and not be rejected for expressing them. Others may not necessarily agree with you, but they will respect the honesty of your views. The licence to speak freely, nominally espoused across the West, is promised by the radical honesty community as an actuality. Lying is considered the main root of all human suffering. It is possible that such communities exist, where truth-telling is genuinely welcome (encounter groups, Quaker meetings?), but it is clearly countercultural. You would probably not survive for long in this civilisation, economically at least, if you always spoke the truth. Jim Carrey's honest lawyer character in the film *Liar Liar* would not survive economically in the real world. It even goes somewhat against the grain in a book of this kind to speak naively about 'the truth'. Opposites of truth – besides fantasy, exaggeration, euphemism – are blatant lies and evasive language; and academic discourse, or sophistry, is an example of the latter. It is ironic that Foucault, who espoused parrhesia but spoke and wrote tortuous and obfuscatory 'theorrhoea', has been the darling of so many academics in the social sciences and humanities.

Drunks, small children and people with Down Syndrome may innocently tell the truth, but the majority of us learn to speak and act in evasive, polite and obtuse ways. 'How are you?' 'I'm fine, thanks,' is the best known example of quotidian evasiveness.

But there may be a form of emotional honesty that the DR has sacrificed in his own life. If the pessimist is one who has suffered severe disappointments and learned to disguise his hurt by outward cynicism and rejection of social norms, then by sheer habit he can become paradoxically resistant to emotional truth and its nuances. What should be his natural ally, unwavering radical honesty, is then avoided. Perhaps he feels that his gloomy views will be automatically rejected by a so-called radical honesty that appears to have its home in a community of humanistic psychologists, themselves surely reflexive supporters of touchy-feely American optimism. One can see these dynamics at work in Yalom's (2006) novel built on dismantling Schopenhauerian ideas. By trusting others, you come to swap your cynical, intellectual isolation for emotional intimacy, and all shall be well. Well, we also have to ask whether the radical honesty community isn't wrapped up in its own fantasy of utopia-by-truthfulness, just as the 1960s hippies' love and peace fantasy died a relatively quick death. All such movements, like early Christianity, start well but cannot persist. The DR-oriented Old Testament is swept aside by the New Testament, which in turn reverts entropically, every time, to perennial human corruption. A DR view of communal radical honesty pictures many drowning people in an ocean of lies, bobbing up and shouting out truths, before drowning. It's worth trying, but it fails to reckon with the gravity of irreversible anthropathology.

Antinatalism and population control

Philosophical and philanthropic antinatalists are sincerely opposed to procreation on the grounds that it knowingly creates and protracts human suffering. They take this responsibility upon themselves by not having children but also advocate it for others, indeed for all other humans. Insofar as it is a voluntary antinatalist agenda it poses no problem for the vast majority who are likely to be dismissive. Clearly, there have been and are groups of humans whose tribal loyalties inspire them to want to see the end of life by genocide for specific other groups, and possibly there are small groups of militant misanthropes who would annihilate the entire human race if they could find the means to do so and could evade government surveillance agencies. We can also see the tendency of small population decreases in some countries, probably on an instinctive basis, guided by a hedonistic or pragmatic philosophy. The majority will probably ignore antinatalist calls and adopt antinatalism only in the event of extensive catastrophes such as chronic famine.

In what realistic ways then can antinatalism have any social policy impact? Demographic changes in recent years have included smaller families and later conceptions; but also in vitro fertilisation, large families among some immigrant groups and extended life spans. Overall, world population continues to rise and many see no inherent problem with this. On the other hand, climate change scenarios drive some predictions of greater disease epidemics and famine, and regional wars show no sign of ending soon. Also, possibilities of spontaneous new epidemics or terrorist generated bacteriological warfare are always present. Genetic research already drives some caution or antinatalism in cases of high risk of genetically transmitted problems. The Chinese government's policy of single-child families, instigated in 1979, has given way to some relaxation in the light of experience. Various eugenic theories and experiments, heavily touted in Britain and elsewhere in the 1930s (Overy, 2010) fuelled extreme Nazi anti-Semitism. In principle we already have the basis for some planned population control but little taste for it in operation. An explicitly antinatalist policy probably has no realistic traction but antinatalism might yet have some influence. A few publicised cases of voluntary sterilisations and principled declarations of personal antinatalism may create some sense that it is not necessarily a weird or selfish course of action, and others may follow. The voice of those gay people who do not wish to have children may have some influence (Edelman, 2004), and increasing secularisation may undermine religious procreative injunctions. As for the finality of such decisions, we may note that the previously unimaginable mass tattooing trend of the early 21st century has shown the willingness of many to embark on irreversible life decisions, and child-free lives could become one of these.

We wait to see if the projected worldwide increase in clinical depression by 2030 will also have an impact on any antinatalist trend. Some may come to instinctively or unconsciously feel distaste for procreation and its responsibilities (recall the Japanese *mendokusai* phenomenon). On the other hand, DR antinatalists may at least unconsciously come to realise that their beliefs are probably not widely shared, and this indifference or hostility to their case would confirm their negative minority status and reinforce a sense of hopelessness. In the currently unlikely event that antinatalism makes a significant impact, we could experience a sea change in perceptions about the quality of life and expectations of the future.

End of life care

So-called end of life matters usually refer to the very last months and weeks of the terminally ill. But here I want to suggest that retirement marks the first significant end stage. This is because most of us cease working, experience a fall in income and concomitant reduction in status and quality of life. Money cannot buy us an escape from death or ageing but it can ward off many of the adversities of ageing. Money can buy holidays and other pleasures that take the edge off suffering. In our retirement years, around 10, 15 or 20 of them, say, we have oceans of time in which to think, something that our working lives minimise. Superannuated academics may enjoy and profit from extensive thinking but it is doubtful if most people do. Given the poverty of distractions available to the

Lessons and possibilities for individuals and society   181

majority, the witnessing of others' deaths and unavoidable reminders of one's own impending demise, it becomes a question of acute ethical significance to ask why only the richest minority can afford to buy themselves the most psychologically as well as physically comfortable end of life. This is about healthcare and companionship, dignity and ease. Currently, we appear to condone the view that people get the (often sad, lonely and penurious) old age they deserve. The elderly with fine homes and holidays, access to the best entertainment and education, presumably deserve what they have, and those who failed to save or invest do not deserve better than the boring and depressing end they have. The older we get, the less we are able to rely on the Zapffean defences of isolation and distraction, and only the most religiously devoted can continue to hold out hope of salvational anchoring. Distraction becomes the key issue. Old age, and compassion for the old, should oblige us to re-examine the balance of capitalist and socialist priorities: can we really allow the wealthy old to enjoy a far better end of life?

We show little commitment to a socialism of old age beyond providing some insultingly small financial benefits. Individual stoicism is the norm. We provide, in those countries with free national health care, reasonable basic healthcare for the elderly, although healthcare and palliative care is always superior for the rich, and we acknowledge the high expense of all old age care. Most astoundingly, obstacles are erected for humane assisted dying for those who are very ill and in pain and who wish to die, all sorts of religious objections and alleged qualms about abuses barring a change in relevant law. From a DR perspective, it makes no sense to insist on keeping anyone alive who is suffering severely and who wishes to die. Public opinion seems to be far from able even to consider it, but a DR position might well be that any adult of any age who is 'of sound mind', uncoerced and wishing to end his or her life for *any* reason should have both the right and the means of doing so. A fearful, superstitious and denial-oriented public is presumably against even considering the idea of state-funded voluntary death facilities. When the novelist Martin Amis talked about the need for 'euthanasia booths', he was vilified by pro-life groups (Davies, 2010). Common thanatophobia drives medical research and treatment, so that our lives become longer and many are kept alive, often in undignified, immobile and dependent circumstances, beyond a reasonable optimal point. Fearful death avoidance could be replaced by the wise recognition that an unwanted, depressing old age should give way to freely chosen termination of life.

A long-range twofold conundrum here for antinatalists is as follows. First, if significant numbers of people stop having children, the old will have far fewer grandchildren to give them comfort, grandparenthood being acknowledged as one of the greatest comforts in old age. Secondly, we are told that the increasing number of old people, who themselves are living longer, need a buoyant population of younger working people to support them financially. It is difficult to see a way around these problems without either revolutionising our economic systems or installing human assisted dying facilities. An optimistic

182 Lessons and possibilities for individuals and society

realism position would argue that old people are in fact much healthier and happier than I claim here, that we all should and can save more from an early age towards larger pensions, breakthroughs in the treatment of old age disease and rejuvenation technologies are just around the corner, the earth can sustain billions more people and so on.

A depressive realist-informed civilisation?

I strongly suspect this grandiose idea is a non-starter. Is a Zapffe-inspired society possible? Presumably not at all, since Zapffe advocated antinatalism. Indeed, following any antinatalist agenda, which is likely to have only the barest minority appeal, it will be the pronatalist population that proliferates all the more. Is a civilisation guided by moderate DR principles possible? To the extent that we equate DR with nihilism, and furthermore a compassionate, pragmatic variety of nihilism, I believe this is a possibility. Think of John Lennon's song *Imagine* which cuts its way through various illusions of meaning to arrive at 'peace, a brotherhood of man, no possessions'. Not exactly a watertight prescription for living, nor was it ever very convincing that a Proudhonian agenda would be proposed by a multi-millionaire, and we may struggle to imagine a truly post-tribalistic world community. But it does propose an illusion-free or illusion-disemburdened world of sorts. A civilisation offering the basics of food, water, housing, safety, medical care, ample distractions and assisted dying might meet DR criteria. If ever a majority accepted DR's arguments against illusions and came to embrace such an outlook, we could perhaps imagine a world slowed down to a post-capitalist tempo, and given to collective stoicism, with sufficient humour and sense of conviviality to survive.

On the face of it, most people do not think of Jesus as a depressive realist. Yet the Biblical Jesus was clearly anything but a facilely happy consumerist, bureautype or bovine citizen. Rather, he espoused an ascetic lifestyle, nomadic, without possessions, possibly without sex, without career anxieties ('consider the lilies') and at best paying lip service to civic authorities and traditional religious institutions. Along with Diogenes, many anarchists, and latter day hippies, Jesus has been regarded as a model of the be-here-now philosophy, and hardly a champion of a work ethic and investment portfolio agenda. Jesus and others did not expect to find fulfilment in *this world* (meaning this civilisation) but looked forward to another world, or another kind of existence. Since that fantasised world has never materialised, we can only wonder about the likeness between early Christian communities and theoretical DR communities. There are certainly some overlaps but one distinctive dissimilarity: the DR has no illusory better world to look forward to, whereas the Christian had (and many Christians still have) illusions of rapture and heaven to look forward to. The key problematic here, however, for Jesus, the early Christians, anarchists, beats, hippies and DRs hoping for a DR-friendly society, is that intentional communities require some sense of overcoming adversity, having purpose, a means of

Lessons and possibilities for individuals and society 183

functioning and maintaining morale in the medium to long-term. It is always one thing to gain identity from opposing society at large, and quite another to sustain ongoing commitment.

A depressive realist-informed view of violence and war

In common with terror management theory, a DR-informed view of species-wide gratuitous violence extending from interpersonal bullying to world wars must ask about causes. Terror management theory posits that mortality salience and our avoidance of it can paradoxically push us to violence, among other irrational behaviours. This is because the horror of consciously focusing on our mortality, or any loss that reminds us of it, makes almost anything preferable. It is fairly easy to accept that religion might be an illusion we marshal for such purposes since on the face of it religious illusions look harmless. But it is admittedly counter-intuitive to suggest that dread of death drives us towards death. However, we have only to witness the risk-taking behaviours of many young men, high suicide rates, violent crime, terrorism and war, to at least pause for thought. On the one hand, the alternative to risk is safety, and chronic safety can feel stultifying to the point of feeling that life is unstimulating and futile. On the other, constant death awareness can trigger such high anxiety levels that rushing *towards* danger and death offers relief (Starrs, 1994).

A DR view resonating with TMT might suggest that confrontation of our mortality, however so effected, holds some hope of reducing violent acting-out. The tragedy of causing death in order to lessen the fear of it is probably readily understood by behaviourists, and psychologists and criminologists might hope for a breakthrough in this direction. However, DR is likely to recognise the law of unintended consequences or anthropathological loops at work here. It would be nice to think we had discovered the secret of violence and how to reduce or end it. But it is much more likely, if tragic, to have to confront the probability that violence is an intrinsic aspect of existence, of all natural phenomena. We *might* reduce violence in some areas of human life but it is likely to appear elsewhere, or the costs of suppressing it are likely to be too high in terms of what else is collaterally suppressed. Can we really imagine a world altogether without danger and violence? The love and peace movement is understandably well motivated, but predominantly male-driven hatred, revenge, risk-taking and war cannot be realistically abolished by a process of taming. But if they were, what unpredictable phenomena would take their place? Can we really think that a future of everlasting peace, guaranteed security, worldwide democracy, economic equality, multicultural harmony, lifelong monogamy, disease-free and extended lifespans and perfect ecological balance is possible and desirable? As we know, bad things happen to good people, and probably always will. In this sense pessimistic observers like Gray (2004) cannot be ignored, and Kaplan (2000) is right, I believe, to say: 'The years that follow an epochal military and political

184 Lessons and possibilities for individuals and society

victory such as the fall of the Berlin Wall are lonely times for realists' (p. xi) insofar as optimism about any final peace is naïve, and could only be guaranteed by a totalitarian world regime.

Acceptance of disenchantment

The nihilism in DR argues that desperation sits at the core of human consciousness, against which many if not most, perhaps all ideologies and social institutions currently act as defence mechanisms. To take religion, there *might* be a common God among the various religions; there *might* be a 'true' Christianity, for example, beneath its churches' distortions; there *might* be *a* God beneath the contortions of theological sophistry; there *might* be a 'spiritual reality' beneath theistic myths; 'spirituality' *might* be real and hold hope for humanity. But the probability is that all such desperate remedies for the meaninglessness of the human condition have only tenuous temporary credibility. The hopeful emotion fuelling them is now challenged by a rationality that inevitably feels disenchanting and threatening. Followers of Frankl may urge psychotherapy clients to find meaning, preferably a godly meaning but almost any ersatz meaning, any anchor in the storm of existence (Frankl, 2010). But any DR – and many besides – knows that having to construct meaning reveals the fictional nature of such meaning.

But rationality, too, will serve only for so long as a defence against our desperation; this doesn't mean that it is false or in equal competition with spiritual mythologies but that our knowledge is always partial. Science is never complete, the theory of the Big Bang, for example, being susceptible to criticism, refinement and eventual replacement. We can say the same about politics, philosophies and psychotherapies, that their remedies 'work' only temporarily, and their function is more to give us hope that we know where we stand – to rescue us from terror and desperation, to stand as epistemological placebos – than to be finally 'true'. Scientific rationality is undoubtedly disillusioning. Something else will sooner or later take its place. If we could learn to accept this uncomfortable epistemological and emotional trajectory, we *might* be better able to navigate our way into a somewhat co-operative and minimally conflicted collective future.

An alternative to despair and defence might be to collectively admit that anthropathological reality underpins everything, and to explore this post-delusional space for as long as possible. By collective I mean a small collective of DR-informed thinkers who might have the capability of deep acceptance without flight and who would engage in dialogue on the question of post-delusional experience. In our ambivalent perseverance we might yet bear fruit.

Researching consciousness

As the jigsaw puzzles of humanity are gradually completed, with the human genome project succeeding in 2003 and the human brain project scheduled for completion in 2023, we should see more and more detail on how we function.

If those of us who believe something markedly dysfunctional happened to the brain of human beings some thousands of years ago are correct, we can hope for evidence of this in the form of an archaeologically-informed anthropathology project. Already there is significant interest in the neurology of epilepsy, stroke, autism, schizophrenia, obsessive compulsive disorder, Tourettes Syndrome and Down Syndrome, as well as creativity and mystical or altered states of consciousness and the workings of psychedelic drugs. The functions and interrelationships here may be of great interest in demonstrating so-called normal neuropsychological functioning but also how other and deeper states operate. Even if no scientists are looking for the 'anthropathology site' in the brain, related research cannot avoid casting light on it and arguably we are more likely to find it than any 'seat of the soul'.

One possible route for discovery may be via probing for the workings of the brain in those deemed enlightened. For example, if something genuinely transformational happened neurologically and spontaneously to U.G. Krishnamurti, as well as to Jiddu Krishnamurti and Suzanne Segal and unknown others, it cannot forever evade investigation. If Dostoevsky found in his epileptic fits some contact with the mystical, and a neuroscientist like Jill Bolt Taylor (2009) found in her stroke some fortuitous experience of nirvana, we may have some important clues to build on. This is not about a search for exotic and possibly non-existent entities but part of the hunt for comparisons between brains, and an understanding of why the majority of humans appear to be so estranged from their 'natural state' in which aggression, deceit and other forms of dysfunctional compulsion and behaviour are absent or minimal. If human consciousness altered profoundly and dysfunctionally, we should want to know how, why and when, if possible. Although important as an aspect of paleopsychology, such research *might* also hold some promise of radically changed human behaviour for the future. I am, of course, bypassing here what I consider to be the silly idea of a science of happiness and optimism. Self-report surveys of happiness, contentment or life satisfaction mean nothing in a society where the required response to 'how are you?' is 'fine thanks'.

Social forecasting

The DR nature of prophets has been noted. DRs tend to look into the future while the majority look to the short-term or *the now*. In the now and the medium term one can see grounds for satisfaction and hope. In the exercise of thinking and forecasting, however, one sees doom and death: death is getting closer to us all individually and collectively, social decay is likely, and the agenda of the posthumanists (probably the best bet for long-term survival) is fraught with dehumanising dangers. As often as not, however, forecasts turn out to be woefully incorrect: no religious doomsday schedule has been met; the population time bomb has not yet exploded; no leisure society ever materialised; extensive communism did not hold the answers and did not work out well where

186 Lessons and possibilities for individuals and society

it was tried. We do not know quite what to expect from the current climate change scenario, how accurate the data are, how bad things will get, when and where disasters will strike.

Inter-tribal wars look set to continue and retain the potential to escalate into worldwide tensions and wars. It is possible that the tribally driven violence that has long evolutionary roots will wither naturally in the centuries to come, or if not strong coalitions will emerge to monitor and foil outbreaks. Dramatic challenges can be dealt with more easily than slow social trends that threaten human sanity and survival. One of these is the acceleration of knowledge and information overload. Analogous to the social brain hypothesis, an information-overloaded world and brain may also be regarded as threatening us from within, as it were, insofar as our own well-intentioned collective actions evolve into unmanageable and portentous conditions. If the Zapffean hypothesis of the over-developed human consciousness is correct (and see Bohm, 1994), we can see a parallel danger in information overload and its neurological and social consequences. But it may be asking too much of us to accurately anticipate and head off our own follies-in-the-making.

In a more generalised sense, DR sees human folly and denial continuing indefinitely. Human civilisation will continue on the basis that we must not have population control; that we must maintain and increase wealth; that all misfortunes, including death, can be conquered. And contrarily the voices of romantic socialism will continue to call for equality, moderation of consumption, governmental control and human rights. Overarching both these is posthumanism which is founded on belief in a need for radically new post-biological solutions that altogether transcend current norms. No-one can accept or build policies on any conception of tragedy. But realism must contain recognition of randomness and negativity: earthquakes, volcanic eruptions, tsunamis, epidemics, asteroid impacts, ice ages all lie in wait, with science doing its best to monitor, predict and forestall. Neophilia and moribundancy (abundancy of the moribund), or negentropy and entropy, the dynamics of will and surrender, continue their dance into future aeons but ultimately entropy must win.

Compassionate nihilism

Much of what is proposed here is from the position that things probably are as bad as the gloomiest picture presented. That is a different position from *knowing* that things are this bad. While a very strong DR belief easily leads to moods of depression, pessimism and social withdrawal, it is possible that a deeply embodied *knowledge that all is suffering* leads to a somewhat different attitude. The Buddha is said to have postponed the fruits of nirvana in order compassionately to help others to exit from the state of suffering. The overwhelming majority of us do not experience nirvana or anything like it, and in fact we have no strong basis, beyond hope, for even believing that any such state of consciousness exists. Some DRs may, however, in a sustained refusal to escape into defensive illusions,

Lessons and possibilities for individuals and society   187

sometimes pass into states of acutely embodied knowledge of the truth of DR. Refusal to escape constitutes a paradoxical loyalty to nihilism. But the DR's nihilism need not be dismissive, bitter or misanthropic; in one form it is compassionate, clearly seeing fellow human beings as suffering from the conditions of existence, and feeling the same compassion for himself. Rosenberg (2012) refers to 'nice nihilism' as the natural state for scientifically informed, Darwinian atheists: it suits us to be nice to each other, not for moral reasons but simply because it works in our current circumstances.

DR 'moods' may shift from bleak nihilism and misanthropy to compassionate nihilism, moments of forgetfulness, peace and humour, to acutely compassionate self-consciousness. You inhabit this programmed and entropic body that is bound for death and it deserves some care. But the mood shifts back to bleakness in a to-and-fro movement through existential seasons with no stable core. You see your existential companions flailing tragicomically around the fractional awareness of the predetermined trap they are in. In our shared folly there is some room for inexpressible pity at how little freedom we have to change anything fundamental about ourselves.

Back to reality

Following an episode of upsetting domestic friction in which two loving adults are temporarily possessed by their ancestral demons ('man hands on misery to man' yet again), I find myself embroiled in an online academic dispute. An ambitious young colleague intends to fail a student; standards must be upheld. I disagree with what I consider his pointless harshness over archaic symbolic systems but can't abide a trivial battle over it, so I reluctantly compromise. Meanwhile, negative newspaper headlines provide perennial DR background in one's mind. Suffering from the aftermath of insomnia, I walk to the local harbour and peer into the sea: jellyfish and man, just a metre or so apart. I am looking across an evolutionary chasm of about 600 million years, just as at night I can look at stars billions of years old. I am kidding myself, but I feel some sort of ironic fellowship with these jellyfish. I imagine they wonder what I am, and I imagine myself ashamed that human beings evolved to this point: clever but crazy and cruel animals, gratuitously hurting each other, living in insanely symbolic systems that also hurt them. The stars, the jellyfish, and us; here we all are, but was any of it worth the trouble? Perhaps. Perhaps not.

References

Blanton, B. (2005) *Radical Honesty (Rev. edn.)*. Stanley, VA: Sparrowhawk.

Bloom, A. (2015) Experts condemn removal of suicide from A-level sociology syllabus. *Times Educational Supplement*, 24 June.

Bohm, D. (1994) *Thought as a System*. London: Routledge.

Bolt Taylor, J. (2009) *My Stroke of Insight: A Brain Scientist's Personal Journey*. London: Hodder & Stoughton.

188 Lessons and possibilities for individuals and society

Cain, S. (2013) *Quiet: The Power of Introverts in a World That Can't Stop Talking.* New York: Penguin.

Case, T.I. & Williams, K.D. (2004) Ostracism: A Metaphor for Death. In J. Greenberg, S.L. Koole & T. Pyszczynski (eds). *Handbook of Experimental Existential Psychology*, pp 336–351. New York: Guilford.

Cvetkovich, A. (2012) *Depression: A Public Feeling.* Durham, NC: Duke University Press.

Davies, C. (2010) Martin Amis in new row over 'euthanasia booths'. *The Guardian*, 24 January.

Davies, M. & Barnett, R. (eds) (2015) *The Palgrave Handbook of Critical Thinking in Higher Education.* New York: Palgrave Macmillan.

Edelman, L. (2004) *No Future: Queer Theory and the Death Drive.* Durham, NC: Duke University Press.

Feltham, C. (2012) *Failure.* London: Routledge.

Frankl, V.E. (2010) *The Feeling of Meaninglessness: A Challenge for Psychotherapy and Philosophy.* Milwaukee, WI: Marquette University Press.

Fromm, E. (2001) *The Sane Society.* London: Routledge.

Gray, J. (2004) *Heresies: Against Progress and Other Illusions.* London: Granta.

Jackson, P.S. & Peterson, J.P. (2004) Depressive disorder in highly gifted adolescents. *Journal of Secondary Gifted Education*, 14 (3), 175–186.

Jardine, D.W., Gilham, C. & McCaffrey, G. (eds) (2014) *On the Pedagogy of Suffering: Hermeneutic and Buddhist Meditations.* New York: Peter Lang.

Kaplan, R.D. (2000) *The Coming Anarchy: Shattering the Dreams of the Post Cold War.* New York: Vintage.

Ormerod, P. (2005) *Why Most Things Fail: Evolution, Extinction and Economics.* London: Faber & Faber.

Overy, R. (2010) *The Morbid Age: Britain and the Crisis of Civilisation 1919–1939.* London: Penguin.

Rosenberg, A. (2012) *The Atheist's Guide to Reality: Enjoying Your Life without Illusions.* New York: Norton.

Scruton, R. (2010) *The Uses of Pessimism and the Danger of False Hope.* London: Atlantic.

Shaha, A. (2014) *The Young Atheist's Handbook.* London: Biteback.

Starrs, R. (1994) *Deadly Dialectics: Sex, Violence and Nihilism in the World of Yukio Mishima.* Honolulu, HI: University of Hawaii Press.

Tallis, R. (1997) *Enemies of Hope: A Critique of Contemporary Pessimism.* Houndmills: Palgrave Macmillan.

Williams, K.D., Forgas, J.P. & Von Hippel, W. (2005) *The Social Outcast: Ostracism, Social Exclusion, Rejection, and Bullying.* New York: Psychology Press.

Yalom I. (2006) *The Schopenhauer Cure.* New York: Harper Collins.

Index

Abrahamic religions 23
academia 7, 42, 71, 76, 152
acedia 29, 59
adolescence 138–9
adulthood 140–2
affect heuristic 168
affect studies 111
ageing 38; *see also* old age
akrasia 161
alienation 65
Allen, W. 61, 156, 159, 163
Alloy and Abramson 1, 68
Amery, J. 146
anarcho-primitivism 26; *see also* Zerzan, J.
anchoring 41, 177
anthropathology 14–15, 32, 128, 161, 179
antihumanism 157
antinatalism 33, 38, 43–5, 119, 179–80;
    see also Benatar, D.
anxiety 31, 147
artificial ape thesis (Taylor) 14, 119, 128
assisted dying 45, 181
atheism 23, 26, 30–1

Bacon, F. 39, 109
Baumeister, R.F. 69–70
Beauvoir, S. de 161
Beck, A. 70, 85–6
Becker, E. 136, 143
Beckett, S. 32, 35, 41, 59–60, 66, 75, 83, 96, 109, 123
Benatar, D. 1, 3, 6, 35, 43–5, 146
Benjamin, W. 111
bereavement 37, 84, 108
Big Bang 20, 119, 184
big history 11, 14–15, 19
Bion, W. 83
birth 15, 133
boredom 50, 149

Bowring, J. 111–12, 159
brain, the human 12, 13, 119, 166, 184
Brassier, R. 39, 119
brutalism 6, 4, 92, 101
Buddhism 27, 31, 32, 38, 158, 170

Camus, A. 46, 47
capitalism 18, 26, 29, 102, 149, 177
Christianity 24, 182, 184
Cioran, E.M. 20, 32, 36, 107, 113, 133
climate change 14, 20, 96, 105, 123, 125, 129
cognitive behaviour therapy (CBT) 74, 83–6, 144, 166
cognitive dissonance 93, 142, 161
consciousness 3, 11, 14, 38, 41, 159, 184
Critchley, S. 33
curmudgeonliness 162
cynicism, philosophy *see* kynicism
cynicism, modern usage 4, 65, 156, 179

Darwin, C. 20, 70, 121–3
death 14, 53, 76, 136, 146, 147–9, 161; and psychotherapy 89–90
democracy 18, 103–4
denial 4, 42, 144, 174
depression 1, 30, 37, 70, 74, 81, 85, 133, 137, 143, 152, 164, 174, 176
depressive position 63
depressive realism: and acceptance 184; arguments against 156–171; definition 2, 3; as enquiry 20; and psychology 68
depressive realists 1, 2, 3, 4, 70, 95; and everyday life 151; and minority status, 5, 49, 164, 176–8
depressogenic thinking 84, 96, 125
determinism 114, 161, 168
Diamond, J. 16, 20, 121
Diogenes 28, 36

190 Index

disenchantment 4, 121
distraction 41, 63, 82, 165, 181
DSM (Diagnostic & Statistical Manual)
   5, 80
dukkha 1, 23, 27
dysthymia 74
dystopia 60, 127

education 175–6
efilism 44
Eliot, T.S. 46, 55, 57, 176
Ellis, A. 4, 84; *see also* REBT
emptiness 25, 54
end of life care 180–2
Enlightenment (historical period) 23, 28
enlightenment (Buddhist) 27, 158
ennui 163
entropy 26, 48, 49, 61, 77, 129
equality and happiness 109–13; and
   Denmark 110
everyday life 149–51
evolution 10, 15, 37, 122, 187; *see also*
   evolutionary mismatch theory 14
evolutionary psychology 71–2, 101
existentialism 2, 32, 175
existential therapy 87, 90, 166
extinction events 12, 119

failure 173
Fall, the 13, 170
fallenness 13, 23
fatalism 26
feminism 17, 26, 108
Ficino, C. 37
film 61–6
Frankl, V. 81, 87, 161, 184
free will 15, 25, 32, 43, 47
Freud, S. 32, 70, 73, 82, 89, 112
futilitarianism 50, 148
future, and DR 124–31

geopolitics 104–5
Gilgamesh 53
God 11, 23, 25, 28, 32, 38, 161, 184
good life, the 47–8
Graham, G. 39
Gray, J. 30, 42–3, 102, 168

Hardy, T. 57
Hecht, J.M. 46
Heidegger, M. 35
Hinduism 26, 28
Holocaust 17, 18, 32, 43, 46, 61

Homo sapiens 12
homosexuality (and gay issues) 17, 45, 95, 180
hopelessness 63, 96, 133, 158
Hopkins, G.M. 55
Houellebecq, M. 2, 23, 58–9, 83, 113, 76
human condition 28, 72, 75–7, 93, 113–14,
   118, 137, 176, 177, 184
humanistic psychology 27, 102
humanistic therapy 86–7
human nature 71, 102
human rights 17, 18, 45, 101, 104

illusion 20, 32, 39, 43, 48, 65, 69, 83, 112,
   126, 141, 163, 182
industrialisation 13, 18, 19, 121
infancy and childhood 134
information overload 3, 20, 186
injustice 100–2
Islam 16, 25
isolation 41, 148

Jacobson, H. 61
James, W. 70
Jaynes, J. 13, 53
Jews 16, 17, 28, 61
Judaism 24
Jung, C. 17, 74, 76, 165

Kane, S. 46
Kierkegaard, S.A. 31, 110
Klein, M. 138
kluge 15, 20, 119
Krishnamurti, J. 29, 38, 185
Krishnamurti, U.G. 28, 59, 170, 185
kynicism 36

Larkin, P. 55
late modernity 18
Layard, R. 73, 85
left-wing politics 7, 111, 157, 176
Leopardi, G. 35, 54
lifespan 132–49
Ligotti, T. 2, 35, 122, 172
logic 36, 45, 48
loneliness 141, 149
lying 135–6, 178

McCarthy, C. 58
McGilchrist, I. 13
Marx, K. 10, 18, 32, 40
marriage 140
maya 23, 32, 126
meaninglessness 8, 19, 24, 37, 61, 161

Index

melancholy 4, 37, 56
mendokusai 45, 141, 180
mental health 5, 80, 91, 94, 112, 177
Michelstaedter, C. 7, 139
middle age 142–3
minority group, DR as *see* depressive realists
misandry 17
misanthropy 59, 109, 157, 186
moribundancy 86
mortality salience 140

nadir experience 4
nausea 57
negativity bias 71
negentropy 76, 160
neophilia 8, 76, 149, 186
neti neti 36
newspapers 99–100
neuroscience 15, 20, 185
Newton, I. 120–1
Nietzsche, F. 28, 35
nihilism 3, 7, 39, 56, 114, 127, 150, 152, 172, 186; compassionate 186
nirvana 186
novels 56–61

old age 143–7
optimism 119, 158, 170
optimism bias 71
original sin 14, 23, 25, 31

parenthood 141
parrhesia 178
patriarchy 12, 107–8
Perry, S. 43, 108, 114, 151
personality dependent realism 48–9, 123, 135, 168
pessimism 2, 4, 24, 25, 27, 35, 39, 40, 54, 61, 99, 118, 150, 158, 167–70
philosophy 35–52, 175; as depressing 39; of mental health 38
Plath, F. 55–6
Plath, S. 55, 99, 108
poetry 54–6
Pollyannaism 71, 86, 174
population control 179, 186
positive psychology 74, 166–7
posthumanism 16, 44, 125, 186
post-traumatic growth 75
progress 126, 170
psychoanalysis 82–3
psychology 68–79; as depressing 72; and fraud 73

psychotherapy 5, 46, 80–98, 161; as depressing 90–92; and ethics 92–94; research 91
purposelessness 33

queer theory 111, 177

radical honesty 178–79
REBT (rational emotive behaviour therapy) 84
re-enchantment 86
religion 13, 23; as negative 29; as worldview 31; *see also* spirituality
right-wing politics 18, 108
Rogers, C.R. 29
Russell, B. 39, 112

sadness 2, 47, 145
Saltus, E. 40
samsara 160
Sartre, J-P. 57
scepticism 156
Scheffler, S. 44, 124
schizophrenia 12, 114
science 118–30; as dangerous 123
schooling 136–7; *see also* education
Schopenhauer, A. 2, 10, 28, 31, 40–1, 82, 100, 132
self, the 132
self-deception 14, 55, 74
Seress, R. 46
Shakespeare, W. 56, 143
Sloterdijk, P. 6, 36, 159
social brain hypothesis 186
social evils 106
social forecasting 185
socialism 102–3
spirituality 28, 184
subhumanism 158
sublimation 4, 54, 56, 152
suicide 4, 32, 36, 45, 88–9, 111, 133, 139, 146, 151, 173
Szent-Györgyi, A. 124

Tallis, R. 1, 15, 43, 122, 167–70, 177
terror management theory (TMT) 66, 75, 141, 183
thanatophobia 129, 169
theory of mind 14
they, the (Heidegger) 49
Thomson, J. 6, 55
Tolstoy, L. 31
Tønnessen, H. 81

tragedy 11
tragic pluralism 105–7
tragicomedy 60, 81
tribalism 16, 18, 48, 179, 186
True Detective 62–3
truth 35–8, 39

violence 12, 113, 139, 183
von Trier, L. 65–6

Wade, N. 13, 16
Weltanschauung 4
worldviews 4, 31, 114, 174

Yalom, I. 81, 161, 179

Zapffe, P.W. 13, 41–2, 182
Zerzan, J. 18, 64, 67, 124, 172